AN INTRODUCTION TO
THE NEW TESTAMENT

UNIVERSITY OF CHICAGO PRESS · CHICAGO 37

Agent: CAMBRIDGE UNIVERSITY PRESS · LONDON

AN INTRODUCTION TO THE NEW TESTAMENT

By EDGAR J. GOODSPEED

UNIVERSITY OF CHICAGO PRESS
CHICAGO · ILLINOIS

v

PREFACE

In dedicating his collected *Letters* to his friend Septicius, Pliny says, "You have often urged me to
collect and publish my letters"—*colligerem publicaremque*. The science of New Testament Introduction has paid too little attention to the part played by publication in ancient life and in the development of the New Testament literature. We must not forget that there was really just as much difference in antiquity as there is now between a letter written and a letter published.

Publication in Antiquity

The scattered letters of Paul had no considerable effect upon developing Christian literature until someone thought of seeking them out, gathering them into a collection, and publishing them. That action had a very marked effect upon the production of further Christian writings, quite apart from the composition of the several letters by Paul a generation before. Of course, the mere undertaking of such a collection implies a developed Christian activity where it was made, and so has a value for the historian as well as for the interpreter.

The Collecting of Paul's Letters

Our concern with it here is for its contribution to the science of Introduction, for which the making of that collection has as much importance as the writing of almost any book in the New Testament. It was, of course, a significant thing for Paul to write his letters to Corinth, send them there, and experience their effects. They fell into the soil of the early Corinthian church and disappeared. But it was a very different thing when, some thirty-five years later, someone had the acumen to seek out those letters and publish them as part of a Pauline letter-corpus. It was that act that made them active as literature and put them in the way of influencing Christian writing as they had never done before.

This long-neglected matter of the collection and publication of Paul's letters is of great significance *A New Or-* for New Testament Introduction, since it *ganization* at once organizes the whole material into *of Intro-* the works written before that event, and *duction* the ones that were written after it and under the influence—many of them, indeed, in imitation—of the newly published collection.

This is no external or mechanical principle of organization; for the forms, views, and groupings of all this subsequent literature show the influence of the published Pauline letters. Not only does the personal letter become the model for the formal epistle, as Deissmann observed, but these later epistles are not for private use but for publication and circulation. Further, the Pauline letter-corpus became the model for a whole series of later letter-corpuses—those of the Revelation, Ignatius, John, the Pastorals. The recognition of this sets all these groups of documents in new perspectives. We perceive that they are not to be considered atomistically, as though they originated one document at a time; they came into being as corpuses and were published as such. This is plain in the case of Revelation, chapters 1–3; it is no less important to observe it in the Johannine and Pastoral corpuses. It is not without significance even for the Ignatian corpus as well.

In the published Pauline corpus, in short, we possess an instrument by which we can effect a new and fruitful reorganization of New Testament Introduction. It is such a reorganization that is undertaken in the present volume.

New Testament Introduction has suffered from a general tendency toward atomistic treatment. Cherished positions of various origins, tradi-
Atomism tional or critical, are found to be attended with what seem difficulties, and these are necessarily dealt with one by one and disposed of. The fault of this procedure obviously is that the investigator falls into the attitude of supposing that, if the one particular objection or difficulty under immediate scrutiny can be disposed of, the desired position is established. But of course it is precisely the cumulative effect of these difficulties that matters. We must not assume that, if this one difficulty be disposed of, the position is established, when nineteen other difficulties just as serious are waiting to be dealt with. In such a situation it is time to recognize that these objections can no longer be viewed as difficulties; they should rather be

regarded as clues to the true solution of the problem. In fact, a host of considerations that have usually been regarded by learning as difficulties to be zealously and ingeniously whittled away, one by one, are really nothing less than invaluable clues to the very solutions the achievement of which is the historical student's sole concern.

Not only is atomism a grave peril in detailed problems of Introduction, but it seriously affects its broader aspects. The individual letters of Paul have absorbed so much attention that their greater and very different value as a collection has been entirely lost sight of in Introduction. The letters, when collected, formed a new literary unit and at once and for the first time began to exert a literary influence. The Four-Gospel corpus has been similarly disregarded, as though it were of no concern for Introduction but only for the history of the canon. The letters to Timothy and Titus have been dealt with severally, as though they had separate origins instead of having originated as a corpus, which makes the study of them quite another matter.

How long it has taken us to perceive that Luke-Acts is not two works, written at different times, but simply two volumes of a single work—a very fruitful finding for all that concerns Introduction! And under the baneful influence of the old chapters and verses we have always interpreted the New Testament too atomistically, so that most people never dream a gospel or a letter has any broad general controlling purpose or message of its own.

Whatever may be said of the historian or the critic, it is the task of the interpreter to understand. The *The Task of the Interpreter* writer on Introduction must take account of the findings of history and of criticism, but his primary concern is interpretation. It is for the understanding of the literature that he labors. Its sources are for him a matter of secondary interest; the rebuilding of history upon it is not his immediate responsibility, though he will be satisfied that a sound history can be built only upon a faithful interpretation.

The interpreter must not, therefore, be drawn aside into the search for sources which might so absorb him as to make him forget his proper sphere. Nor should he become so engaged with historical reconstruction as to neglect his own task. His peculiar business is to understand and make understandable the literature he deals with, to appreciate and appraise the use his authors have made of their sources, and to find out the ends to which they used them.

What some antique sentence taken up into Revelation or Acts may have meant when it was first framed does not matter for his present task; what does matter is the use to which it is put in the New Testament book in which it now stands. Form criticism is, therefore, not the province of the introductionist; the discernment of the origins of the materials behind the sources is not a part of his immediate task. Much may be learned from such studies for the history and life of the early church, but it must of course be remembered that the fact that a saying fits a particular historical situation does not always mean that the situation created it.

The rise of the New Testament canon I have not dealt with in this introduction, inasmuch as I have treated it elsewhere, in my *Formation of the New Testament*, and I feel that brief accounts of it as adjuncts to volumes on Introduction are likely to be unsatisfactory.

Within twenty years after the death of Jesus the Christian movement was entering the Greek world. *Greek Readers* It was a reading and a writing world. Greek settlers were scattered along the shores of the Mediterranean, and everywhere they went, as the Greek papyri from Egypt have shown us, they read Greek books, old and new.

Into this Greek atmosphere of books and writing Christianity entered with astonishing vigor. Paul *Christian Writers* wrote his letters in Greek for Greek converts; Mark wrote his gospel for Greek Christians in Rome. Soon a Greek took up the pen and wrote a two-volume work on the history of the movement. John recast the Christian message for the Greek world, and the Rylands Library fragment shows that within a generation his gospel was circulating in Egypt in the new codex or leafbook form which was just coming into fashion. It now seems probable that Christianity, which had a huge religious literature to circulate, was among the leaders or actually took the lead in adopting that ingenious innovation in book forms. Certainly the earliest leafbooks which we possess are Christian documents—John, Paul, Hermas, the Oxyrhynchus Sayings, the British Museum gospel.

The New Testament may be described as the literary precipitate deposited by the Christian movement when it impinged upon the Greek world.

ACKNOWLEDGMENT

This book owes much to many hands and many sources—notably, to the men and women who have studied with me at the University of Chicago. But I must especially acknowledge the kindness of Professor Henry A. Sanders, of the University of Michigan, in permitting us to publish in facsimile the first page of Ephesians in the Michigan papyrus of the Pauline Epistles, showing the absence of the words "in Ephesus" from this oldest extant copy of that epistle. I wish also to thank Mr. Harold H. Hutson, Fellow in the Department of New Testament and Early Christian Literature in the Divinity School of the University of Chicago, who has very obligingly read the whole book in manuscript and nineteen chapters of it in proof.

EDGAR J. GOODSPEED

TABLE OF CONTENTS

xvii

I

THE FIRST LETTER TO THE THESSALONIANS

+

Occasion. Twenty years after the death of Jesus, and about the middle of the first century, a man sat down in the Greek city of Corinth to write a letter, and with his letter Christian literature began. Beyond a doubt a new spirit there and then began to inform the written word—that spirit which sets Christian writing apart from all other and which now so largely pervades the world's best literature.

For the writer was Paul, a Jew, brought up in the Greek city of Tarsus, a member of the pharisaic party, educated in Jerusalem to be a rabbi, but won over to faith in Christ through an experience so deep and transforming that it made him the greatest Christian missionary of the first century.

He had just been through an anxious experience. Only a few months before he had taken the momentous step of crossing from Troas into Macedonia, thus carrying the gospel from Asia, the continent of its origin, to Europe, the continent of its destiny. These first undertakings in the new field were full of promise but attended with no little difficulty. No sooner was an impression made and some success achieved than jealousy and opposition developed in town after

town, and Paul had to hasten on, leaving his work
only begun.)

It was so at Philippi, and it was so at Thessalonica.
Jewish hostility developed, and Paul had to leave,
sometimes under a cloud and at the demand of the authorities. What must have been the effect of these
ignominious nocturnal departures upon the little
groups of believers that he had been able to gather in
the course of four or five weeks? He could not help
being anxious over that question, as he went on to
Berea and later, when the old hostility which had
forced him out of Thessalonica drove him on to take
refuge in Athens.

In his anxiety over the little groups he had so pre-
cipitately abandoned, he sent his two lieutenants back
to see them, explain his disappearance, and conserve
what might remain of his work in Thessalonica and
Philippi. Acts speaks as though he sent them back
when he left Berea and set out for Athens (Acts 17:14,
15). Paul's own words in I Thess. 3:1, 2 are not incompatible with this, though they sound rather as if
his messengers did not leave him until he had reached
Athens: "I made up my mind to stay behind alone at
Athens and I sent my brother Timothy, ... to
strengthen you in your faith, and encourage you not
to be led astray, any of you, in all these troubles."

From Athens, Paul soon proceeds to Corinth, and
there finds employment at his trade, resumes his work
of preaching, and is soon embarked upon one of the
great ministries of his life. But his thoughts still turn
anxiously back to Thessalonica, and doubtless Philippi

too. What is going on there? Have his few converts retained their new faith and held together in a little church? Or have they been disheartened and disillusioned by the abrupt flight of their teacher and returned to their old religious and social affiliations?

It made an enormous difference to Paul and his prospects. For if a missionary must settle down in a Greek city for years of steady labor to establish a Christian church there, it will be a slow business taking the gospel to the Greek world. But if a few weeks' work in a place will suffice to form a lasting Christian group in it, the gospel is going to go through the Greek world like wildfire. Which is it to be? Timothy and Silvanus will give the answer when they come down from Macedonia to rejoin Paul.

The books of the New Testament are most of them definitely occasional in character; they connect themselves immediately with some particular situation or event that called them forth. This is true of the First Letter to the Thessalonians. It states its occasion very specifically and crisply. Timothy has just come back to Paul, 3:6, brought him good news of their faith and love, and told him how kindly they think of him and that they are just as anxious to see him as he is to see them.

So the news, when at last it comes, is good news—the very news Paul has been so anxiously hoping for. Not only are his apprehensions about his new Christian friends at Thessalonica relieved, but his hopes for the whole Greek mission are brightened. Paul is immensely encouraged. He can really live once more,

now that he knows they are standing firm in the Lord.
No doubt Silvanus brought equally good news from
Philippi. The Philippians seem always to have been a
comfort and stay to Paul, and we cannot help wishing
we had the letter he must have written them at the
same time that he wrote I Thessalonians.

In his relief and gratitude Paul sits down and dic-
tates a letter, probably to one of those public letter-
writers that were to be found on every hand, in eastern
cities especially, in the Greek world. Sometimes his
amanuenses were brothers in the church: "I, Tertius,
who write this letter, wish to be remembered to you
as a fellow Christian," Rom. 16:22. Paul had a way
of adding a few words in his own hand, which looked
large and awkward beside the swift, regular hand of
the professional letter-writer. Paul felt this. "See
what large letters I make when I write to you with
my own hand!" he says to the Galatians, 6:11. But
the body of all his letters was written by the professional writer, to whom Paul dictated it, sentence by
sentence.

Contents. So we may picture the apostle, after a
long day spent at his trade in Aquila's shop, seated by
his amanuensis or pacing to and fro and pouring out
the paragraphs of his letter in his animated style, almost as though the Thessalonians were right before
him. It is a classic of Christian friendship. He wonders now that he ever doubted the steadfastness of the
Thessalonian brothers. When he recalls the welcome
they gave his preaching when he first appeared in
Thessalonica, the way they followed his example, and

what we should call the Thessalonian revival that broke out there during his short stay, he can only thank God for them. He should never have had any doubts about them. Their acceptance of the gospel he had preached to them had been so spontaneous and joyful that it had become famous all over Greece, and Paul was known as the man who had led them in it.

For though our message brought you great trouble, you welcomed it with joy inspired by the holy Spirit, so that you set an example to all the believers in Macedonia and Greece. For the Lord's message has rung out from you not only over Macedonia and Greece, but the story of your belief in God has gone everywhere, so that we never need to mention it. For when people speak of us, they tell what a welcome you gave us, and how you turned from idols to God [1:6–9].

These extraordinary words conjure up a remarkable picture of what the Thessalonian response to Paul's preaching had done for his work in this new continent he was just entering. The story of it had gone before him, paving the way for him in the Greek cities about the Aegean, 1:2–10.

But the news Timothy has brought from Thessalonica is not all good. The old stock slanders so often brought against the bearers of a new religion have appeared there and are faithfully reported to Paul. Nowadays, when a man appears in a modern community with a new religion, he is generally suspected of being either immoral, mercenary, or inordinately vain, and just these slanders were being circulated in Thessalonica about Paul.

Paul often had occasion to defend himself against charges of one kind or another, and most of his letters contain an apologia, long or short. The second paragraph of I Thessalonians is such a defense.

Our appeal does not rest on a delusion, nor spring from any impure motive; there is no fraud about it. . . . . We never used flattery, as you know, or found pretexts for making money, as God is our witness. We never sought praise from men, either from you or anyone else, though as Christ's apostles we might have stood on our dignity. We were children when we were with you; we were like a mother nursing her children. . . . . You remember, brothers, how we toiled and labored. We worked night and day, when we preached the good news to you, in order not to be a burden to any of you. You will testify, and God will, how pure and upright and irreproachable our relations were with you who believed [2:3–10].

The Thessalonian Christians have indeed had their difficulties since Paul's visit. Their acceptance of a new faith had cost them a great deal. It had meant breaking off old and valued social and religious associations. But the Thessalonians had felt that the gospel was peculiarly a message from God himself, and that conviction had fortified them to endure such misunderstanding and ill-treatment as had overtaken them. To their old friends and neighbors they now appeared as renegades, just as the Christian Jews had seemed to their people. Paul rejoices that the Thessalonians had stood fast.

For you, brothers, followed the example of God's churches in Judea that are in union with Christ Jesus, for you in your turn had to bear the same ill-treatment from your neighbors as they did from the Jews, who killed the Lord Jesus and persecuted the prophets and us; [2:14, 15].

Paul has thus far dealt with three matters: his relief at the Thessalonians' steadfastness, 1:2–10; the slanders against him that have been circulated among them, 2:1–12; and the annoyance to which they have been subjected because of their change of religion, 2:13–16. He now admits the great anxiety he had felt about them, his desire to revisit them in person, and the suspense he felt while he waited for Timothy to go to them and bring him word of their state, 2:17—3:10. For when the suspense had become unendurable, he had sent Timothy to them to strengthen and encourage them:

That was why, when I could not bear it any longer, I sent to find out about your faith, for I was afraid that the tempter might have tempted you and all our labor might be lost. But now that Timothy has just come back to me from you, and brought me good news of your faith and love, and told me how kindly you think of me, and that you long to see me just as much as I long to see you, I feel encouraged, brothers, about you, in spite of all my distress and trouble, at your faith, for now I can really live, since you are standing firm in the Lord. For how can I thank God enough for you, for all the happiness you make me feel in the presence of our God, as I pray night and day with intense earnestness that I may see your faces and supply what is lacking in your faith? [3:5–10].

This affectionate passage is followed by a great benediction:

May our God and Father himself and our Lord Jesus open my way to you! May the Lord make your love for one another and for all men wide and full like my love for you, so that your hearts may be strong and faultlessly pure in the sight of our God and Father, when our Lord Jesus Christ appears with all his saints! [3:11–13].

This concludes the first part of the letter.

It has sometimes been said that Paul regarded the Christian salvation as an *opus operatum*, a thing completed or at least accomplished in the very act of faith. In a sense this is true. And yet in every letter Paul shows his solicitude that Christian believers should not rest content with this assurance but strive to develop their moral sense and perfect their characters in every possible way. Toward the end of each letter he turns to practical moral admonition, in no dry formal way but with great vitality and vigor.

In just this way he now appeals to the Christians in Thessalonica to go on trying to live in such a way as to please God. He does not suggest that they are not doing this already; they are doing it, only they must do it more and more, 4:1, 2.

Nothing in the pagan system was more in need of elevation than the relation between the sexes, and Paul's first admonition has to do with marriage. It must be honorably and purely entered into and sacredly respected, 4:3–8.

The early Christians were always ready to help one

another in material ways, when any need arose, and the Thessalonians are cheerfully doing this. But some of them are in danger of taking advantage of this disposition and of relaxing their own efforts to support themselves. Paul has something to say to each of these groups at Thessalonica, 4:9–12.

The Thessalonians, like Paul, confidently expected the early return of Jesus on the clouds of heaven in messianic state. But they feared that their friends who did not survive until then might miss the glorious experience of witnessing it. Paul reassures them. In his picture of the messianic advent those who had fallen asleep were to rise first and be ready to meet the Lord at his coming, 4:13–18.

When all this was to be, was of course the great question. Paul can say only that it will be when it is least expected. Their task is to be vigilant and composed. If they are armed with faith and love and the hope of salvation, the Day when it comes will not take them unprepared, 5:1–11.

Paul bespeaks respect and co-operation for the leaders of the Thessalonian church, 5:12–13. He also has something to say to these same leaders, 5:14. And then, in a wonderful series of crisp appeals, he gives us glimpses of the Christian life as he saw it. "Treat everyone with kindness. Always be joyful. Never give up praying. Thank God whatever happens. . . . . Do not stifle the Spirit," 5:15–22.

A second benediction, with greetings to all, and then a third conclude the letter, 5:23–28. Verses 25–28 probably form the concluding paragraph in Paul's own hand which, in II Thess. 3:17, he says is his mark in every letter.

Problems. New light has been thrown upon the date of I Thessalonians by the letter of Claudius to the city of Delphi imperfectly preserved in an inscription, fragments of which have been unearthed at Delphi. It mentions Gallio as proconsul of Greece (Achaea) at the time of Claudius' twenty-sixth imperatorial acclamation, which was not earlier than the closing months of A.D. 51 or later than the spring of 52; for he received his twenty-seventh such acclamation before August 1 of A.D. 52. That is, Gallio was proconsul during some part of the time between summer, 51, and summer, 52. But since proconsuls came out about June and held office for one year, his incumbency must have been from June of 51 to June of 52.

The reference to Gallio in Acts 18:12–17 reads as though he had only recently arrived in Corinth, whereas Paul's stay there is nearly over; "Paul stayed some time longer, and then bade the brothers goodbye and sailed for Syria," Acts 18:18. But he had spent a year and a half in Corinth. If Gallio came to his province in the summer of 51—the natural time for him to arrive—and Paul had been there eighteen months, Paul must have arrived in the winter of 50.[1] We have seen that he wrote I Thessalonians very soon after his

[1] As Deissmann puts it, "If Gallio entered on his office in the middle of the summer of 51, and if the accusation of Paul by the Jews took place soon afterwards, then *since he had already been working for approximately eighteen months in Corinth, Paul must have come to Corinth in the first months of the year 50, and left Corinth in the late summer of the year 51*" (*Paul*, p. 282).

arrival. We can therefore say with a good deal of confidence that it was written in the spring of A.D. 50. It is a matter of no little satisfaction to be able to date so closely the earliest of Paul's letters and the first book of the New Testament.

Some scholars have felt that Galatians must be given the honor of being the earliest of the letters of Paul that has come down to us, instead of I Thessalonians. But, while McGiffert has wisely warned us against acting as though we possessed a complete file of Paul's letters, and hence knew the ebb and flow of his thoughts and interests with any continuity and fulness, yet it is hard to understand Paul's neglect of the Judaizing problem in I Thessalonians, if it had risen so acutely and so recently in Galatia as would have been the case if Galatians had been written only a year of two before. We can see the overhang of the Galatian and the Corinthian conflicts in Romans, written some years after the trouble in Galatia and very soon after that in Corinth, and if Paul had had his trouble with the Galatians only a few months or a year or two before, we should expect some reminiscence of it to appear in I Thessalonians, as it does long after in Romans. Since it does not, we may rest assured that the Galatian controversy has not occurred and Galatians has not been written.

People used to approach the New Testament for its contribution to theology; that was their main interest and concern. But now we are interested in all it has to teach us about early Christian life and thought. All the problems, situations, emotions, and aspirations of that amazing age are of interest and of value to us. The New Testament has far more than a theology for us.

And, so considered, this first book of the New Testament is of wonderful interest and worth. What light it throws upon the relations between this first great missionary and his converts! His attitude to them is not in the least official or perfunctory. He and they are friends, and friends in a new and particularly Christian sense, for they are all friends of Christ, members of one great household of God. Paul does not say this in I Thessalonians, but the friendship and kinship in Christianity which were afterward expressed by Paul, and later by John, are unmistakably here. I Thessalonians is a great document of Christian friendship. Here, already, at the beginning of Christian literature, is that church life which we all know so well, which is unlike any other social relationship in the world, being based upon self-forgetting devotion to the good of all. A new kind of friendship had come into the world.

LITERATURE

DEISSMANN, ADOLF. *Paul* (2d ed.; New York, 1911), pp. 261–86.

DOBSCHÜTZ, ERNST VON. *Die Thessalonicher-Briefe* (Göttingen, 1909).

FRAME, JAMES E. *Epistles of St. Paul to the Thessalonians* (New York, 1912).

MILLIGAN, GEORGE. *St. Paul's Epistles to the Thessalonians* (London, 1908).

II

THE SECOND LETTER TO THE THESSALONIANS

+

Occasion. The eagerness and zeal with which the Thessalonians had welcomed the gospel (I Thess. 1:5-9) had actually run away with some of them. These persons were so convinced that a new age had dawned that they had given up work and were absorbed in waiting for the return of the Messiah on the clouds of heaven. This threw a heavy burden upon their more practical brothers in the church, who felt obliged to provide for their material wants. Paul had been warned of the danger of this development before he wrote I Thessalonians and had touched upon it in I Thess. 4:11, 12, hoping to prevent it from becoming acute. But a few months later it developed into more serious proportions.

It had its origin in the idea which had sprung up in Thessalonica, perhaps from something Paul had said or was reported to have said, that the Day of the Lord, foretold by the prophets, had now come. In a sense this was true. For if the great messianic Day was to be that on which the Christ came to the earth, one might well think it had come, since he had come, in the person of Jesus.

The group at Thessalonica thought of it in other

terms, however. They believed the messianic age had begun, and that the messianic reorganization was now so imminent that they might better give themselves to religious reflection and contemplation than to mundane matters like earning their daily bread. This threw a heavy strain upon their more practical fellow-Christians, who had to support them as well as themselves. This was not all. Not all of those who had given up earning their living devoted themselves to spiritual exercises. There was just as much human nature in the first century as there is now, and leisure as well as labor has its temptations. So the Thessalonian drones became a cause of scandal in the community, not only because they let their Christian brothers support them but because they were getting to be loafers and busybodies.

News of this situation soon came to Paul at Corinth, and he dealt with it promptly and energetically in a second letter to Thessalonica, written not long after I Thessalonians, probably in the year 50. There was no place in his practice or teaching for such a proceeding. His own life was a marvel of efficient, independent energy. He earned his living by his trade and preached the gospel in his leisure hours. So far from looking to the Jerusalem church to support him in his missionary travels and labors, he himself used to raise money to send back to them for their Christian poor. He was about the last man in the world to have any sympathy for the present course of these Thessalonian adventists.

Of course, he was an adventist too; he believed in the speedy return of Jesus in messianic splendor, to judge the world and adjust its wrongs. He also believed that the Messiah had already come, but he held that, as he had not performed the characteristic messianic function of judgment, he must come again to perform it. That would indeed be the Day of the Lord, foretold by the prophets, for with them that Day had always been described as a Day of Judgment.

Of the use to be made of the short interval between these two messianic comings, the coming of Jesus and the Day of Judgment, Paul and the Thessalonian adventists took opposite views. They thought it had better be spent in reflection, religious exercises, and self-preparation. Paul thought it should be spent in making the Christian salvation known as widely as possible in the Greek world. His aim was to become everything to everybody, so as by all means to save some of them. The Thessalonian idlers looked within and saw their own sinful hearts, all unready for the messianic advent. Paul looked without and saw a world of men and women who might be saved in time.

Paul had already written the Thessalonians that the Day was coming without any warning and like a thief in the night, I Thess. 5:2. In the stress of the new situation, however, he somewhat modifies that opinion. Out of his Jewish inheritance, which had already given him his doctrine of the coming of the Messiah to judge the world and usher in the Day of the Lord, he now brings forward another apocalyptic doctrine—the Antichrist.

It is true the word "Antichrist" is not used by Paul, either here or elsewhere in his letters, nor has it ever been found in earlier literature, Jewish or Christian. Its first recorded occurrences are in I and II John (I, 2:18, 22; 4:3; II, 7), which were written probably sixty years later than II Thessalonians. But Jewish messianic thought dramatically pictured the long conflict between right and wrong, good and evil, as culminating in a gigantic duel between the two embodiments of the rival forces. Evil would indeed wax worse and worse, until at length the champion of wickedness, the Antichrist, would appear and assume control. And then the Christ would come and in a great conflict with Antichrist overthrow him and his whole regime. This Antichrist some believed would arise out of the tribe of Dan; it is a curious fact that in Rev. 7:4–8 Dan is not included among the tribes of Israel. *The Testaments of the Twelve Patriarchs, Dan* 5:6, 10 (100–50 B.C.), also rather suggest this: "I have read in the book of Enoch, the righteous, that your prince is Satan, ... And there shall arise unto you from the tribe of Judah and of Levi the salvation of the Lord, and he shall make war against Beliar." We should compare also Gen. 49:17, Jer. 8:16, and Dan. 11:36. But the fact remains that the classical passage for this Antichrist doctrine is the second chapter of II Thessalonians.

To this very Jewish idea Paul now appeals to convince the Thessalonian idlers that the Day of the Lord has not come, at least in the sense that they suppose. For the Antichrist has not yet appeared and made the triumph of evil really complete. It is true his work is developing, and he is soon to come, but just now for a time something and someone are holding him back. When these restraining forces are withdrawn, he will come in all his pretension and deception and for a time prevail, only to be destroyed by the Messiah at his coming.

But since this Embodiment of Disobedience has not yet unmistakably appeared, and since his appearance must, according to the messianic program, precede that of the Messiah, then evidently the final coming of the Messiah cannot have taken place.

This curious doctrine is worked out with Paul's usual trenchant boldness in II Thessalonians, chapter 2. He proceeds in chapter 3 to draw from it some practical inferences.

Contents. As in the first letter, Silvanus and Timothy are associated with Paul in writing II Thessalonians, 1:1, 2. The opening expression of thanksgiving for the Thessalonians' faith, love, and steadfastness in persecution leads to denunciation of their persecutors, who will be terribly punished in the approaching messianic judgment, 1:3–12.

They must not suppose that the Day of the Lord has come; that will not be until the Embodiment of Disobedience appears, for his coming is to precede that of the Messiah who is to overthrow him. He is, in fact, already at work but is being temporarily held in check. Presently he will make his appearance, with all his pretended signs and wonders, only to be destroyed by the Lord Jesus, the true Messiah, when he in turn makes his appearance upon the scene, 2:1–12. After renewed thanksgiving for their divine election and an exhortation to steadfastness, the main part of the letter closes with a benediction, 2:13–17.

Paul asks them to pray for his work in Corinth and expresses his confidence in them, 3:1–5. The practical side of their situation is then dealt with: they are not to countenance idlers in their number. They must remember Paul's own course. He ate nobody's bread without paying for it. He worked night and day to keep from being a burden to any of them. He might as their teacher have claimed the right to be supported by them, but he would not do this, for he wanted to set them an example by his own conduct. He repeats the rule he had given them when he was at Thessalonica: "If anyone refuses to work, give him nothing to eat." In the most solemn way he charges the idlers to go to work again and earn their own living. The brothers who have been supporting them are not to get tired of helping the really needy. But any who will not obey Paul's order, they are to have nothing to do with. Not that they are to look upon them as enemies; they are still to warn them as brothers, 3:6–16. Paul's autograph greeting concludes the letter, 3:17, 18.

Problems. Two objections have been brought against the authenticity of II Thessalonians. One is the apocalyptic objection. It is pointed out that in I Thessalonians Paul declares that the Day is coming without any warning at all; it will be like a thief in the night. Everyone will be saying "What peace and safety!" when suddenly destruction will be upon them. All anyone can do is to be vigilant and composed. But now, in II Thessalonians, he declares that there will be some warning, in the coming of the Antichrist with his pretended signs and wonders and his claim of being God himself. Some scholars feel that the inconsistency between these two positions is so great that they cannot have been held by the same man.

If we were to view Paul's writings dogmatically and to assume that he could never alter his position under the stress of circumstances, but must always and everywhere have agreed with himself, this objection might be valid. But if we view Paul historically, as a man of great power and sincerity and strength, grappling vigorously with immediate personal conditions that were constantly changing, we shall find no difficulty here. Paul's letters are not to be viewed like a textbook on mathematics or even dogmatics. And it is precisely the best and wisest of men who honestly and sincerely shift their ground as circumstances may demand. Moreover, this is simply another piece of that same Jewish apocalyptic messianism—the Messiah coming on the clouds of heaven to execute judgment and usher in the Day of the Lord—with which Paul was clearly saturated.

The idea of a restraining influence, that is now holding the Antichrist back, is another important element in the situation. The way in which it is mentioned— now as impersonal, 2:6; now as personal, 2:7—somewhat suggests that the Roman Empire and emperor are thought of as holding the forces of evil in check for a time, until this restraining force is overridden by the powers of evil. Paul shows in Romans that he believes in obeying the emperor and his governors, 13:1-

10. But after Nero's outbreak against the church in Rome, in August of 64, it is difficult to see how anybody could any longer have conceived the Empire as a beneficent force restraining the full triumph of evil. Even I Peter, loyal as it is, takes a comparatively chastened view of it.

We must not be content to set aside an ancient writing as not authentic; some better place in the history of early Christian literature must then be found for it, for we are seeking to interpret these documents, and to do that we must discover their place in history—the date and circumstances of their composition. No one has found a better place or date for II Thessalonians than Corinth about A.D. 50. In view of these considerations most serious students of II Thessalonians now give little weight to the apocalyptic objection.

But another objection has been raised of a very different kind; in fact, it is almost the exact opposite of the apocalyptic objection. It is the psychological objection. The two letters, we are told, are too much alike to have been written by one man, especially a man so full of originality and freshness as the author of Galatians, Corinthians, and Romans. Not only are the letters alike in plan with a sonorous benediction, perhaps two-thirds or three-fifths of the way through, marking the close of the doctrinal part—I Thess. 3:11–13; II Thess. 2:16, 17—but many sayings of the first letter are repeated in the second. Thus I Thess. 2:9 is practically repeated in II Thess. 3:8, and in both letters much is said about thanking God for the Thessalonians, I, 1:2; 2:13; 3:9; compare II, 1:3; 2:13.

References to Jesus' messianic return are met with in both letters, I, 1:10; 3:13; 4:13–17; 5:23; compare II, 1:7–10; 2:1, 8, 14. In both letters the church is suffering ill-treatment and persecution, I, 2:14; compare II, 1:4–6.

But in writing again within a few months to the same group, some repetition would be inevitable, and the contrasting character of II Thessalonians, chapter 2, certainly makes the second letter anything but a feeble copy of the first. The second letter has too much of the characteristic Pauline trenchant vigor (see chap. 2) to be dismissed as an imitation, and the developed situation above described sufficiently accounts for such resemblances as there are. So the psychological objection, like the apocalyptic, fails to disturb the authenticity of II Thessalonians.

Paul must, of course, have written many private letters before I and II Thessalonians, but they are the earliest of his letters that have been preserved. The Thessalonians read them and valued them so much that they preserved them, perhaps with the rolls of the Greek Old Testament which were their first scriptures. But forty years were to pass before these letters were published and made any impression upon the general Christian thought of the first century. To the Thessalonians they were just private letters to them from their great teacher, worth preserving, indeed, and occasionally re-reading but never meant for a wider circulation. So these letters, like all of Paul's, fell into the soil of the early church, did their work, and for a time disappeared.

The fact that our earliest Christian writings are personal letters carries with it two considerations that bear upon their interpretation and use. For one thing we must expect to find them difficult to understand. Professor Grenfell once remarked that of all papyrus documents private letters were the most difficult to understand and interpret. This is entirely natural, of course, for they necessarily assume a common background of situation and information possessed only by the writer and the particular person or group to which he writes. On the other hand, such letters are also the most trustworthy of all historical sources, for they are written not to be published but simply for the people addressed in them. They actually reflect immediate historical situations. If, then, there are in Paul's letters some things hard to understand, as II Peter long ago pointed out,[1] we shall be more than compensated by the original, first-hand character of their contents, which constitutes them historical documents of the first order.

LITERATURE

BOUSSET, W. *The Antichrist Legend: A Chapter in Jewish and Christian Folklore*, trans. A. H. KEANE (London, 1896).

BROOKE, A. E. *The Johannine Epistles* (New York, 1912), pp. 69–79.

DOBSCHÜTZ, ERNST VON. *Die Thessalonicher-Briefe* (Göttingen, 1909).

FRAME, JAMES E. *Epistles of St. Paul to the Thessalonians* (New York, 1912).

MILLIGAN, GEORGE. *St. Paul's Epistles to the Thessalonians* (London, 1908).

[1] II Pet. 3:15, 16.

III

THE LETTER TO THE GALATIANS

✠

Occasion. Paul had hardly reached the shores of Syria, on his return from his long residence in Corinth, when he was met by bad news. Someone had been spreading a narrower type of Christianity among the churches he had organized in Galatia a few years earlier, and the Galatians were swinging away from Paul's simple doctrine of faith.

The Galatian mission had been the most fruitful part of the work Paul had done in company with Barnabas four or five years before, on what is usually described as his first missionary journey. They had first preached in Cyprus and then crossed to the south coast of Asia Minor, where Paul seems to have been prostrated by illness, perhaps one of those fevers still so severe along that coast. From the lowlands his companion had taken him up into the high-lying interior to Galatia, so that Paul could afterward remind the Galatians that it was because of an illness that he had preached the good news to them the first time.[1] So the gospel came to Antioch in Pisidia, Iconium, Lystra, and Derbe. Again, on his second journey, these Galatian churches were among the first ones visited by Paul and Silas after setting out

[1] Gal. 4:13.

23

from Syrian Antioch; indeed, it was at Lystra that a young man named Timothy became a member of their missionary party. So Paul knew these churches well; in fact, he was peculiarly bound to them through Timothy, who had developed into a trusty lieutenant. It was Timothy whom he had sent back to Thessalonica to steady the Thessalonians, and who had brought back the good news that called forth I Thessalonians.

Paul's party had called at Ephesus on their way east from Corinth, but there was as yet no Christian body there, and it is difficult to see how he could have learned of the disturbed state of things in the little Christian groups in Galatia before he reached Antioch in Syria, which was his headquarters in so far as he had any. In Antioch, Paul had many friends, and the work he had done in Galatia was well known. There at any rate he might learn what had been going on in the Galatian churches while he had been so far away.

Into these little bodies had come Christian teachers of a more rigorous and Jewish type. They considered Jesus the fulfiller and completer of the old agreement between God and Abraham. The blessing promised in that agreement was to be for Abraham and his descendants, and for nobody else. In order, then, to profit by the spiritual blessings Jesus had brought, one must be a descendant of Abraham, or become one, by being incorporated into the Jewish people. In short, one must become a Jewish proselyte. The synagogue was the only door to the church.

The first step was, of course, the acceptance of the

rite of circumcision, to be followed by the observance of at least a minimum of the Jewish Law. Christianity so understood would be a kind of modified Judaism, with none of the spiritual freedom which Paul so greatly enjoyed and so ardently taught.

As for Paul, he was not really an apostle at all— that is, one of the Twelve Apostles—nor was he authorized by them to offer the Christian salvation to Greeks on such easy terms. These Jewish-minded teachers felt that he was cheapening their old prerogative and throwing open the blessings of their cherished faith to all the heathen. They thought of religion in terms of privilege, of which they were the custodians, and it is a fair question whether they were more concerned to win the Gentiles to the Jewish salvation or to keep it from them.

The Jews had, it is true, translated their scriptures into Greek (the Septuagint Version) and sent Jewish missionaries about the Greek world before the time of Christ.[1] But, on the other hand, by the formal demands they made upon converts and by their superior and exclusive spirit they repelled more than they attracted. To this day, as in the time of Ezra, in orthodox Jewish circles a man or woman who marries a Gentile is cast out of his or her family as a renegade, and something of this condescending spirit marked the work of the Judaizers in Galatia. The blessings of true religion seemed to them their exclusive property, all that was left to them of their old national glory, and

[1] F. M. Derwacter, *Preparing the Way for Paul* (New York, 1930).

the terms on which the Greeks might share them were still the same as they had always been.

The logic of this teaching was really unassailable, once its premises were granted. But Paul had found in the Christian life something that entirely transcended the old scribal dialectic—a great, vital, inward experience which he described as faith, before which such mere legalistic logic shriveled away. That the Galatians who had once had this sublime experience should now lapse into the dull, lifeless, formal kind of religion their new teachers offered them was more than he could bear.

This is the situation that confronts Paul immediately upon his arrival at Antioch, for bad news travels fast and his friends would not be slow in letting him know the fate of what must have seemed his most successful mission east of the Aegean. It would have been quite unlike Paul to accept such a defeat. Yet he cannot immediately leave Antioch, where he had only just arrived after a long absence. It may seem to us at this distance of time that the main thing Paul had to do was to write his letters, but of course as a matter of fact they were a very minor part of what he did. This is a point often lost sight of by students of his work.

Much as he would like to face the Galatians and show them the truth, 4:20, he cannot do so, and so he writes a letter. Paul's letters are probably the most extraordinary letters in the world, but none of them is more remarkable than Galatians. Its vigor, variety, audacity, and self-revealing frankness, together with its deep and direct insight into religious truth, put it in a class by itself among the books of the New Testament. Conventional proprieties and courtesies are forgotten, for tremendous issues are at stake and Paul is writing under very great excitement. He cares deeply for the Galatians, and their religious welfare is a matter of the utmost personal concern to him. They are the children of his Christian ministry, and he will not let them fall into blindness and folly without a struggle.

Contents. With his first words he attacks. He *is* an apostle, whatever the Judaizers may say of him; not commissioned by the Twelve, indeed, but with higher credentials than they could give, for Christ himself has commissioned him. Paul had realized the great truth that the indispensable authorization in religion is that of inward experience and conviction, and that without that no formal election or laying-on of hands amounts to anything.

With himself he associates, in all he has to say, all the brothers that are there with him. This must mean the whole church at Antioch—the one great missionary church of the New Testament. It was from that church, so rich in prophets and teachers—Barnabas, Symeon, Lucius, Manaen, and Saul—that Barnabas and Saul had first been sent forth into the Greek world of the West, Acts 13:1–4. Paul puts the authority not of Jerusalem but of Antioch back of his message to the Galatians.

He addresses not a single church, as he usually did, but all the churches of the Galatian series—Derbe,

Lystra, Iconium, Pisidian Antioch, as his messenger from Syria would come to them. There is not time for individual letters, and so Paul for once writes a circular letter to all four, 1:1–5.

He is amazed that they are turning to a different gospel from the one he preached to them. For it is no true gospel they have now been given but an upside-down one, the very reverse of the one he had given them. No matter who preaches it to them, even if he be an angel from heaven, it is false! In his indignation Paul calls down curses upon its preachers, 1:6–9.

They have charged him with flattery and cajolery; he calls the Galatians to witness that this does not sound much like it. Paul's gospel, he would have them know, was not something he had received from other men but came to him out of a great inward experience—a revelation of Jesus Christ, 1:10–12.

He now turns to deal with the charge that he was not recognized or commissioned by the Twelve Apostles. He does not deny this; rather he reviews his whole Christian life to show how little he had seen of Jerusalem or the Twelve. Three years after his conversion he had indeed spent a fortnight with Cephas, as he calls Peter, but saw no other apostle. Fourteen years later he went to Jerusalem again, with Barnabas and Titus, and explained to the leaders of the church the work he was doing among the Greeks. The Jerusalem leaders did not even require his Greek companion Titus to accept circumcision. On the contrary, they pledged Paul and Barnabas their co-operation and definitely assigned to them the mission to the Greeks, 1:13—2:10.

On a later occasion Paul had met the same problem in Antioch, when Peter came there. At first Peter had eaten with the heathen—the Greek Christians—without scruple, but the arrival of some overscrupulous Christian Jews from Jerusalem led him to give up this liberal practice for fear of the "party of circumcision," as Paul calls the Judaizers. Paul then brought up Peter's former course with devastating effect: "If you live like a heathen and not like a Jew, though you are a Jew yourself, why should you try to make the heathen live like Jews?" The fact that Peter had eaten freely with Greeks, regardless of the ceremonial regulation against it, showed that he really held the same position that Paul did about that and similar regulations and could not consistently demand that Greek Christians observe them, 2:11–14.

Paul goes on to show that men born Jews had found their way to the Christian salvation only by the exercise of faith; they had not found it through the observance of law. So for Jew and Greek alike the way to the Christian salvation is the way of faith. The Law has no part in it. Yet it was to the Law that the Judaizers were trying to recall the Galatians, 2:15–21.

In a passage of the utmost boldness, 3:1–6, Paul points out the illogical folly of their conduct. The early Christians experienced a great release of religious intuitions when they came into the attitude of faith. Had a set of legal observances given it to them? Was it not the simple exercise of faith that had done so?

If, then, their new religious life began on the high levels of inward spiritual experience, do they expect it to conclude and culminate on the low levels of external precept and statute? The Judaizers had made much of the agreement with Abraham. But what was Abraham's experience? He had faith, and it was credited to him as uprightness.

With these words Paul really snatches the sword from the Judaizers and turns it against them. Abraham on whom they had built so much now turns out to be Paul's ally. The men of faith are the real descendants of Abraham. The Scripture said all the heathen should be blessed through him, and here they are, experiencing that blessing, 3:7-9.

In a kaleidoscopic series of arguments Paul now rakes the Judaizers' position from every side. He pours them forth in a torrent that must have swept it all away. What had the law achieved? It only left all its devotees under the curse, for none of them had fully observed it. From that curse Christ's death had ransomed us all, in order that the blessing promised to Abraham might indeed through Christ reach the heathen as the Scripture had promised it would, 3:10-14.

The mere fact that the Law was not given until centuries after Abraham's time shows that it cannot possibly be read into the promise made to him. "An agreement already ratified by God cannot be annulled and its promise cancelled by the Law, which arose four hundred and thirty years later," 3:17. The Judaizers cannot claim the promise and then try to combine the Law with it, as though the Law were a kind of belated codicil to the promise. Paul holds the Judaizers strictly to Abraham and the promise. If they wish to drag in the Law, then they must let go the promise, 3:15–18.

This leaves Paul with the difficult question of the Law. It was subsequent, subordinate, and temporary. It was like the attendant who, in the ancient world, took the boy through the streets to school and there turned him over to his teacher. (To render *paidagogos* "schoolmaster" spoils the figure entirely. Jesus was the "schoolmaster," not the Law.) Now that we are, through faith, in the presence of the teacher himself, we have no further need of the Law, 3:19–25.

This figure of the noble child being conducted to school reminds Paul of the noble condition of the Christian believers. They are all sons of God through their faith. The old distinctions of race, sex, condition are no more; they are no more Jew or Greek, slave or free, male or female; one with Christ, they are all one. If they belong to Christ, they are true descendants of Abraham and heirs of the promise made to him, 3:26–29.

The noble boy suggests to Paul another telling figure. The Christian is like the heir to some great inheritance. Through the years of his minority, under tutors and guardians, he is little better than a slave himself. But a day arrives when he comes of age and is free and master of it all. So we are sons and heirs, with a spirit in our hearts that makes us call God "Father," 4:1–7.

From such a prospect how can the Galatians turn back to the old dull, mechanical views of religion that are now being offered them? Paul begins to fear that the labor he had spent on them was wasted, 4:8–11. He turns from argument to impassioned emotional appeal. What friends they had been once! With what understanding sympathy the Galatians had once received him when he came among them, miserable in his illness! They would have done anything for him then. What has changed them so? It is these Judaizers who have done it, and for their own ends, 4:12–20.

Paul's final argument has in it more than a touch of allegory. But the wonder is that his letters contain so little of that favorite ancient type of thinking. Let the Judaizers remember that Abraham had two sons: one, of the flesh, by a slave; the other, of the promise, by a free woman. Let those who make so much of physical descent from Abraham remember that Ishmael was just as much his physical descendant as Isaac was. For we who share Abraham's spiritual experience and so inherit his promise are in Isaac's line and children of no slave but a free woman, 4:21–31.

"This is the freedom with which Christ has freed us. So stand firm in it, and do not get under a yoke of slavery again." This is the trumpet call to religious freedom in which Paul's argument reaches its climax. Men cannot progress in religion half slave and half free, winged with faith on one side and limping on a crutch of law on the other. In union with Christ neither circumcision nor the want of it counts for anything but only faith acting through love, 5:1–12.

Paul knew well enough the dangers of freedom—how easily it becomes an excuse for laxity and license, for just following impulse. The Galatians will not do that, however, if they really admit the Spirit to their hearts and listen to what it directs. For what the Spirit produces is love, joy, peace, patience, kindness, goodness, faithfulness, gentleness, self-control. If Paul's argument culminates in his call to freedom, his exhortation reaches its climax here, 5:13–24.

"If we live by the spirit, let us be guided by the spirit." We must not be censorious but bear one another's burdens. The old law of retribution still holds: a man will reap just what he sows, 5:25—6:10.

Paul's closing paragraph in his own hand stands out curiously from the swift, even writing of the letter-writer who had penned the letter. "See what large letters I make, when I write to you with my own hand." He repeats in his own hand the main theme of the letter. The scars of his beatings in Philippi he describes as the brand he wears as a slave of Christ, for the ancients would sometimes brand their slaves. No one can say now that Paul is not a slave of Christ. We are left to wonder whether the Judaizers had any such honorable scars to show, 6:11–18.

So ends Galatians, a perfect torrent from the first word to the last, a blaze of fiery eloquence, strongly charged with emotion from beginning to end. Paul was never greater than in this letter. Its great doctrine of freedom of religion, set forth here almost at the beginning of the New Testament, has again and again awakened the church from formalism and conven-

tionality to religious life and vigor. It is not an anti-
quated ideal but one which we have never overtaken,
which still beckons us onward toward the higher
possibilities of religion. One thing is certain; we shall
never go beyond it.

Problems. One serious problem about Galatians is
the location of Galatia as Paul understood it and as
he used the word, Gal. 1:2. It was Paul's usual practice (as distinguished from Luke's) to use, and to use
accurately, the regular Roman provincial designations
—Asia, Macedonia, Greece (Achaea), Judea, Syria,
Cilicia, etc. We may expect that he uses Galatia in this
way. But the region into which the Pergamenes under
Attalus I had herded the invading Kelts, or Galatae, in
239 B.C. was that about Tavium, Ancyra, and Pessinus
in north-central Asia Minor. If that is the region intended by Paul by the word Galatia, the Galatian
churches were founded not on the first missionary
journey but on the second, in the hurried tour described in Acts in 16:6: "They crossed Phrygia and
Galatia." They would probably be located in Tavium,
Ancyra, and Pessinus. But there is no record of any
very ancient Christianity in these places, and it would
have meant a far swing to the northward in Paul's
itinerary, as a glance at the map will show, though of
course there is nothing impossible in that.

Recent studies in Roman provincial organization
have shown that Lycaonia was included with Galatia
in Roman administration. Tacitus says that Galba
made Asprenas governor of Galatia and Pamphylia,[1]

[1] Tacitus *Histories* ii. 9.

which strongly implies that those provinces were contiguous. This shows that, soon after Paul's day at least, it was customary to speak of the district of Derbe, Lystra, and Iconium as part of Galatia; Galba was emperor in A.D. 68, and Tacitus wrote his *Histories* about A.D. 115.

It has been urged by some that Paul would hardly have addressed people of Derbe, Lystra, Iconium, and Pisidian Antioch as "Galatians," even though their country had for years been combined with Galatia proper as one administrative district. Still, he does speak of his friends in Thessalonica and Philippi as "Macedonians," II Cor. 9:2, 4, certainly with no suggestion that they were of Macedonian stock or descent. Luke's usage is less strict than Paul's, but he speaks of Paul as a "Roman," Acts 22:25, 26, 29 (cf. 23:27), of course in no ethnographic but in a very technical political sense. Trophimus of Ephesus is classed with Tychicus as an "Asian" in Acts 20:4, and no one imagines that they must have come from the Lydian town of Asia from which the province and then the continent of Asia had already taken their names. If Paul could refer to the brothers in Philippi, Thessalonica, and Berea as "Macedonians," he could quite reasonably speak of those of Derbe, Lystra, Iconium, and Pisidian Antioch as "Galatians." For at least seventy-five years—that is, since the death of Amyntas in 25 B.C.—these towns had been a part of Galatia, and it is fantastic to suppose, as Jülicher does, that they would not in that length of time have come to be referred to as Galatians; when, as we have seen,

Thessalonians could be called Macedonians; Ephesians, Asians; and a Tarsian like Paul, a Roman. It is a mistake to think that it would have taken a hundred years to accustom a Lystran to the fact that he was also, provincially speaking, a Galatian.

The mention of Barnabas as though well known to the Galatians, 2:13, accords better with the view that they were first evangelized by Barnabas and Paul, hence on the first missionary journey and in south Galatia, rather than on the second, by Paul and Silas, so summarily sketched in Acts 16:6. Moreover, when the money collected by Paul for the Christian poor in Jerusalem was carried there, representatives of the various contributing groups were to take it, I Cor. 16:3; as the party was finally made up, there were two from south Galatia, Gaius and Timothy, but nobody from north Galatia.

It is difficult to see under what other name Paul could have grouped the Christian residents of Derbe, Lystra, Iconium, and Pisidian Antioch. On the whole it is reasonable to conclude that his Galatians were the inhabitants of those south Galatian cities, especially as there is no record of any Christian churches in the northern part of the province until long after Paul's day.

To Paul's argument in 3:10 it is sometimes objected that the Jewish Law nowhere demands full obedience to itself in all its details. But that is just what it seems to do in Deut. 28:58: "If you are not careful to observe all the provisions of this code [Torah], written in this book, ... then the Lord shall bring extraor-

dinary plagues on you and your descendants." At
the end of the last code, that of Deuteronomy, the
observance of the whole legislation seems to be en-
joined: "At the end of every seven years, ... you
must read this code [Torah] in the hearing of all
Israel, ... that they may hear it . . . . and be careful
to observe all the provisions of this code [Torah],"
31:10–13. The word "all" is indeed absent from the
Hebrew text of Deut. 27:26 (the passage Paul quotes
in 3:10), as we have it, but it is present in the Septuagint Greek version. That this is the clear intention of
the passage is shown by the frightful curses pronounced immediately after, in 28:15–68, upon all who
are not "careful to observe all his commands and
statutes which I am commanding you today," 28:15.
These passages amply support the contention of Paul
that the Law demanded full obedience to all its particulars. For in Jewish use these predicates were of
course extended to the whole Law, all of which it was
understood Moses had written.

A somewhat different situation has been proposed
by Lütgert[1] and developed by Ropes[2] to explain
Galatians. On the basis of a number of passages in the
letter, especially 3:6—4:7; 5:11—6:10, it is claimed
that there were in the Galatian churches not only persons of the extreme Judaizing type but, over against
them, a group of spiritualistic radicals, *pneumatikoi*,
who thought Paul too much inclined to find the roots

[1] Wilhelm Lütgert, *Gesetz und Geist* (Gütersloh, 1919).

[2] J. H. Ropes, *The Singular Problem of the Epistle to the Galatians* (Cambridge, 1929).

of Christianity in Judaism, from which they wished to detach it altogether, being for their part entirely satisfied with faith and the religious endowments which it brought. It was these radicals who were out of sympathy with those who taught the word, 6:6, and were inclined to disdain the flesh and its temptations and fall into the libertinism and perfectionism of which Paul speaks in 5:13–17. There were, therefore, on this view two kinds of errorists in Galatia, each of whom had seized upon a part of Paul's teaching and exaggerated it. It is against the contentions of these perfectionist radicals that Paul in 1:11—2:14 shows that his gospel has not been influenced by the Jerusalem authorities. In fact, throughout the letter, he seems to be facing now one party and now the other.

Such is the theory. But it seems that, if there had been two groups so diametrically opposed to each other in Galatia, Paul could hardly have failed to make the fact clear instead of generally addressing the Galatians as though they were all of one stripe.

LITERATURE

Burton, E. D. *The Epistle to the Galatians* (New York, 1920).

Lightfoot, J. B. *St. Paul's Epistle to the Galatians* (10th ed.; London, 1890).

Ropes, J. H. *The Singular Problem of the Epistle to the Galatians* (Cambridge, 1929).

IV

THE FIRST LETTER TO THE CORINTHIANS

+

Occasion. Dr. Stalker once said that the letters of Paul take the roofs off the meeting places of the early Christians and let us look inside,[1] and this is peculiarly true of the letters to the Corinthians. Paul had again journeyed westward, through Asia Minor, to the Aegean and was settled at Ephesus for what was to prove the longest missionary activity of his life. He had previously reconnoitered Ephesus as a place for missionary work, Acts 18:19–21, when he left Corinth after his eighteen months' stay there, described in Acts 18:1–17, and set out for the east. We are to think of him as settled in Ephesus, working as usual at his trade and preaching in his leisure hours with such success, Acts records, "that everyone who lived in Asia, Greeks as well as Jews, heard the Lord's message," 19:10.

Just across the Aegean, almost opposite Ephesus, lay Corinth. It was not the old luxury-loving city of classical times; that had been destroyed by the Romans in 146 B.C. The new city had been founded just a century later by Julius Caesar and had developed rapidly. The notorious Astarte-Aphrodite worship of the older

[1] James Stalker, *The Life of St. Paul* (Edinburgh), § 129.

city was revived but never regained its old proportions, when it had claimed a thousand hierodules. The
new Roman Corinth was pervaded by the mystery
religions, and their practices of initiation and religious meals, their universalism and sense of individual salvation, and their mystical experience of
identification with a Lord and Savior, form part of the
background of I Corinthians and had an undoubted
influence upon Paul's ways of describing the religious
significance of Jesus to them. To the Corinthians the
Christian faith must have appeared another, but
superior, mystery religion.

Corinth was only a couple of days' sail from Ephesus and must have been in constant communication
with it. Visitors from Corinth were frequent in
Ephesus, and among those who came and went were
some who knew the little group of Christians in
Corinth and indeed probably belonged to it. They are
referred to by Paul as "Chloe's people." Perhaps they
were her slaves or her freedmen or were employed by
her in some way. At any rate they had brought Paul
news about his Christian friends in Corinth, and it
was very disturbing.

The Corinthians it seemed, according to these visitors, were breaking up into cliques or factions; not
about anything of moral or doctrinal significance but
merely about their favorite teachers. Perhaps Apollos
with his polished Alexandrian style had caught their
fancy and struck them as a better man than Paul. At
any rate Acts speaks of his coming to Corinth, 18:24—
19:1, and of his being there when Paul reached

Ephesus and settled there, and Paul repeatedly speaks in I Corinthians as though he were being compared with Apollos, 1:12; 3:4; 4:6. Certainly a distaste for Paul's style had developed. The Corinthians considered him "rude in speech" and wished he would give more attention to the refinements of expression, like the Stoic philosopher-preachers to whom they were accustomed. But Paul insisted upon talking simply and directly in the plain speech of everyday life. That he used the vernacular in his letters the Greek papyri discovered in the sands of Egypt in the last forty years have abundantly proved. These are documents of common life, written by all sorts of people—men, women, and children—and they exhibit the same linguistic features as Paul's letters. Paul made no effort to be "literary" in writing his letters.

Not only did Paul seem less gifted than Apollos but the Corinthians had come to think him inferior in position to such Christian leaders as Cephas, that is, Peter. Possibly Judaizing Christian teachers from Jerusalem had come among them, as they had among the Galatians, and aroused these suspicions.

But more serious evils than these were reported to Paul by Chloe's people. There were cases of immoral conduct among the Corinthian Christians. One man had married his widowed stepmother. And in their business disagreements among themselves the Corinthians were actually going to pagan courts to have their differences settled.

Another matter brought to Paul by his Corinthian visitors was the shocking way in which the Lord's

Supper was being kept in Corinth. It was the custom there for each one to bring his own food and drink for the occasion and to join some congenial group to share it, so that some had not enough to eat and drink and others had too much, and the Supper degenerated into a carouse.

Paul's mind was seething with all this distressing information, when three men from Corinth sought him out in his lodgings at Ephesus or perhaps at Aquila's workshop, where he was probably employed, Acts 18:2, 3, 24, 26–28; 19:1, and put into his hands a letter, I Cor. 7:1. Paul must have received hundreds of letters, for the papyri show that the Greeks were great letter-writers, and Paul himself has lived in history chiefly as a writer of letters. But this is the only one that we definitely know of his receiving. It was from the Christians at Corinth and was brought to him by Stephanas, Achaicus, and Fortunatus as representatives of the Corinthian church. Stephanas may have been the leader of the Corinthian church, for Paul seems to speak of him in that way, in I Cor. 16:15–18.

Paul had already written a letter to Corinth, charging the Corinthians not to associate with immoral people who were supposed to be Christians, I Cor. 5:9–13. This letter was probably short and must have been lost, unless it is preserved, perhaps in part, in what we know as II Cor. 6:14—7:1. That section seems quite detached from its more spirited context; in fact, the context gains greatly in coherence and movement without it. And while Paul often interrupts himself, he usually interrupts a less animated passage with a more animated one. But here it is the less animated passage that interrupts the more animated one. It reads:

Do not get into close and incongruous relations with unbelievers. What partnership can uprightness have with iniquity, or what can light have to do with darkness? How can Christ agree with Belial? Or what has a believer in common with an unbeliever? What bargain can a temple of God make with idols? For we are a temple of the living God, just as God said,

"I will live in them and move among them,
And I will be their God and they will be my people."[1]

Therefore,
    "Come out from them,
        And separate from them, says the Lord,
        And touch nothing that is unclean.[2]
        Then I will welcome you,
        I will become a father to you,[3]
        And you shall become my sons and daughters,
        Says the Lord Almighty."[4]

So since we have promises like these, dear friends, let us cleanse ourselves of everything that can defile body or spirit, and by reverence for God make our consecration complete.[5]

The passage deals with just the matter with which Paul's missing letter evidently dealt; except that it has to do with the Christian's relation with unbelievers, and the lost letter dealt with immoral people inside the church, I Cor. 5:9–13. But it must be noted that it required some explanation in Paul's next letter to

[1] Lev. 26:11, 12.   [3] Jer. 31:1.
[2] Isa. 52:11.   [4] Hos. 1:10; Isa. 43:10.   [5] II Cor. 6:14—7:1.

make this distinction clear. We cannot be by any means sure that II Cor. 6:14—7:1 is the lost letter, or even a part of it, but II Corinthians is certainly not a single letter but a combination of letters, and the passage is a difficult interruption where it now stands.

Whatever may have become of that first letter to Corinth, the Corinthians now had a host of other questions for him to answer. They had not been Christians very long, and there was no Christian literature to guide them in their new life. Yet problems were constantly arising. One was the age-long question of the sexes and their relations, which each new generation discovers for itself with delight and surprise. What is the meaning of marriage? Is it wrong to marry? What about divorce? What about engaged people? Shall they proceed to marry?

Another question that greatly concerned the Corinthinans was where they should buy their meat. The best meat in Corinth was to be had at the markets connected with the great idol temples. It was from specially bred and fattened animals, in prime condition and properly slaughtered, and may be compared with the prize beef from a modern fat-stock show, which is so much better than even the best beef one can ordinarily buy. The Corinthians knew what good living was, and they had been accustomed to buy this meat. But now that they were Christians, what ought they to do?

One party at Corinth, knowing that an idol was nothing and the meat had suffered nothing from being offered in sacrifice, maintained its right to buy and

eat this meat, as it had always done. But there was
another group in the church that had grave misgivings
about it. They pointed out that this proceeding made
the Christians supporters of the heathen cultus, which
was, of course, in part maintained by the profits of
these temple markets. And when Christians were
found attending dinners given in the clubrooms attached to the idol temples, other Christians might
easily be led into semi-idolatrous practices.[1]

How men, and especially women, should conduct
themselves in church was a matter that gave rise to a
whole series of questions at Corinth. One was whether
women should wear veils in Christian meetings. The
early Christians of course had no church buildings and
held their meetings in private houses. Some brother
with a large house would open it for Christian worship. In such a place should a woman dress as she
would in a private house or as in a public place?
Eastern and Western proprieties were also involved.
Paul was a Jew by education, and women had no part
in Jewish worship; it was carried on by the men and
boys. Even to this day, in orthodox Jewish syna-
gogues, the women witness the service from a gallery
or from behind a screen. In Herod's temple the women
could not advance beyond their own court into the
Court of the Men of Israel. But, through the influence of the mystery cults and other forces, women in
the Greek world had more freedom and a greater place
in religion, and capable Greek women in Corinth felt
quite equal to taking part with the men in the meet-

[1] Cf. Oxyrhynchus Papyri 110, an invitation to dinner at the Serapeum.

ings of the church. The Corinthians are not sure which practice to follow in their meetings.

But the great problem in their worship was occasioned by ecstatic speaking. This familiar religious phenomenon, not unknown today in unsophisticated circles, was disturbing the Corinthian meetings and giving the brothers great concern. There is always something infectious about it, and when one brother under great religious excitement broke out into an unintelligible babble, others were almost sure to follow his example. The result was bedlam; a stranger coming in would have said that they were mad. Still Corinthian leaders like Stephanas hesitated to forbid ecstatic speaking altogether, for they recognized it as in a sense, though a very primitive one, a religious expression.

Another question on which the Corinthians needed Paul's counsel was the matter of the Resurrection. To the Greek mind, immortality was a familiar idea, but the Jewish way of describing it as "Resurrection," which formed part of Paul's apocalyptic teaching, created grave difficulties. These they seem to have laid before Paul in their letter, which was, in short, a veritable question box.

Contents. Paul's answer is our I Corinthians. But, before he begins to deal with their list of questions, he takes up the matters of which he had been told by Chloe's people, which had been preying upon his mind for some time, chapters 1–6. He seems unable to talk over the Corinthians' questions until he has got the matters of hearsay off his mind, and, first of all, the Corinthians' objections to his literary style.

The vigor and informality of Paul's style in his letters give us some faint idea of how trenchant, swift, and informal he must have been as a speaker. He does not deny the familiar, conversational style of his preaching. On the contrary, he admits it and declares that he will never attempt fine language in preaching, lest his diction come to have more of his attention than his message and so the cross of Christ may seem an empty thing. It is just here that the modern discoveries of Greek papyrus documents in Egypt have come to our aid in translating and understanding Paul. These papers of common life—deeds, letters, leases, contracts, notices, invitations, accounts—have given us for the first time a complete picture of the familiar spoken Greek of New Testament times. We actually possess at least one dated Greek document from every single year of the first century, and they have proved that Paul meant just what he said. His style was not literary, it was colloquial. The New Testament was written in colloquial Greek. The modern-speech translations that have resulted from this discovery have made Paul's letters more coherently intelligible and continuously readable than they have ever been in English before.

Paul condemns the Corinthian factions and explains what his relation to other teachers really is. He presented the gospel to them in simple direct terms, for they could not have grasped anything more advanced. He had done the planting, Apollos the watering, but it was God who had made the plants grow. Their belittling of his work stirs Paul to compare himself to the men condemned to death in the arena, who trudged along at the very end of the procession that passed through the streets to the amphitheater. He still feels toward them like a father, he declares, 4:14, 15, but he closes this discussion of the factions and parties at Corinth, chapters 1–4, on a threatening note: "Which will you have? Shall I come to you with a stick, or in a loving and gentle spirit?"

In chapters 5 and 6 he takes up the case of immorality at Corinth, insisting upon the Christian duty of purity and truth. Business differences are not to be taken before heathen tribunals for settlement; the Christians are to judge the world, how much more ordinary matters? The Christian is the temple of the Spirit of God; they must honor God with their bodies.

The matters of hearsay brought to Paul by Chloe's people having been mostly disposed of (with the exception of the Lord's Supper, 11:17–34), Paul turns to the Corinthians' letter which he has not thus far even mentioned. The procedure here is like that in the Letter of Claudius to the Alexandrians, written soon after his accession, in reply to a letter from them, proposing certain honors for him and asking certain favors.[1] The phraseology with which new topics of their letter are introduced is like that with which Paul passes to each new subject raised by the Corinthians, 7:1, 25; 8:1; 12:1.

---

[1] H. I. Bell, *Jews and Christians in Egypt* (London, 1924), p. 24.

The first of their questions has to do with marriage, chapter 7. We are so accustomed to think of the church as the one great force favoring and fostering marriage that it seems strange that it is here so depreciated. Once entered into, it is of course to be sacredly respected. But Paul feels that the single life is the one more likely to be pleasing to God. "It is an excellent thing if they can remain single as I am."

Two things must be remembered in dealing with Paul's letters and especially with the letters to Corinth. One is his half-oriental background—his Jewish upbringing. The other is his vivid expectation of Jesus' speedy messianic return. It was Paul's Jewish background that led him to refuse support from his churches, for the rabbi taught without pay, while the Greek lecturer expected a fee from his class.[1] Paul's Jewish background also held him in spite of himself, as revealed in Gal. 3:28, to a low view of the place of women in religion: "Women are to keep quiet in church," I Cor. 14:34.

But it was his messianic expectation that largely controlled his views on marriage and slavery. The time is short. The Lord is at hand. Let the unmarried remain unmarried, the married not seek to separate, the slave disdain emancipation. Not that it is a sin to marry, but the unmarried man or woman is freer to do the Lord's work. Young people who are engaged may marry if passion is getting too strong for them; but the better course is for them to remain as

[1] Justin *Dialogue* ii. 3.

they are.[1] A widow may marry again, if she marries a Christian; but she will be happier, Paul thinks, if she does not.

It may seem that no problem could have been more unpromising than where the Corinthians should do their marketing, 8:1—11:1, and yet nowhere does Paul show his greatness as a teacher more than in this and the next discussion—that on order in public worship. He might have dismissed these petty questions with curt answers, but instead he states them fully and fairly and then debates them until he reaches some great principle of Christian conduct, vastly more far-reaching than the petty question in hand might seem to call for.

The positions of the party that has knowledge and the party that has scruples are both fairly stated, chapter 8. Then Paul seems to forget all about the question and to wander off into a long series of rhetorical questions about his own procedure in a variety of matters, which at first appear to have little to do with the Corinthians' questions, chapter 9. The chapter is suggested by the claim of the party of knowledge that it has a perfect right to buy meat at the temple markets, as it had always done. Paul admits this but points out that he had relinquished a whole series of cherished rights in order to do a greater service for the Kingdom of God. In so doing he actually works out the program of civilization, for it is only by the voluntary

[1] This position has recently received strong Jewish support from Samuel Belkin, "The Problems of Paul's Background," *Journal of Biblical Literature*, LIV (1935), 49.

relinquishment of natural rights that man has been able to rise out of barbarism.

So when Paul returns to the problem of where the Corinthians are to do their marketing, chapter 10, there is nothing more to be said. He has freely admitted the Corinthian claim to certain rights but has then shown by his own experience and example that sometimes the best possible use we can make of our rights is to relinquish them when a great cause will be furthered by our doing so. They must follow his example in this as he follows Christ's.

When the matter of dress and behavior in church is reached, 11:2—14:40, Paul's Jewish training is again involved. Paul had already come to see that in union with Christ differences of sex no longer mattered, Gal. 3:28. But old social inheritances are not easily cast aside, and it still seemed to him indecent for a woman to appear in church without a veil—not, indeed, over her face, but on her head and shoulders. And it must be remembered that from a strictly Jewish point of view it was a great concession when Paul admitted women to any share in public worship. While Paul says farther on in the letter, 14:34, that women are not allowed to speak in church, here he speaks of them as offering prayer and explaining the will of God, 11:5, 13, apparently in church. They evidently had some speaking privileges, and the prohibition of 14:34 is probably much less sweeping than is usually supposed.

The matter of dress and behavior in church seems to remind Paul of what he has heard, doubtless from

Chloe's people, of the abuse of the Lord's Supper at Corinth. It had evidently degenerated into a sort of carouse. This was not so strange in a Greek world, accustomed to the rites of Bacchus, which found something religious even in intoxication. Paul interrupts his answers to the Corinthians' questions to correct this matter with a good deal of sternness. He takes occasion to repeat, evidently from the Oral Gospel familiar to them in its Greek form, the oldest account of the Last Supper and tells them to make every observance of it the occasion of a serious self-examination, 11:17–34.

Returning to the topics of their letter, he comes to the question of spiritual endowments, and particularly the disturbing matter of ecstatic speaking, which was apparently wrecking their public worship and mutual instruction, chapter 12. Paul deals with this matter patiently and fairly, not denying it a place in religion, and pointing out what varied manifestations there are of the Spirit. Then, in chapter 13, he seems to turn aside again, as he had done in chapter 9, and talk of other things. He breaks forth into an encomium upon love, the supreme endowment, one of the three really enduring ones, and the greatest of the three. And here as in chapter 9, he carries the Corinthians through with him to a great Christian attitude which will settle the matter of ecstatic speaking and most other problems besides. For here Paul has worked out nothing less than the principle of Christian courtesy— one of Christianity's chief endowments. In the light of that principle even ecstatic speakers will first con-

sider whether their meaningless speaking is going to
be helpful to the brotherhood, and if it is not, they
will of course be silent.

So Paul comes back from the praise of love to the
matter of ecstatic speaking, chapter 14, with the
matter really settled, just as he came back from his
discussion of the voluntary relinquishment of personal
rights for a larger good at the beginning of chapter 10.
It is these great principles to which Paul leads the
halting and perhaps rather small-minded Corinthians
that make his letters live so fruitfully today.

Whether the Resurrection was also one of the matters about which the Corinthians asked has been much
debated, but the place it has in the letter and the tone
in which Paul discusses it seem to prove that it was.
In a magnificent series of paragraphs Paul argues for
it, chapter 15, as no one among his Jewish predeces-
sors had ever done.

The letter draws to a close with what may be
called business and personal matters, chapter 16. Well-
to-do Jews out in the Greek west were accustomed to
send money to Jerusalem to help maintain the Jewish
group there, just as they do today. Paul and the
Christian leaders at Jerusalem were anxious to continue such aid to dependent Jerusalem Jews who became Christians, Gal. 2:10. He now invites the Corinthians to join in this contribution, as the Galatians
were doing, 16:1-4. He is planning a visit to Corinth,
for his work in Ephesus is nearing its end, 16:5-9.
There are personal messages, interspersed with crisp

epigrams, 16:10–20. He closes as usual with his autograph farewell, 16:21–24.

No document of the New Testament is more closely and convincingly integrated with the church life of its time than I Corinthians. It reveals it frankly and fully, in its imperfections and in its strength. In mountain regions one sometimes wanders through dark, intricate defiles and then suddenly emerges, surprised, upon some vast and dazzling prospect. It is so with I Corinthians. One is led through intricate antique discussions of petty and insignificant matters of ancient life, like marketing and speaking with tongues, to sudden, vast outlooks upon human life, its motives and its possibilities, that still command the assent of all thinking people.

LITERATURE

Lietzmann, Hans. *Handbuch zum Neuen Testament: An die Korinther I–II.* (2d ed.; Tübingen, 1923).

Robertson, Archibald, and Plummer, Alfred. *First Epistle of St. Paul to the Corinthians* (2d ed.; New York, 1916).

V

THE SECOND LETTER TO
THE CORINTHIANS

✝

Occasion. First Corinthians has always stood so high in popular esteem, especially by reason of the thirteenth and fifteenth chapters, that it is difficult for us to understand why it should not have been welcomed by the Corinthians whom it immortalized. But it was not. Its effect was not at all what Paul intended. So far from ending the opposition and hostility to himself and the Corinthian factions, it intensified both. The parties opposed to Paul united in opposition to him, as the party of Christ, and matters there went from bad to worse.

It is only when we examine the letter from what must have been the point of view of its original recipients that this development can be understood. If we look at it for a moment from the Corinthians' position, the situation soon becomes clear. To begin with, Paul hardly acknowledges their letter. He is so full of what Chloe's people have told him that he does not mention it until he is a third of the way through. Imagine the effect upon the assembled Corinthian church of the reading of this long criticism of themselves, based upon what some third party had told Paul about them! Whatever steps Paul may have

taken to satisfy himself of the truth of all these
charges, the Corinthians would have been very much
annoyed at them. In fact, the truer the charges were,
the more vexed they would have been.

Paul's tone in dealing with them was also far from
conciliatory. Again and again he seeks to bring the
Corinthians into line with the practice of other
churches, or asks them whether they think they are
the only Christian church in the world, 11:16; 14:33,
36. It was no doubt quite true that not many of them
were what men call wise, or influential, or of high
birth, and that Paul had to treat them like babies in
Christian living, 1:26; 3:1, but we should not have
liked being reminded of it, if we had been the Corinthians, and they evidently liked it just as little as we
should have done. The severity of Paul's rebuke, 5:1;
6:1–11; 11:17, 22, and his threat in 4:21, "Shall I
come to you with a stick?" coupled with his steadily
depreciatory way of speaking of them—"Who sees
anything special in you? And what have you got that
you have not been given?" 4:7—must have stung the
Corinthians and put them in no mood to think reasonably and patiently of Paul's instructions. At any rate,
as compared with what Paul meant it to accomplish
in Corinth, I Corinthians seems to have been a failure,
no matter how greatly it has been prized elsewhere
ever since the first century.

The next stage of the correspondence is reflected in
Paul's words in the early part of II Corinthians, where
he tells them of his distress in Asia, when he was so
utterly and unendurably crushed that he actually

despaired of life itself and felt in his heart that the end must be death, 1:8, 9. It is not like Paul to use strong language like this of physical hardship or peril, but where sacred personal loyalties and understandings were at stake, he might well speak in this way. It there appears that, in the effort to straighten out matters with them, in view of their reaction to I Corinthians, he has made them a visit, for he says he had made up his mind not to make them another painful visit, 2:1; compare 12:14; 13:1. He had finally written another letter, 2:3, 4, so painful and distressing that it was bound to hurt their feelings; in fact, after it was sent, Paul regretted having written it, 7:8. He had sent it to Corinth by the hand of Titus, and then completed his long ministry at Ephesus and proceeded to Troas, where he expected to meet Titus with news of how the letter had been received, 2:12, 13. It was evidently one of those letters which most of us have sometimes to write—letters which are so frank, personal, and severe that we know they will either mend matters or make the breach irreparable. That seems to have been Paul's feeling about this harsh, painful letter, written with many tears and regretted after it was sent, 7:8.

What has become of this third letter of Paul's to the Corinthians? For this description will not fit our I Corinthians at all. It cannot be described as particularly painful to Paul, or hurtful to the Corinthians' feelings, or likely to have been regretted by him after he had sent it. I Corinthians is not the letter written with many tears.

Problems. The problem of II Corinthians is its unity; is it one letter? From the beginning through chapter 9 it is pervaded by a sense of harmony, reconciliation, and comfort. Paul's mind is at last completely at rest. The Corinthians and he are fully reconciled. The letter opens with a commanding statement of the comfort he feels, 1:3-7; the Corinthians are not only on Paul's side, they are in danger of going too far in their enthusiasm for him, 2:5-11. Paul cannot say enough about their present devotion to him, 7:7, 11, 12. "I have the greatest confidence in you. I take the greatest pride in you. I am fully comforted. After all my trouble, I am overjoyed," 7:4.

But suddenly, without any warning at all, this mood of harmony and reconciliation gives place to the very opposite. With the beginning of chapter 10 we are once more in the midst of personal misunderstanding and bitterness, and these continue to dominate the letter to the end. This sudden change of tone is the greatest problem about II Corinthians. Efforts have been made to explain how Paul could have felt so differently in the two parts of the letter. If the parts were arranged in the other order, with the harshness first and the reconciliation second, the matter might be somewhat easier. As it is, it seems impossible that Paul should have sent by the same messenger and as parts of one letter two representations of his own frame of mind so fundamentally contradictory. He cannot have felt as thoroughly satisfied with the Corinthians as he declares in chapters 1-9 and at the same time have been so deeply injured and profoundly incensed as he appears in chapters 10–13. It is psychologically impossible.

This undeniable incongruity between the two parts of II Corinthians naturally suggests that we have in it two letters instead of one—one conciliatory and gratified, the other injured and incensed. And as the early part of II Corinthians clearly looks back upon a painful, regretted letter, the possibility suggests itself that we actually have that letter in chapters 10–13. As we proceed to examine it with that possibility in mind, the possibility grows to a probability. We cannot say a certainty, but no other explanation meets the peculiar conditions so well—the manifest incongruity of the two parts of II Corinthians and the fact that a harsh and painful letter intervened between our I Corinthians and the early part of our II Corinthians. Let us examine the latter part, chapters 10–13, on the theory that it is the missing letter or part of it, always remembering that, when we really hit upon the historical situation that called forth an ancient document, especially a personal letter, it should gain greatly in intelligibility and meaning.

Contents. This four-chapter letter is one long apologia. Paul is on the defensive. Chapter 10 opens with an ironic reference to what was evidently a Corinthian slur upon Paul—that he was humble enough when face to face with them but bold in dealing with them when he was far away. The claim of the Christ party at Corinth that it "belonged to Christ" leads Paul, 10:7, to declare that he "belongs to Christ" just as much as any of them. Other charges and criticisms gleam through these paragraphs: that he boasts too much of his authority, 10:8; that his letters are impressive and telling, but his personal appearance is insignificant, and as a speaker he amounts to nothing, 10:10; that he is beyond his proper missionary field when he tries to control the Corinthians, 10:13; that their present religious authorities are his superiors, 11:5.

The Corinthians are annoyed because Paul will not follow the Greek practice of accepting a fee or at least his support for his preaching, 11:7, 8. And we can understand this, for most of us would much prefer to pay our minister a salary to having him earn his living as a neighborhood artisan or by working in some brother's shop. But the sting of this matter at Corinth lay in the fact that they believed that Paul had accepted money from other churches; in fact, while he was at Corinth, brothers from Macedonia had brought him money. This made them feel that their standing was inferior to that of the Macedonian churches— probably Philippi, in particular, for we know from the letter to the Philippians that they had sent him money repeatedly. Paul probably felt that a gift from his friends there was not at all the same thing as accepting his support from week to week from the Corinthians or anybody else.

The Corinthian way of putting it, however, was that he robbed other churches, letting them pay him to work for the Corinthians, 11:8. But Paul insisted that he would not give up this policy; he would never become a burden to them, and by following this course he would expose their new religious masters, their superfine apostles, for the unprincipled masqueraders they were, 11:12, 13.

The situation roused Paul as he was probably never roused before. The ungrateful belittling of his work by the Corinthians, for whom he had done so much, stirs him to boast like his rivals, foolish as it is to do it. The result is a passage of the most amazing force and vigor—the catalogue of hardships, 11:21–33, which leaves the reader simply breathless at the end. These few informal lines, deeply imbued with Paul's intense feeling, have a power and effectiveness seldom equaled in any literature. Paul will not tell of visions and revelations of the Lord; that would be a profanation of them. He will rather boast of his weaknesses, for it is when he is weak that he is really strong, 12:1–10.

The fires of his indignation have not yet burned out, however, and he resumes his invective against the superfine apostles and his ironic defense of his financial course at Corinth, 12:11–13. They must forgive him that wrong! He insists that neither he nor his lieutenants have ever taken any financial advantage of the Corinthians: "I was clever about it, you say, and took you in by a trick! Yet did I make anything out of you by anybody that I sent to you? . . . . Did Titus make anything out of you?" 12:16b–18.

These piercing thrusts alternate strangely with emotional outbursts of great affection for the Corinthians; indeed, it was clearly his deep personal attachment to them that made him feel their defection so deeply. "It is not your money but yourselves that I want.

. . . . I will be glad to spend all I have and all I am for your sakes," 12:14*b*, 15*a*. But in general the severe tone is maintained almost to the end of the thirteenth chapter. Yet Paul has no desire to be proved right at their expense. "Be what you ought to be, listen to my appeal, agree with one another, live in peace," 13:11*b*.

It is at once apparent that this letter, or part of a letter, was a painful one to write and must have hurt the feelings of the Corinthians. We can also easily understand that, after writing it, Paul might well have felt regret and misgivings about it. In short, it fits remarkably well the picture of the lost intervening letter given us in the early part of II Corinthians. Moreover, without it, chapters 1–9 (with the exception of 6:14—7:1) form a thoroughly intelligible and harmonious unit, ending in chapters 8, 9 with business and personal matters. To recognize in chapters 10–13 the lost third letter to Corinth relieves II Corinthians of its greatest difficulty—the incongruity of its two parts with each other—and restores to us the missing letter or the bulk of it. And so understood the two letters at once take on new clearness and significance. For there are some things in II Corinthians, chapters 1–9, which become clear only as the sequels of other things in chapters 10–13. Thus the catalogue of hardships in II Cor. 6:4–10 (cf. 4:7–11) is a milder form of the great catalogue in 11:21–33.

Such in all probability was the letter sent by the hand of Titus (2:13; 7:6–9, 13, 14) and reflected in II Cor. 2:3, 4; 7:8–12. After writing it, Paul stayed on for a time in Ephesus, concluding his work there, and then proceeded to Troas where he expected to meet Titus with news of the effect the letter had had upon the strained situation. But Titus did not appear, 2:12, 13. There was a good opening for the Christian mission in Troas, but Paul had no heart to establish new churches when his old ones were crumbling beneath his feet, so he said goodbye to them and went on in great distress of mind to Macedonia. His poor human nature could get no relief—there was trouble at every turn, fighting without and fear within, 7:5.

It was then and there in Macedonia that God, who comforts the downcast, comforted him by the coming of Titus, and not only by his coming but by the comfort the Corinthians had given him, for he told Paul how they longed to see him, how sorry they were for what had happened, and how they now took his part, 7:5–7. The long, painful misunderstanding was over. Paul and the Corinthians were reconciled.

So somewhere in Macedonia, perhaps among his loyal Philippians, Paul wrote the fourth letter in this extraordinary correspondence, the letter of reconciliation. From the first sentence it breathes the serene air of harmony, understanding, and comfort. It is no conventional commonplace that it begins with a cry of gratitude to God. The fact that the same great expression was repeated later in Ephesians and I Peter has made it seem little more than a form, but it was more. It was a heartfelt outburst of relief and thanksgiving. "Blessed be the God and Father of our Lord Jesus Christ, the merciful Father and the God always ready to comfort! He comforts me in all my trouble, so that I can comfort people who are in any trouble with the comfort with which I myself am comforted by God." He goes on striking this note of comfort until in this paragraph he has used it, as verb or noun, ten times, 1:3–7, and he returns to it again later in 7:6, 7, 13, 14.

The letter is addressed to the Christians not only of Corinth but of all Greece, 1:1, 2; as though Paul wanted the widest possible circle to share in his joy over his reconciliation with the Corinthians. His jubilant expression of relief and comfort, 1:3–7, is followed by a dark picture of the anguish of spirit he endured before that relief came, 1:8–11.

Just as after any heated controversy it seems necessary to review the main points of misunderstanding in a gentler vein, before cordial personal relations can once more be happily resumed, so to cement the new understanding Paul reviews some of his differences with the Corinthians in a milder tone. They do not need to read between the lines of his letters; there is no ulterior meaning in them, 1:12–14. He is not vacillating, as they have sometimes thought, though he had planned to go to see them before visiting Macedonia and then to revisit them after leaving Macedonia, 1:15–22. As it is, he has stayed away from Corinth and gone to Macedonia first simply to spare them what, before their misunderstandings were cleared up, would have been a painful visit, 1:23—2:3. He refers to his previous letter, 2:4, almost in an apologetic tone: "I was in great trouble and distress of mind, when I wrote you, and I shed many tears as I did it, yet it was not to hurt your feelings, but to make you realize the extraordinary affection I have for you."

The Corinthians have turned about so completely that their former leader in attacking Paul must now be protected by the apostle from their indignation. Paul has forgiven him, and they must restore him to his place in their affections, 2:5–11.

Paul proceeds to tell of his anxiety at not hearing from them through Titus, and soon finds his way, informally and naturally, into one of the most remarkable things anywhere in his letters—an account of his motives and methods in his ministry, 2:12—6:10. This statement of the ideals of the Christian missionary as they appeared to the greatest Christian missionary of the first century, though generally overlooked, is certainly one of the great treasures of Christian literature.

Paul thinks of himself as one of those incense bearers who accompanied triumphal processions through the ancient streets, filling the air with a divine fragrance. He is no peddler of God's message, but like a man of sincerity, commissioned by God and in his presence, in union with Christ he utters Christ's message, 2:12–17.

He needs no credentials with the Corinthians. His authorization is from God, who has qualified him to serve him in the interests of a new agreement, not in writing but of the Spirit, 3:1–6. A greater splendor than shone on Moses' face attends this new revelation, 3:7–18. In such a service Paul never loses heart. He disowns disgraceful, underhanded ways. He will not practice cunning or tamper with God's message, "It is by the open statement of the truth that I would commend myself to every human conscience in the sight of God." It is not himself but Christ Jesus that he is proclaiming as Lord. Paul is the bearer of the heavenly light, 4:1–6.

Much as he has suffered, he has never really known defeat, 4:7–15. He never loses heart. His eyes are on the unseen, eternal values, 4:16—5:5. His hope of a heavenly dwelling gives him confidence, 5:6–10. Christ's love controls him. In union with Christ we are new beings. God has commissioned Paul to proclaim reconciliation—how God through Christ reconciled the world to himself and intrusted Paul with the message of reconciliation, 5:11–21.

In a gentler but still vigorous and dramatic way Paul reviews his hardships, 6:1–10, another grander catalogue of which had formed the climax of the third letter (11:23–33). We can hardly suppose he would have put two such lists into the same letter. Then he looks back and realizes how he has laid bare his inmost emotions and calls upon them to reciprocate. Yet they have already done so; he has the greatest confidence in them; he takes the greatest pride in them. He is fully comforted. After all his trouble he is overjoyed, 6:11–13; 7:2–4.[1]

In a more matter-of-fact tone he resumes the account, broken off at 2:13, of his movements after leaving Ephesus and Troas. At last, in Macedonia, Titus

---

[1] This paragraph is interrupted by the fragment of the first letter to Corinth, 6:14—7:1, which seems to have no possible connection with it.

had rejoined him, and his long suspense was over. The Corinthians had come over to his side without reserve. The harsh letter had indeed hurt their feelings but to good purpose, for it led them to repent. "See how earnest this God-given pain has made you! how eager to clear yourselves, how indignant, how alarmed, how eager to see me, how zealous, how avenging! At every point you have proved that you are clear of this matter." Titus shares his gladness over their changed attitude. Paul can now feel perfect confidence in them. The reconciliation is complete, 7:5–16.

Paul is preparing to return to the east, to Antioch and Jerusalem, and the fund for the Jerusalem Christians, mentioned in I Cor. 16:1, must be ready for him to take with him. It is decidedly interesting for us moderns to see Paul as a money-raiser, chapters 8, 9. He has already told the Corinthians of his instructions to the Galatians about this fund, and now he tells of his efforts to interest the Macedonians in it. It was destined to have a decisive influence upon Paul's life and fate.

As we look back over this correspondence with Corinth, the fullest that we possess from Paul's hand, we therefore recognize four letters written by Paul to the Corinthians:

1. The letter mentioned in I Cor. 5:9, written from Ephesus about A.D. 54 and probably preserved in part in II Cor. 6:14—7:1. The Corinthians replied with a letter asking further questions, which is mentioned in I Cor. 7:1.
2. I Corinthians, written from Ephesus in answer to this letter from Corinth about A.D. 54.

3. The painful letter, mentioned in II Cor. 2:3, 4, 9; 7:8, written from Ephesus about A.D. 55, probably preserved, at least in part, in II Corinthians, chapters 10–13.
4. The letter of reconciliation, written from Macedonia about A.D. 55, preserved in II Corinthians, chapters 1–9.

The intensity of feeling revealed in the third letter has been obscured by traditional forms of translation and even more by its location at the end of II Corinthians, where its sharpness of tone is blanketed and masked by the opposite character of chapters 1–9. It is a proof of the completeness of the Corinthians' repentance that they preserved in their church chest a letter that so gravely reflected upon them. When, a generation later, some great admirer of Paul undertook to assemble what could still be found of his letters, it was natural to mask the indignant reproof of the third letter with the serenity and friendliness of the fourth. Historical situations and chronological sequence did not so much interest the collector of the letters as practical religious values.

As for Paul himself, nowhere else have we such a full-length self-portrait as in the Corinthian correspondence. Its length, variety, and intensity, together with the heights to which it sometimes rises, give it a unique place in the Pauline literature.

LITERATURE

LIETZMANN, HANS. *Handbuch zum Neuen Testament: An die Korinther I–II.* (2d ed.; Tübingen, 1923).

PLUMMER, ALFRED. *Second Epistle of St. Paul to the Corinthians* (New York, 1915).

VI

THE LETTER TO THE ROMANS

✛

Occasion. Paul's work in the Eastern world was done. It had begun in Syria and Cilicia, extended to Galatia, and then passed beyond the borders of Asia into Europe, to the provinces of Macedonia and Greece. The foundations he had laid in Philippi, Thessalonica, Corinth, and Ephesus, and his conviction that his work was to pioneer and break new ground for the Christian mission, now led him to turn his eyes to the West, to Rome and the western Mediterranean, even to Spain.

The name of Spain sounds strange in the New Testament, and especially here in these earliest writings in it. But Roman roads and aqueducts, amphitheaters and bridges, had made Spain a new world. Some of the bridges, built under Augustus, still stand, as solid and serviceable as ever, and the great aqueducts which so awed the medieval Spaniards that they called them "miracles" still fill the traveler with wonder.

It was not only in material progress that Spain was coming to the front in the first century. It is a curious fact that, in the very years when Paul was writing his letters, the torch of Latin literature was passing from Italian to provincial hands, and men from Africa and Spain were beginning to write Latin books. First among these Spanish writers stands Seneca, Nero's tutor, a contemporary of Paul. Martial, Lucan, Columella, Pomponius Mela, and even Quintilian, the great authority on Latin style, were all from Spain. Materially and culturally Spain was, in Paul's day, a new world.

This was the Spain that so attracted Paul as a field of missionary pioneering. He stood now on the pinnacle of the third journey at Corinth—Corinthus Bimaris, Corinth on two seas—with its two ports, Lecheum and Cenchreae. From one he could take ship for the East, for Antioch and Caesarea. From the other he could sail away over the Gulf of Corinth to Brundisium and the Appian Way, which led to Rome.

Paul is poised upon a momentous decision. The West is calling him. He wishes to visit the Roman church and have a hand in shaping its religious life. Galatia and Corinth have shown him into what mistaken attitudes Christian groups might suddenly veer, and his great conception of faith as the central thing in Christian experience must be put before the Roman Christians, if they are to be safeguarded against grave errors. With his vivid messianic expectations Paul can hardly have foreseen much of the vast future that lay before the Roman church. But its immediate importance for the Greek mission was evident enough.

The founding of the Roman church is lost in obscurity. The legend connecting Peter with its foundation is clearly unhistorical. We are left to suppose that Roman visitors to Corinth, Ephesus, or Antioch had carried the gospel back with them to Rome, or that visitors from those places or others like them had carried the good news to Rome and it had taken root there. Paul's friend and employer Aquila was from Rome, Acts 18:2, and he and his wife Priscilla may have had a hand in it. Or perhaps Paul, in his slow voyages about the Mediterranean, had sowed the seed of it in conversation with strangers from Rome on the moonlit deck of some coasting vessel. At any rate, Paul had learned that there were already believers there. He would have liked to lay that foundation himself; but if it was already laid, he would want, above everything else, to go there and make his views and presence felt in the formative period of the church that was taking shape in the capital of the world.

Everything, in short, draws Paul westward, first to Rome and then to Spain. At Corinth he is already well on his way to the West. Only one thing holds him back, but that is a decisive thing—the collection for the poor brothers in Jerusalem. The churches of four provinces—Galatia, Asia, Macedonia, and Greece —have raised the fund Paul had asked for, and now he must take it to Jerusalem.

He might, of course, have sent a draft.[1] The bankers of his day were quite capable of transmitting credits about the Mediterranean. But that would not do. This money was not simply to feed so many hungry mouths; it was to bind the two parts of the Christian body together, to satisfy the Jerusalem group of the reality of their union with the Greek churches of the

[1] M. Rostovtzeff, *Social and Economic History of the Roman Empire* (Oxford, 1926), p. 170.

West. The fund had to be interpreted by Paul in person if it was to do the thing he most hoped for, that is, to reconcile Jerusalem to the Greek mission.

Raising money in the first century or the twentieth carries with it grave responsibilities, and it was these that now controlled Paul's movements—most unfortunately, too, as it turned out. For it was this fatal collection that took Paul to turbulent Jerusalem, already seething as he knew very well, 15:31, with that mad unrest that ten years later was to break into open war. It was this charitable fund that cast him into prison and terminated the missionary work of the best missionary of them all. We may talk as we like about Paul the prisoner and what he could accomplish talking to his guards or writing his letters, but common sense tells us that what a man shut up in prison can accomplish is nothing to what the same man, free and at large, can do.

So Paul must turn his face eastward once more, with the representatives of the contributing churches whose names are given in Acts 20:4. But he cannot turn his back upon Rome and the West without some gesture indicative of what he felt and desired about them. So he writes the letter to the Romans.

Burton called it "prophylactic," designed to safeguard them against dangers he had seen other churches experience. Sanday called it "testamentary," the compressing of his gospel into a letter and bequeathing it as a last will and testament to their keeping. There is truth in both interpretations. The echoes of the Galatian controversy, chapters 3–5, and the manifest allusions to the kind of thing that had happened at Corinth, chapter 14, show that the letter was designed to safeguard the Roman believers against similar errors. And the more ordered manner of presentation that distinguishes Romans from the other letters of Paul, together with the constructive character of the letter, justifies Sanday's description of it as testamentary. Paul may well have felt that he might never be able to reach Rome. Certainly it has, in fact, become what Sanday said it was intended to be—Paul's bequest of his gospel to the Roman Christians and to the world.

Contents. No book of the New Testament appears more formidable to the modern reader than Romans. It is positively awe-inspiring, and this fact considerably impedes the understanding of it. At the risk of violating sound principles of pedagogy and interpretation, let us turn aside for the moment from the front of the letter and see if the student's apprehensions may not be appreciably lightened if we approach it from the rear.

We are here confronted by one of its problems. Chapter 16 is a letter of introduction for Phoebe, an assistant of the church at Cenchreae, who is about to make a journey, apparently to Rome. There is nothing impossible or improbable about that, of course; Aquila and Priscilla had come from Rome to Corinth and established their business first there and then at Ephesus, Acts 18:1, 2, 18, 19, 26. Here in Rom. 16:3 they are mentioned as at the place which Phoebe was about to visit. It would seem that they have gone back to Rome, though at last accounts they were in Ephesus, I Cor. 16:19, where one congregation met in their house. The fact that greetings are sent to Epaenetus, the first man in Asia to turn to Christ, 16:5, rather suggests, however, that Ephesus is Phoebe's destination, not Rome, unless he too has, like Aquila and Priscilla, betaken himself to Rome. The extraordinary number of persons greeted in the chapter, twenty-six in all, is surprising if it is addressed to Rome. Not that Paul might now know that many people in a city he had never visited (he has never been in Rome) but because he is so familiar with their domestic or religious groupings; he knows that Rufus has his mother with him, that Philologus and Julia are together. Nereus has his sister with him, and they form the nucleus of a Christian congregation. So do Asyncritus, Phlegon, Hermes, Patrobas, and Hermas; a group of brothers meets with them. No less than twenty-four people—men and women—are greeted by name, not to mention Rufus' mother and Nereus' sister, 16:13, 15. The Christian record of some of these people is also emphasized. Some of them had worked very hard in the Lord's service: Tryphaena, Tryphosa, Persis. Paul knows of three different congregations and the individuals that they rally around, perhaps in whose houses they meet, 16:5, 14, 15. Some of the people greeted are old comrades of Paul's in missionary work; some have shared imprisonment with him, 16:7.

All this makes it seem extremely probable that Paul is not writing to a strange city but to his well-known and greatly loved Ephesus. Acts records that, on his final journey to the East, he had a special farewell for the elders of Ephesus, 20:17–38. Having just spent more than two years in Ephesus, Acts 19:8–10, he would, of course, have just such knowledge about people and groups there as chapter 16 exhibits and, if a friend were crossing at once to Ephesus, would naturally send them his greetings. On the other hand, it is difficult to see how he could know so much in detail about the Christians in Rome, or how so many of his old friends could so suddenly have removed to Rome. The warning against departing from "the instruction you were given," 16:17, fits Rome poorly if Paul has never been there, and on the whole it is very probable that chapter 16 was written not to Rome but to Ephesus. Short journeys are more numerous and hence more probable than long ones, and it is likely that Phoebe was making the short voyage to Ephesus, not the longer journey to Rome. It may be added that Cenchreae was the Aegean port and slightly favors contacts with Ephesus rather than with Rome. Not that a resident of Cenchreae might not undertake a journey to Rome; only that a woman of Cenchreae would be rather more likely to have contacts—business or social—with Ephesus than with Rome.

The separation of the bulk of the sixteenth chapter from the rest of Romans has very recently received striking support in the Ann Arbor papyrus manuscript of Paul's letters,[1] published by Professor Henry A.

---

[1] Ten leaves of this very ancient papyrus codex of Paul's letters were published by Sir Frederic G. Kenyon in London in 1934 (*Chester Beatty Biblical*

Sanders in 1935 and dated by Wilcken and Gerstinger about A.D. 200. The Michigan leaves include Romans and place the great doxology, 16:25–27, at the end of chapter 15. This so fully accords with the main facts about the sixteenth chapter that it may be said to complete the evidence. The Letter to the Romans ends with the fifteenth chapter and the doxology; the sixteenth chapter is not a part of it; it is a letter of introduction, one of those letters so frequent in the ancient world, referred to by Paul in II Cor. 3:1. There are numerous examples of them in the Greek papyri,[1] and Christians must have made use of them constantly, for in moving about the ancient world, where the inns were so often places of ill-repute and questionable morals, the Christians on their journeys formed the practice of stopping with some Christian brother, to whom they carried letters of introduction. III John is such a letter. So Romans, chapter 16, makes Phoebe known to Paul's old friends, the Christians of Ephesus. That it contains so little in the way of instruction, coupled with the references to instruction previously given, verses 17–20, is natural enough in view of the fact that Paul has so lately come from there by way of Troas and Macedonia.[2]

Papyri, Fasc. III). Thirty others from the same codex were published at Ann Arbor by Professor Henry A. Sanders in 1935, and forty-six others, also from the same codex, have been published by Sir Frederic from the Chester Beatty Collection, in 1936, as Fasc. III, Suppl.

[1] Milligan, *Greek Papyri* (Cambridge, 1910), p. 24.

[2] The objections raised by C. H. Dodd (*The Epistle to the Romans* [New York, 1922], pp. xix and xx) yield readily to this approach: (1 and 2) If Phoebe is going to a city from which Paul has just come, after spending

If we pursue our plan of beginning Romans at the end, we find that the next main portion of it is concerned with an account of Paul's situation and prospects, 15:14–33. Much that has just been said about his situation when he wrote the letter is drawn from these lines. The next preceding section, 12:1—15:13, tells what the Christian's conduct ought to be in the world, the state, and the church. This is our longest statement from Paul's pen of his ideal of Christian behavior and deserves to stand next to the Sermon on the Mount among such statements.

It is, in turn, preceded by a discussion of the hardening of Israel or, as we should say, the Jews' rejection of Christianity, chapters 9, 10, and 11. The fact that the Jews did not accept their own Messiah must have greatly embarrassed the efforts of Paul and other missionaries to interest Greeks in Christianity and called for a good deal of explaining on their part. This is

almost three years preaching in it, it is natural that he should take advantage of the opportunity to greet many old friends there, thus also introducing Phoebe to them personally; that he has no new body of instruction to impart is entirely natural in the situation. The preponderance of greetings creates no difficulty; cf. the letter of Sempronius to his mother (second century A.D.), in which in a letter of seventeen lines eleven persons or groups are saluted; cf. also Deissmann, *Light from the Ancient East* (New York, 1927), pp. 192–94. This sort of thing is a marked and well-known feature of ancient Greek letters. (3) Dodd's excellent solution of 16:16b, "All the churches of Christ wish to be remembered to you," fits Ephesus quite as well as Rome: "Paul was at the moment in close touch with the churches of Galatia, Asia, Macedonia and Achaia, over the business of the relief fund, and it may be that their delegates had already assembled" (*op. cit.*, p. 240). (4) It is no longer necessary to suppose that the letter ended at 15:33; the Ann Arbor papyrus shows that the great doxology, 16:25–27, originally stood after 15:33.

Paul's chief effort to deal with that problem, which was still acute when the Gospel of Matthew was written, some twenty-five years later.

The formidable letter is thus reduced to more feasible proportions when we temporarily dismiss these last two-fifths of it as supplementary matters, not intimately related to its main argument. And the three chapters next preceding may also be detached as setting forth the relation of those who possess faith to sin, law, and the new life, chapters 6, 7, and 8.

The commanding part of Romans, its great argument, is really in what remains—chapters 1-5. The rest is largely sequel to what is established there. Let us now approach this main trunk of the letter from the beginning.

Paul addresses his letter to those in Rome whom God loves and who are called to be his people, describes himself as commissioned in Jesus' name to preach obedience and faith among the heathen, and declares Jesus to be the long-foretold Messiah. And here one cannot forget the epigrams of Matthew Arnold: "The first chapter is to the Gentiles—its purport is: You have not righteousness. The second is to the Jews—its purport is: No more have you, though you think you have."[1] The third chapter goes on to show that, with sin and guilt thus shown to be universal among Jews and Greeks, there has now been revealed through Christ a way of becoming upright and accepted with God; it is the way of faith. Faith with Paul means an attitude of vital dependence upon

[1] *St. Paul and Protestantism* (New York, 1883), pp. 78-79.

God—of repentance, obedience, and spiritual union with him. As such it was in simple fact the germ of all true uprightness, for it accepted his will and made it its own. This new uprightness comes through having faith in Jesus Christ, and it is for all who have faith without distinction. For all men sin and come short of the glory of God, but by his mercy they are made upright for nothing, by the deliverance secured through Christ Jesus.

The relation of the death of Christ to this is set forth in two ways: It is an expiation for man's sin, and it is a revelation of God's own righteousness. It is the fashion nowadays to belittle sin and represent it as a sort of theological fiction. But one does not have to look very far about us in the modern world to find plenty of conduct which cannot be called by any less serious name. And if the modern world were all virtuous, the death of Jesus is by itself enough to prove that sin once existed on the earth, for how else could such a man be brought to such an end?

Paul somehow saw in the death of Christ a great gesture of reconciliation on the part of God. Man deserved the penalty; Jesus took it. He was a sacrifice of reconciliation, to be taken advantage of through faith.

The foes of this doctrine of faith were wont to appeal to Abraham and God's agreement with him. Christ was the completer of that old agreement which promised blessings to Abraham and his descendants. So, in order to benefit by this new salvation, one must be a descendant of Abraham. This was the battle fought out in Galatians. Here again, in Romans, Paul takes the sword from the hands of his Judaizing opponents and turns it against them. For it was by his faith, the Scripture says, that Abraham won God's approval. So for Greeks and Jews, as for Abraham, salvation comes by the way of faith. The story of Abraham is no obstacle to Paul's doctrine of faith; it has become one of its chief supports, chapter 4.

As in chapter 4 Paul has shown how Abraham illustrates his teaching, now in chapter 5 he turns to another great figure of the Jewish theology—Adam. It was a Jewish commonplace that Adam's sin had infected mankind with guilt. Over against this unitary source of condemnation Paul now puts Jesus as a unitary source of acquittal. He has hardly accomplished this, however, when he pulls down the scaffolding, which the figure of Adam had afforded, to leave Christ standing alone.

There is no comparison between God's gift [of salvation] and that offense [of Adam's]. For if one man's offense made the mass of mankind die, God's mercy and his gift, given through the favor of the one man Jesus Christ, have far more powerfully affected mankind. Nor is there any comparison between the gift and the effects of that one man's sin.

This plainly means that the good Christ did far outweighs the harm Adam did, and that can mean only that Paul perceived that good was more fruitful than evil. So the great idea of the superior fruitfulness of good gleams through this paragraph. Once more Paul has brought us, by devious intellectual paths, to a great spiritual outlook.

So in chapters 4 and 5, as Matthew Arnold put it, Paul employs the history of Abraham and Adam to illustrate his doctrine of faith. The great idea that shows now and again through the text is that God has forgiven the world. All man has to do is to accept that forgiveness in faith. This is the great undercurrent of chapters 3, 4, and 5, which form the heart of Romans.

The consequences of this great amnesty are presented, as we have already seen, in chapters 6, 7, and 8. The man who adopts this attitude of faith is saved from sin; it no longer has control of him, chapter 6. He is freed from law, chapter 7; and did anyone ever probe more deeply into the eternal conflict in man's moral nature than Paul does here? The man of faith lives a new life on a new spiritual level, as a son of God, with God's spirit in his heart. It is a tremendous thought, but the fact is he has in some way, however imperfect, attained God's point of view. He views himself and mankind and life itself just a little as God himself views them. God's will becomes his. He has found the river of the love of God. He is at one with the deepest life of the universe, chapter 8.

These are magnificent concepts in religion. No wonder Paul bursts forth at the end into exultation: "If God is for us, who can be against us? . . . . Who can separate us from Christ's love? Can trouble or misfortune or persecution or hunger or destitution or danger of the sword? . . . . In all these things we are more than victorious through him who loved us."

Nothing can separate us from the love of God, shown in Jesus Christ.

So the great letter, in its essential argument, really ends. But Paul must add an appendix to explain the failure of the Jews to accept the culmination of their own religion. To this he devoted chapters 9, 10, and 11. The Jews have indeed failed to see the values in the religion of faith, although Jesus was in truth the Messiah foretold by their own prophets. But it is their reluctance that has given the Greeks their opportunity, and it is the plain duty of the Greeks to seize it and not debate about it; otherwise they in their turn, wild olives as they are, may be pruned away. Still Paul is not without hope that Israel may yet turn to the gospel. "Only partial insensibility has come upon Israel, to last until all the heathen have come in, and then all Israel will be saved." The section on the hardening of Israel ends with another outburst. "How inexhaustible God's resources, wisdom and knowledge are! . . . . For from him everything comes; through him everything exists; and in him everything ends!"

The series of exhortations and moral instructions that follows, 12:1—15:13, is by itself a commanding statement and would attract far more attention if it were not overshadowed by the rest of Romans. But it still amazes us by its penetration, elevation, and breadth. Here is a morality that does not grow old or obsolete. And it is all so inward, so little concerned with the accidental or the temporary. Chapter 12 has to do mostly with relations in the church, while chapter 13 deals with relations to the state. "Love never wrongs a neighbor, and so love fully satisfies the Law."

Chapter 14 reviews some matters already worked out with the Corinthians, for the strong and the weak parties reappear—the party that has knowledge or the emancipated party, on the one hand, and the over-scrupulous party, on the other. "It is the duty of us who are strong to put up with the weaknesses of the immature, and not just suit ourselves. . . . . Christ did not please himself. Therefore treat one another like brothers." The same splendid ideal of Christian courtesy set forth in 1 Corinthians, chapter 13, reappears here. The section of moral instruction ends with a quartet of Old Testament oracles showing the place the heathen were to have in the Kingdom of God and a final benediction. It is in its own way fully equal to the great argument that begins the letter, chapters 1–5.

Paul turns in closing to personal plans and movements. As one peculiarly commissioned to the heathen, he has been moved to write them pretty boldly on some points. He reviews his work in the East and declares that it is now done, and he is looking toward Rome and Spain, but that his visit to them must be postponed until he has taken the collection to Jerusalem. Paul knows that this is a dangerous thing for him to do. "Pray that I may escape from those in Judea who are disobedient, and that the help I am taking to Jerusalem may be well received by God's people, so that, if it is God's will, I may come with a glad heart to see you and enjoy a visit with you," 15:31, 32.

This was the letter Paul sent from Corinth to Rome about A.D. 56. It is almost as though he had carried his gospel as far as he could toward Rome, and then, when he could go no farther, had rolled it into this letter and sent it the rest of the way.

Problems. Romans has its problems. Was it really addressed to a single body of Christians, or was it meant for a wider circle? There seems no reason to suppose that it was more than what it claims to be— a message to the Roman church, written when Paul's responsibilities obliged him to postpone the visit to Rome he had planned. Paul wrote long letters to his friends, as I Corinthians shows.

Lake has assembled evidence that a form of Romans without chapters 15 and 16, and perhaps also without the name of Rome in 1:7 and 1:15, was known in antiquity;[1] it is reflected in the list of chapter headings of the Codex Amiatinus of the Latin Vulgate and finds color in the apparent neglect of these two chapters on the part of Tertullian and Cyprian. Origen seems to have preferred manuscripts that omitted Rome in 1:7, 15. The abbreviated form of the letter may have been produced by Marcion or later hands by reduction—a common practice even today[2]—but its existence in antiquity is by no means certain, and the recent discovery of the Ann Arbor–Chester Beatty papyrus of Paul's

---

[1] *The Earlier Epistles of St. Paul* (London, 1914), chap. vi.

[2] In a recent publication entitled *The Bible, Designed To Be Read as Living Literature: The Old and the New Testaments in the King James Version, 1936*, the Letter to the Romans breaks off with 14:12, followed by the Doxology, 16:25–27. Such reductions are frequent nowadays, and they were not unknown in antiquity.

letters in Greek, dating according to the best paleographers from about A.D. 200 and designated P 46 bears most unfavorably upon it, for the closing chapters are present in the manuscript. This is the oldest of our manuscripts of Paul; it goes back to the time of Tertullian and to the boyhood of Origen.

It is, moreover, agreed that chapter 15 is closely linked in thought with chapter 14. Now, while most manuscripts have the Doxology, 16:25–27, at the end of chapter 16, many have it at the end of chapter 14; some have it in both places, and some omit it entirely. But the new papyrus text (P 46) has it at the end of chapter 15—a strong corroboration of the suggestion that chapter 16, the letter of introduction for Phoebe, is an addition to the great letter. This is the obvious testimony of our oldest witness to the text of Romans.

It is altogether probable that the original form of Romans, as Paul sent it to Rome, consisted of chapters 1–15, plus 16:25–27. When the Pauline corpus was formed at Ephesus about A.D. 90, the Phoebe letter which had been written to Ephesus and preserved there, was appended to it. This is the form of Romans contained in the new papyrus text, about A.D. 200. The benediction was afterward variously shifted, on literary or liturgical grounds, from the end of chapter 15 to the end of chapter 14, or to the end of chapter 16; with the result that some later copyists omitted it in both places, while others inserted it in both.

Kenyon argues that "the difficulty still remains of understanding how a letter of introduction for Phoebe should have been extant without preface or conclusion, and should have been attached to the great Epistle to the Romans."[1] But if the Phoebe letter was originally directed to Ephesus, and the first collection of Pauline letters was made there, as I have sought to show,[2] that might very well have happened. The collectors of the letters would possess in their own church chest an unimportant letter of Paul's, which they might well wish to include in the corpus they were forming; they would be reluctant to publish so meager a letter as a separate unit, as the Letter to the Ephesians, to stand beside the massive letters to Rome and Corinth. Yet they would feel that they must not leave it out altogether. It would not be unnatural for them to append it to one of the longer letters, especially if they knew from Acts that Priscilla and Aquila had a Roman connection. It is enough to say that it was attached to Romans to insure its preservation and circulation, which is precisely what it has done. It could not possibly have been added to either of the letters to Corinth, for a woman of Cenchreae, a suburb of Corinth, would be well known already to the Corinthian Christians; she was, in fact, one of them. As one surveys the Pauline letters, it is difficult to find a better one to which to attach it, and the first collectors and editors of Paul's letters had no hesitation about combining two letters into one, as II Corinthians and Philippians show. Moreover, they seem to have been holding the collection to seven churches, the *typus septiformis ecclesiae;* certainly the collection

[1] *Chester Beatty Biblical Papyri*, Fasc. III, Suppl. (London, 1936), p. xviii.
[2] *Formation of the New Testament* (Chicago, 1926), pp. 28 and 29.

has always contained letters to seven and only seven churches, though they are not always the same seven.

There is something very impressive about Paul as we see him in Romans. To the eye, he may have seemed just a Jewish artisan, wandering from one Mediterranean port to another. But what great concerns were occupying his mind! Carrying a conciliatory gift to the Jewish believers of the East with one hand, with the other he dispatches westward a masterly account of the Christian faith in a letter to the new Greek church at Rome; heroically striving to bring East and West, Jew and Greek, together in the Kingdom of God. Such is the giant figure that shines through the pages of the Letter to the Romans.

LITERATURE

Lake, Kirsopp. *The Earlier Epistles of St. Paul* (London, 1914), chap. vi.

Sanday, William, and Headlam, Arthur C. *The Epistle to the Romans* (New York, 1895).

VII

THE LETTER TO THE PHILIPPIANS

✝

Occasion. Paul was in prison. His years of free wandering about the eastern Mediterranean, carrying the Christian gospel far and wide, were over. His apprehensions about the perils that might await him in Jerusalem, Rom. 15:31, had been only too well founded; compare Acts 20:25, 38; 21:4, 13. He had been mobbed in Jerusalem, arrested there, and transferred to Caesarea, and finally, when he appealed as a Roman citizen to the emperor's court, had been removed to Rome for trial.

All this came to the ears of his faithful friends, the Philippians, and they prepared to stand by him as usual. They had been his partners in this gospel business, Phil. 4:15, 17, ever since he had first come among them. Even when he was at Thessalonica, his next stopping place after leaving Philippi, they had sent money more than once for his needs, Phil. 4:16, and after he left Macedonia and went on to Athens and Corinth, no church but theirs had helped him, 4:15. Indeed, this willingness of his to accept Macedonian— that is, Philippian—aid had been one of the grievances of the Corinthians, II Cor. 11:9. It seems to have made them jealous of the Philippians.

It is clear that the Philippians were a very practical

group, and news that Paul was a prisoner and on his way to Rome, or already there for trial, would stir them at once to aid him. If he had needed their help before, when he was an able-bodied artisan busy at his trade, how much more he must need it now that he was shut up in prison. Ancient prisoners needed money, especially prisoners awaiting trial, for they must have counsel, and the Philippians evidently resolved that what money could do should be done for Paul. So they raised a fund and sent one of their number, a man named Epaphroditus, to wait on Paul, attend to his various wants, and stay with him until his matters were settled. Acts says that Paul lived in Rome for two full years in rented lodgings of his own (28:30), and it is very likely that the rent was paid by the Philippians.

It has been assumed that the Philippians would not know of Paul's being dispatched to Rome until he had arrived there, but of course this is not necessarily true. They may have known of it very soon after he did and have made their arrangements for helping him during the winter that he and his companions in shipwreck spent on the island of Malta, Acts 28:1, 11. It is not at all impossible that Epaphroditus was already in Rome when Paul reached the city, and that the deputation that went out from Rome as far as Appius' Forum and Three Taverns (Acts 28:15) to meet Paul as he approached the city included him; he may even have been their leader. Someone in Rome knew that Paul was coming, and Epaphroditus is the likeliest person we know of to have been informed.

These observations are made because some have sought to date Philippians by calculating how long it would take news of Paul's presence in Rome to reach Philippi, how long it would have taken the Philippians to raise their money and find their man, how long it would have taken him to reach Rome, etc.[1] But when we consider that some time elapsed after Paul's appeal to the emperor's court before he actually started for Rome, and what a slow and unfortunate voyage he had, being shipwrecked and delayed for three months on Malta, Acts 28:1, 11, it is clear that such calculations are futile. The Philippians had begun to help Paul with money immediately after he left their town for Thessalonica, years before, Phil. 4:15, 16. They were prompt in taking action. They would not have waited now to hear that Paul had actually arrived in Rome before taking measures for his relief.

Problems. The problem of Philippians is its unity. Considered as a single letter, it presents a most disorderly series of materials—teachings, warnings, news about himself, acknowledgments, accounts of Epaphroditus. In chapter 1 he is making the best of his imprisonment; in chapter 2 he is sending Epaphroditus back to them; in chapter 3 he bursts forth against the Judaizers; in chapter 4 he acknowledges the gift Epaphroditus has brought him. Paul is usually much more orderly than this.

Moreover, there is between 3:1 and 3:2 a break so harsh as to defy explanation. In 3:1 all is serene; they

---

[1] J. B. Lightfoot, *St. Paul's Epistle to the Philippians* (4th ed.; London, 1878), pp. 36 f.

must not mind Paul's repeating himself, for it is for their good. But in the next verse he breaks out against the Judaizers with an intensity unsurpassed even in Galatians.

Look out for those dogs, those mischief-makers, with their amputation! We are the true circumcision who worship God by his spirit. . . . . If anyone thinks he can rely on his physical advantages, still more can I! I was circumcised when I was eight days old, I am a descendant of Israel. I belong to the tribe of Benjamin. I am a Hebrew, and the son of Hebrews.

It reminds one of II Cor. 11:22: "If they are Hebrews, so am I! If they are Israelites, so am I! If they are descended from Abraham, so am I!"

This sharp change after 3:1 (where Paul seems to be closing his letter and saying goodbye) raises the question whether our Philippians does not break at this point into two letters: 1:1—3:1 and 3:2—4:23. This division would entirely relieve the disorder of treatment we have noted. 3:2—4:23 reflects the coming of Epaphroditus with the Philippians' gift, 4:10–19, which Paul gratefully and somewhat playfully acknowledges. The Philippians are his partners in the gospel enterprise, entitled to the profits—of course, spiritual—that it will produce. It is a long time since he has needed their help, but he welcomes it now as an expression of Christian interest. The tone of the paragraph suggests that Epaphroditus has only recently come.

He seems to have brought bad news of the activities of the Judaizers at Philippi, so that Paul bursts out in condemnation of them with his first words, 3:2, 3, just as he does in Gal. 1:6. We must suppose the salutation of this letter was omitted when it was combined with 1:1—3:1. If so, the parallel to Gal. 1:6 is complete.

The idea that our Philippians combines two letters of Paul to Philippi finds some corroboration in the fact that Polycarp of Smyrna, writing to the Philippians some fifty years later, reminds them of the blessed and glorious Paul, "who when he was among you in the presence of the men of that time taught accurately and steadfastly the word of truth, and also when he was absent wrote letters to you, from the study of which you will be able to build yourselves up into the faith given you," 3:2.[1] Some knowledge or consciousness that Paul had written more than once to Philippi may have lingered in Asia, where the Pauline letters were first collected and published. It is of course possible that Polycarp is speaking generally; he knew Philippians and supposed that Paul wrote more than once to the Philippian church. But he clearly implies that the Philippians still have the letters and can study them, though he probably knew very well that they had only the published collection of Paul's letters. On the whole, the more closely one examines the passage, the more it seems to favor the recognition of two letters in our Philippians. Certainly this first direct allusion to our Philippians in Christian literature speaks of it as "letters."

Contents. We may, therefore, regard 3:1—4:23 (or 4:20, if vss. 21–23 be grouped with 1:1—3:1) as

[1] K. Lake, *Apostolic Fathers* (London, 1912), I, 287.

Paul's letter of thanks to the Philippians, written on receiving their gift through Epaphroditus. It opens with a vigorous denunciation of the Judaizers, contrasting their legalistic attitude with Paul's reliance upon Christ and his aspiration toward Christian perfection through him, 3:2–16. On the other hand, the Christian profession must not be made a mask for passion and vicious self-indulgence; we belong to a higher realm, 3:17–21. Personal instructions, crisp admonitions, and farewells follow, 4:1–7.

In the disappointment and bitterness of his imprisonment, Paul had learned the great lesson of directing his thoughts. He might so easily have fallen into resentment, discontent, and despair. Here he was, the most competent missionary of the new cause, shut up in a meaningless imprisonment, while less capable men quarreled over the missionary task. That way madness lies! Instead, he tells the Philippians what he had found out himself, in the hardest possible school: "Let your minds dwell on what is true, what is worthy, what is right, what is pure, what is amiable, what is kindly—on everything that is excellent or praiseworthy. Do the things that you learned, received, and heard from me, and that you saw me do. Then God who gives peace will be with you," 4:8, 9.

He goes on, in conclusion, to acknowledge what the Philippians had sent him. Not that he really needed anything; he can adjust himself to short rations or long; he can do anything through him who gives him strength. "But it was very kind of you to share my difficulties." It reminds Paul of the repeated help they had given him in former years. They have been his business partners in this gospel enterprise. "I am fully supplied with what I have received from you through Epaphroditus," 4:10–20.

Paul must have written the Philippians a letter of acknowledgment of their gift when he received it, and this must be either that letter of acknowledgment or a repetition of it. But there is no suggestion of the latter; it is altogether more probable that this is the original letter sent to Philippi to acknowledge the coming of Epaphroditus with the fund they had provided for Paul's needs and trial.

There is nothing improbable in the idea that two short notes to Philippi should have been combined into one longer letter; we have already seen the same thing done in II Corinthians and in Romans—two letters joined together or a short letter appended to a long one. The men who first assembled and published the letters of Paul were more interested in a few long units than in a long series of short notes. They were practical men with immediate religious uses in mind, perhaps occasional church reading, not as Scripture but as preaching; they were not scholars or pedants, absorbed in the technique of publication.

So Paul condemns the Judaizers and thanks the Philippians. Time goes on and Epaphroditus, who has become very useful to Paul, falls sick. Rome is not a very healthy place, and Epaphroditus may have had the Roman fever, still so familiar. At any rate he is very sick and at death's door. News of his illness reaches Philippi, and the Philippians are greatly distressed. Their representative, who they had hoped would be so useful to Paul, has now become an added care to him. But at length Epaphroditus recovers, at least sufficiently to be sent home. And then lest, when he reappears on the streets of Philippi, the Philippians blame him for leaving Paul still a prisoner, Paul puts into his hand a letter which will silence any criticism of him and make the Philippians respect what he has done for Paul. This second letter is preserved in Phil. 1:1—3:1, to which some think may be added 4:21–23. It begins with an expression of his deep attachment to the Philippians, who certainly seem from first to last to have been the most loyal and understanding friends he had, 1:3–11. He tells them reassuringly of the effect his arrest and imprisonment have had in rousing the courage of Christian preachers. He is clearly facing his trial and confidently hopes that his courage may be equal to the occasion, 1:12–20. He is fully reconciled to his fate whatever it may be. Yet he believes that he will live to be of further service to them. They for their part must not waver, 1:21–30. They must make Christ and his humility and obedience their model. They must be all the more harmonious and obedient now that Paul cannot come and train them. If his life is to be a sacrifice, he is glad to have it so, 2:1–18.

He means to send Timothy to them soon, but now he is sending back Epaphroditus, who has been so very sick but is now able to travel back to Philippi. He calls him his fellow-laborer, his fellow-soldier, and says he had risked his life to serve Paul. "So give him a hearty Christian welcome." And so goodbye, 2:19—

3:1. Since the letter of 3:2—4:20 seems rounded out by the doxology in verse 20, verses 21–23 probably belong to the other letter and should be read immediately after 3:1.

What we possess in Philippians is, therefore, not just a single letter but a section of Paul's correspondence with Philippi, covering two situations: the coming of Epaphroditus with their gift and the return of Epaphroditus weeks or months later, after he had been incapacitated by illness. Some time certainly elapsed between these two situations, perhaps a year, for news has gone to Philippi that Epaphroditus is sick and word has come back that Epaphroditus has heard of this, 2:26. The two letters may have been written as much as a year apart. As they now stand, the later one precedes the earlier, just as is the case with the two letters preserved in II Corinthians.

The Philippian letters were probably written from Rome about A.D. 59, or 59 and 60, respectively. (The question of their origin in an imprisonment at Ephesus will be considered among the "Problems" of Colossians.) They give us significant glimpses of Paul in his relations with the one of all his churches which seems to have stood nearest to him and done most to support and cheer him in his missionary journeys and in his subsequent imprisonment.

LITERATURE

Lightfoot, J. B. *St. Paul's Epistle to the Philippians* (4th ed.; London, 1878).

Vincent, Marvin R. *The Epistles to the Philippians and to Philemon* (New York, 1897).

VIII

THE LETTER TO THE COLOSSIANS

✠

Occasion. Between the material world and the divine spirit the ancients felt that there must lie a great gulf almost impossible to bridge. Yet man must cross it if he was to realize his religious destiny and enter into communion with God. Some thinkers found a way through the doctrine of Aeons, intermediate qualities or even beings, probably derived from the Platonic "Ideas." These aeons were conceived as rising, tier above tier, toward God; and by communing with one after another one might, through reflection, asceticism, and self-discipline, rise from material things into full fellowship with the Divine. It was like climbing a vast spiritual ladder.

When such thinkers entered the Christian church, they of course brought much of their old philosophical thinking with them and fitted it to their new Christian faith and experience. To them Christ became at once one of these divine aeons—the greatest, perhaps, but still only one of many. Communion with him seemed perfectly natural to them. So their old philosophy and their new faith fitted together. Their communion with these aeons was stimulated, they believed, by ascetic practices—fasts, vigils, and the observance of set days.

This type of Christian thought and life had appeared at Colossae, one of the cities on the Lycus River in the Roman province of Asia. Christianity had probably reached Colossae and the near-by cities of Hierapolis and Laodicea as a result of Paul's work at Ephesus, when, as Acts says, everyone in Asia heard the Lord's message, Acts 19:10, 26. The leader of the Colossian church was Epaphras, and in his distress at the philosophic views of these Colossian brothers he sought out Paul in his prison at Rome and laid the situation before him, Col. 1:7, 8; 4:12, 13.

Not only did this system rob Christ of his supremacy in Christian experience; it also created within the church an esoteric group of Christians, claiming superiority over the rank and file of the brotherhood. It created classes within the fellowship and was at variance with the strong democratic strain that marked the early church. In the face of these difficulties Epaphras would very naturally seek out the man who had brought the Christian gospel to the province of Asia in the first place, and ask his counsel.

Contents. So to Rome, to those rented lodgings which Acts mentions and which the Philippians probably paid for, came Epaphras with his problem, 1:7, 8. Paul deals with it in a letter written probably in A.D. 60 or 61. He begins with a paragraph of thanksgiving and prayer for them, going on to describe the place Christ has in the Christian experience. He sees in Christ the embodiment of the divine Wisdom, through which God had made the world and which was the reflection of his nature.[1] Paul had realized the important fact that thought, feeling, conviction, and truth have only a very limited reality unless they are embodied in someone. In Jesus he saw the very Wisdom of God embodied in a human life. Christ was the sole head of the church and possessed all the divine fullness. Christians needed no other intermediaries, or mediators, to help them scale the heights and make their way into the presence of God, 1:3–23.

This idea of the reincarnation of Christ in them is the supreme mystery, the central inner secret, of Christianity. The Colossians were familiar with mystery religions, with their dying and rising savior-heroes in whose life and experience the initiate, through initiatory rites and a sacred meal, was made to participate. Such faiths had their "mysteries"— not only their rites of initiation but their disclosures of secret spiritual truths. Here, then, is indeed such a "mystery" or secret—Christ within them, in their hearts, the promise of a future glorification.

There is nothing aristocratic or exclusive about this possession; it is the property of all. There are to be no classes in the church, no superior and inferior groups. The highest levels of Christian achievement are open to all. They must not be misled by specious arguments but live in vital union with Christ, rooted and built up in him, 1:24—2:7.

What these specious arguments were is indicated in the following paragraph. No one must be allowed to exploit them through philosophic pretensions. In

[1] Wisd. of Sol. 7:26; 9:9.

Christ all the fulness of God's nature lives embodied, and in union with him all believers will be filled with it too. He is the head of all their principalities and dominions, their intermediary aeons, and makes them all superfluous. They have been united with him in the rite of baptism, buried with him there to rise again to life with him. His death is the token of their forgiveness and the defeat of all these imaginary powers which were absorbing their attention, 2:8-15.

On the practical side, no one could call them to account for what they ate or drank or did about fixed days—external matters with no meaning or value for the spiritual life. Petty rules, such as "You must not handle," "You must not taste," "You must not touch," are mere human regulations, of no religious value. The Colossians must not let themselves be imposed upon by the conceit of philosophic pretensions and ascetic poses. These self-imposed devotions, self-humiliation, and self-mortification are really only a catering to the flesh they seem to deny, 2:16-23.

Having disposed of the ideas and practices of the Colossian errorists, 1:1—2:23, Paul proceeds with some practical admonitions. As they have died with Christ, they must fix their thoughts on things that are above. They must treat their physical nature as dead, as far as evil is concerned. They have put on a new self. Old distinctions of Greek and Jew no longer matter, for Christ is in them all. They must clothe themselves with kindness, forbearance, and love. They must live their whole life as followers of the Lord Jesus, 3:1-17.

Special instructions are given to wives and husbands, children and fathers, slaves and masters. It has been suggested that these reflect existing household rules, but thus far no substantial evidence has been produced for the existence of such household rules in antiquity. The reappearance of these injunctions in Ephesians and I Peter is of course due to the direct literary influence of Colossians upon their writers, 3:18—4:1.

Tychicus is the bearer of the letter and with him travels the young Onesimus, a runaway slave, who is returning to his master Philemon. But a notable band of Paul's lieutenants is gathered about him at Rome; Aristarchus of Thessalonica—who had gone with him when he carried the poor fund back from the shores of the Aegean to Jerusalem—Mark, Jesus Justus, their own minister Epaphras, Luke the doctor, who had been with Paul on his voyage and shipwreck, Demas— all these are with Paul at Rome. The presence of such a significant group of his close friends with him possibly suggests that his affairs are nearing a crisis, when as many of his intimates as possible would naturally want to gather about him. Paul himself is clearly facing an examination or trial, when he must try to make the authorities understand his message and mission, 4:2–14.

Colossians closes with a reference to a "letter from Laodicea," which they are told to read. The Colossians are to share their letter with the church at Laodicea and to read the letter that is coming from there. They are also to give a message to Archippus, who seems from the connection to belong to the Laodicean church and to have some special responsibility, 4:15–18.

What was this letter from Laodicea, and what has become of it? What was the special responsibility that belonged to Archippus, and why should the Colossians join in urging him to perform it? These are questions that Colossians does not answer, but on which important light is thrown by its companion letter, Philemon.

Problems. The problem of Colossians is its authenticity—its genuineness as actually a work of Paul himself. Some scholars have felt that the almost Gnostic character of the views that are opposed in the letter points to a time considerably later than Paul's day, while the doctrine of Christ that it presents in order to correct these views is out of keeping with the Christology that marks Galatians, Corinthians, and Romans. The letter is certainly unlike Paul's accepted letters in some ways, but it is a mistake to suppose that he always talked about the same things or talked in the same way. This unlikeness, so far as it exists in Colossians, is naturally explained by the novelty of the problem set before Paul by the situation at Colossae. This reflects the existence there of what may be considered an incipient form of that Gnosticism that ran riot in second-century Christianity. But it may just as well be viewed as a phase of Neo-Platonism, with its system of intermediary aeon-ideas. Indeed the Colossian error, as Paul considered it, may be thought of as standing midway between that older philosophy and its later reflorescence in Christian Gnosticism.

But, further than this, the supposition that someone was imitating Paul and writing letters in his name implies that Paul was already well known as a writer of letters, and this would come about only through the collection and publication of his letters, which would lead people to think of him as a letter-writer and be prepared to respect a letter that bore his name. But he was not so regarded until long after his death, indeed until after the publication of Luke-Acts, which knows nothing about him as a letter-writer. This point has been neglected in the consideration of the authenticity of II Thessalonians, Colossians, and other items in the Pauline literature, but it must be steadily borne in mind. No one would think of putting forth a letter of his own written under Paul's name unless he had somehow become accustomed to respect letters bearing Paul's name and to think of him as characteristically a writer of letters. But that would come about only through the collection and publication of his letters.

And Colossians, so far from being subsequent to the first collection and publication of Paul's letters, was a part of that first collection and was freely drawn upon by the writer of Ephesians, as we shall see, along with the other genuine letters of Paul, in writing his letter.[1] The possibility that Colossians was not written by Paul is reduced by this fact almost to the vanish-

[1] I Clem., chap. 46; cf. Lightfoot, *Clement of Rome* (2d ed.; London, 1890), I, 397; II, 140.

ing-point. Paul's references in II Thessalonians to a possible letter purporting to be from him, 2:2 (cf. 3:17), do not mean that pseudo-Pauline letters are going about—only that he is determined not to be misquoted at Thessalonica on the point he is making. Paul's early fame in the church was as a missionary and preacher, as Acts plainly shows. It was not until some of his letters were collected for publication that people would begin to think of him as characteristically a writer of letters, and so it would occur to anyone to produce letters in his name.

Neither Philippians nor Colossians is explicit about where it was written; it is clear only that Paul is in prison. He was in prison often, however, as he states in II Cor. 11:23—he had known "far more imprisonments" than his rivals had experienced. Acts, however, records only one imprisonment of Paul up to the time when he wrote this part of II Corinthians—that at Philippi, Acts 16:22–40. Of course, Acts is not a biography of Paul and, if it has the apologetic interests that are often claimed for it, would bear lightly upon Paul's prison record. But some scholars maintain that Paul was imprisoned for a time in Ephesus and wrote some or all of the prison letters there.

It is true that Paul was, even according to Acts, the subject of a serious disturbance in Ephesus, 19:23—20:1. He also speaks in his final letter to the Corinthians, II Cor. 1:8–10, of the heartbreaking experiences of his last days in Ephesus; he had been utterly crushed, actually despaired of life, felt the end must be death, so deadly was the peril. In his second letter to

Corinth, I Cor. 15:32, written from Ephesus, he speaks of having fought wild animals at Ephesus. All these touches are interpreted by some as pointing to an imprisonment at Ephesus.

Moreover, Ephesus would be a much more convenient and natural place for the slave Onesimus to take refuge in, when he ran away from Laodicea, and for Epaphras of Colossae to journey to, to consult Paul, and for the Philippians to send Epaphroditus to, with their funds for Paul's defense and other needs.

Certainly Paul experienced more imprisonments than we know of, and one of these may very well have been in Ephesus, though his words in the first paragraph of II Corinthians more probably refer to his inward agony of mind over the hostility of the Corinthians. The fight with beasts at Ephesus certainly must be figurative, perhaps referring to his encounter with the mob, Acts 19:29–31.

It does not however follow that Philippians, Colossians, and Philemon were written from his Ephesian prison. As for the flight of Onesimus, he may just as well be thought of as wishing to get to Rome and see the world, and to get a safe distance away from his injured owner; to take refuge in Ephesus might have been easier for him, but it would not have been half so effective. I know a runaway German boy whose first stop was Australia, and an Edinburgh runaway of my acquaintance brought up on the Mississippi River; it is a mistake to judge runaways by the sober standards of us stay-at-homes.

Nor is it unlikely that Epaphras would be sufficiently in earnest about consulting Paul to journey from Colossae to Rome. Paul had traveled from Antioch to Ephesus to preach the gospel there, and his converts were, many of them, his equals in zeal if not in power.

The vital question is in which of the two atmospheres each of these letters reads most appropriately. The references in Philippians to the imperial guard, 1:13, and to the emperor's household, 4:22, to the rival preachers, 1:14–18, to the representative character of Paul's case, 1:7, 30, and to the seriousness of his situation, 1:20–26; 2:17, 18, rather favor Rome as the place of Paul's prison. Nor would there be anything like the need for Philippian aid if Paul was in prison in Ephesus, surrounded by his Ephesian friends; to send Epaphroditus to him to wait on him at Ephesus would be gratuitous, to say the least. It is safe to say Philippians is not written from Ephesus.

As for Colossians and Philemon, Col. 1:24, 29; 2:1; 4:3, 4, seem to reflect a similar view of his trial as a test case, more appropriate in the Roman situation than at Ephesus. On the whole, the letters seem to fit better in Paul's final imprisonment at Rome than in a hypothetical one at Ephesus.

The researches of Weidinger into earlier lists of household rules (*Haustafeln*) have failed to disclose any serious literary parallels for Col. 3:18—4:1; the Wisdom of Phocylides (second century B.C.), to which he appeals, lacks precisely the balance—wives, husbands; children, fathers; slaves, masters—which is the distinctive feature of the Colossian passage (cf. Karl

Weidinger, *Das Problem der urchristlichen Haustafeln* [Leipzig, 1928]; *Die Haustafeln* [Tübingen, 1928]).

As Dr. John Knox has suggested, the passage is probably best explained on the ground that the matter of the relations of masters and slaves has been raised in an acute form by the return of Onesimus to his master, Col. 4:9 (cf. Philemon, vss. 10, 16). The very meager and inadequate statement of the duties of wives and husbands and of children and parents is no more than a foil for the really acute matter of slaves and masters to which they lead up, and which is given twice as much attention as both of them together.

In his interesting and valuable *Preface to Morals* (1929), Mr. Walter Lippmann has expressed the opinion that no great ancient teacher of high religion ever thought of teaching the highest wisdom to everybody. But this is just what Paul expressly sought to do: "In spreading the news of him, we warn everyone and teach everyone all our wisdom, in order to bring everyone to Christian perfection," Col. 1:28. Paul could hardly have been more explicit or emphatic: everyone—everyone—all—everyone—perfection. But Mr. Lippmann says: "Yet no teacher has ever appeared in the world who was wise enough to know how to teach his wisdom to all mankind. In fact, the great teachers have attempted nothing so utopian. They were quite well aware how difficult for most men is wisdom, and they have confessed frankly that the perfect life was for a select few. It is arguable, in fact, that the very idea of teaching the highest wisdom to all men is the recent notion of a humanitarian and romantically democratic age, and that it is quite foreign to the thought of the greatest teachers" (*Preface to Morals*, p. 199). It is interesting to find Paul in Colossians emphatically teaching the very thing modern progressive thinkers have found out for themselves and consider new. So timely and modern is this central idea of Colossians.

LITERATURE

ABBOTT, T. K. *Epistles to the Ephesians and to the Colossians* (New York, 1909).

LIGHTFOOT, J. B. *St. Paul's Epistles to the Colossians and Philemon* (3d ed.; London, 1879).

IX

THE LETTER TO PHILEMON

✝

Occasion. One of the chief features of life in the Roman Empire was slavery. It was everywhere and all-embracing. Christianity must have been constantly in contact with it from the beginning, but in the New Testament slavery as a living issue meets us first in the Letter to Philemon.

The Roman road that ran most directly east from Ephesus passed through Magnesia and Tralles to Laodicea, and eleven miles farther up the valley of the River Lycus reached Colossae. Six miles north of Laodicea and in full view of it, across the Lycus Valley, was Hierapolis. Hierapolis, Laodicea, and Colossae were thus very near neighbors and in constant communication. There were Christians in all three, and Epaphras who had come to Paul about the difficulties in the Colossian church felt a responsibility for them all. "I can testify," Paul wrote to the Colossians, "how anxious he is about you and the brothers in Laodicea and Hierapolis," Col. 4:13. It is clear that these Christian groups were in close relations.

Some of these Christian brothers in Phrygia were slaveowners, of course, and from one of them a slave named Onesimus had run away, taking with him such valuables as he could lay his hands on, Philemon, verse

18. Such occurrences were frequent in antiquity. Of course, rewards were offered for the return of such runaways as Onesimus, as the Greek papyri show. Here is one circulated in Egypt in 156 B.C.:

The twenty-fifth year, Epeiph 17th. A slave belonging to Aristogenes, son of Chrysippus, an envoy from Alabanda, has run away. His name is Hermon; he is also called Nilus. He is by birth a Syrian of Bambyce, eighteen years old, of middle height, smooth face, strong calves, cleft chin, mole to the left of his nose, scar over the left corner of his mouth, two foreign letters tattooed on his right wrist. He has three minas in gold coin, ten pearls, and an iron collar with an oil-flask and shaving tools on it, and is wearing a short cloak and apron.

Whoever brings him back will receive two talents of copper; if he reports him at a temple, one talent; if with a responsible and law-abiding person, three talents. Anyone so desiring give information to the governor's representatives.

With him ran away Bion, a slave of Callicrates, one of the chief officers at the court; short, broad-shouldered, thin-legged, with light-blue eyes; when he ran away wore a cloak and slave's leathern girdle, and took a woman's cosmetic box worth six talents, and five thousand copper drachmas.

Whoever brings him back will receive the same reward as for the above mentioned. Inform the governor's representatives about this one also.[1]

Rewards were doubtless offered for Onesimus' return, but it was Paul who sent him back. He seems to have made his way as far as Rome, where he had some-

---

[1] Goodspeed and Colwell, *Greek Papyrus Reader* (Chicago, 1935), No. 59.

how gotten acquainted with Paul and become a Christian. Paul had learned that he was a slave and had persuaded him to return to his master, and when Tychicus made his journey to Colossae with the Letter to the Colossians, in A.D. 60 or 61, Onesimus went with him.

Perhaps it was the coming of Epaphras from Colossae, Col. 1:7; 4:12, 13, that had precipitated matters. He may have recognized Onesimus from having seen him in his master's house in Phrygia, at Colossae or Laodicea. He knew the Christians of all three cities. Perhaps his coming had led Onesimus to tell Paul the whole story. At any rate Paul feels obliged to send him back to his master. But he puts in his hands a letter to Philemon, intended to protect Onesimus from punishment and reinstate him with his master.

The letter is addressed to "our dear fellow-worker Philemon, and our sister Apphia and our fellow-soldier Archippus, and the church that meets in your house." The "your" is singular, and it is evident that Philemon's house is meant. The usual ancient way, and certainly Paul's way, was to put the important member of a group of two or three first: Paul and Sosthenes, I Cor. 1:1; Paul and Timothy, II Cor. 1:1 and Philemon, verse 1; Paul and Silvanus and Timothy, I, II Thess. 1:1; Stephanas and Achaicus and Fortunatus, I Cor. 16:15, 17.

Philemon, it appears, has a house large enough to accommodate the meetings of a Christian congregation and so becomes, as Paul sometimes puts it, the host of the church, Rom. 16:23. At Ephesus one congregation met in the house of Aquila and Prisca, I Cor. 16:19, Rom. 16:5. At Corinth the church met in the house of Gaius, Rom. 16:23. At Laodicea one congregation met in the house of Nympha, Col. 4:15.

Apphia is apparently the wife of Philemon, and Archippus, Paul's "fellow-soldier," is probably the minister of the church. He is also referred to in Col. 4:17, where a message is sent him by way of the Colossians: "Tell Archippus, 'See that you perform the Christian service you have been assigned.' " In the preceding lines Paul has been speaking about the neighboring city of Laodicea: "Remember me to the brothers in Laodicea. . . . . When this letter has been read to you, have it read to the church in Laodicea also, and see that you read the letter that is coming from there. And tell Archippus, ..." This plainly implies that Archippus is in Laodicea. If he were in Colossae, why should the Colossians have to "tell" him? He would be present at the meeting of the church and hear the message without being told.

But if Archippus is in Laodicea, then Philemon and Apphia are also, and so is the church that meets in Philemon's house. The letter to Philemon was a letter to Laodicea,[1] and it must not be overlooked that it was addressed not only to Philemon and Apphia but to Archippus and the church that met in Philemon's

---

[1] The damage done to Laodicea by an earthquake about A.D. 60, according to Tacitus *Annals* xiv. 27, seems to have done the city no lasting injury (W. M. Ramsay, *Letters to the Seven Churches of Asia* [New York, 1905], p. 173).

house. And yet it is a personal letter, for it concerns Philemon's personal affairs—his treatment of his slave Onesimus who had run away from him and was now being returned to him by Paul. The letter deals with the matter of how Philemon is to receive the runaway and what he is to do with him. Under the cruel ancient system a master could do anything he liked with a runaway slave. Slaves were regularly examined under torture and might be compelled by their masters to fight with wild animals in the arena. Slaves who provoked their masters were unmercifully beaten. The whole picture is so terrible that modern attention instinctively turns from it.

It was a very serious thing to put Onesimus once more into the power of his injured owner; Philemon could do almost anything he pleased with him and still be within the Roman law and in line with the attitude of his contemporaries. Paul is putting Onesimus in the utmost peril. Even if Philemon were himself humane and kindly, he might think he owed a duty to other slaveowners to safeguard the institution by making an example of Onesimus. He might think he had a duty to his "class." The enormous number of slaves in the Roman world made the fear of a slave uprising very real.

Of course, sending a slave back to his owner seems strange to the modern mind. We remember the Underground Railroad of the northern states of the Union, in the fifties and sixties, with its "stations" in the cellars of courageous abolitionists who abhorred slavery and sought in every way to defeat it. But slavery was far more deeply intrenched in Paul's world than in the United States of eighty years ago. Onesimus would never be safe anywhere until his status with his master was rectified.

Paul took a fearful risk when he sent Onesimus back with Tychicus, and, while we instinctively think of Colossians as the main item in Tychicus' mission, Paul was probably much more anxious about what would happen to Onesimus when he presented himself at Philemon's door. So he puts into his hand a letter, courteously appealing to Philemon on behalf of Onesimus, especially as the young man is now a Christian and should be received by Philemon as a brother in Christ.

Contents. It is to be noted that the letter is addressed not only to Philemon, Apphia, and Archippus but to the church that meets in Philemon's house, and so the matter of the treatment Philemon gives Onesimus will have to be settled in the presence of the congregation. Paul lines up the moral sentiment of this whole Christian group in support of his appeal for Onesimus. And while he speaks throughout in a most courteous tone, the note of authority is not lacking; he does not fail to remind Philemon that he is no less an ambassador of Christ, though just now a prisoner for him, verse 9. Whatever Onesimus may have stolen Paul undertakes to make good, verses 18, 19. Dark as his position is at Rome, he still hopes to revisit Asia and come to Laodicea, verse 22. The same circle reported in Col. 4:10–14 is listed as sending greetings, verses 23, 24. Only Jesus Justus is omitted.

It seems clear that this is the letter referred to in Col. 4:16 as to come from Laodicea, and that the same motive that led Paul to include the whole Christian group that met in Philemon's house in the address of that letter would lead him to wish the Colossian church to be aware of the case of Onesimus and what he had asked of Philemon. The case of Onesimus is to be settled not by Philemon alone, in private, but in the presence of the Christian congregation that meets in his house at Laodicea, and also with the full knowledge of the Colossian church as well. The social pressure of these two congregations is being brought to bear upon Philemon. And why not, if a man's life was at stake? Could Paul have done less? Had he any business to gamble with another man's life, even though that man was only a runaway slave?

Problems. This is the answer to Lightfoot's question, "Why should a letter, containing such intimate confidences, be read publicly in the Church, not only at Laodicea, but at Colossae, by the express order of the Apostle?"[1] Of course, this question is automatically disposed of by the undoubted fact that the letter, however intimate, is itself specifically addressed to "the church that meets in Philemon's house," verse 2. If it was to be read before one church, by Paul's own order, the addition of another church cannot be said to introduce any new element. Certainly Paul himself manifestly disclaims any such intimate character for the letter as Lightfoot proposed. It was no time for

[1] *St. Paul's Epistles to the Colossians and Philemon* (3d ed.; London, 1879), p. 279.

punctilio; it was a matter of life and death. Wieseler, the leading advocate of this view, was right in describing the identification of Philemon with the Letter from Laodicea as "scarcely open to a doubt."[1] The view gains additional probability from the fact that Paul does not describe the companion letter as the Letter to the Laodiceans—it was only secondarily to them; it was primarily to Philemon, the master of Onesimus, so it is simply "the letter from Laodicea," Col. 4:16.

The whole matter seems quite plain. The Colossians are to get in touch with Archippus, tell him to perform his Christian duty unflinchingly, and say that Paul wishes the Laodiceans to see the Colossians' letter and that they understand that a letter from Paul has also been received at Laodicea, which Paul wishes them to see, Col. 4:16, 17. This would inevitably lead to an exchange of letters between the two churches, just as Paul desired.

[1] "The opinion of Wieseler," says Vincent (*Epistles to the Philippians and to Philemon*, p. 157), "that both Philemon and Archippus belonged to Laodicea, and that the epistle was therefore sent to that place, is entitled to no weight." If, as Vincent supposed, the same persons (with one exception) were saluted in Philemon as in Colossians, it would be natural to assign the two letters to a common destination. "All the persons saluted," he declares, "are named in the salutations of Colossians except Jesus Justus" (p. 192). But the fact is, he has mistaken the middle for the passive voice. It is the persons *sending* the greetings that are so largely the same, so that all that they prove is that the letters came from the same circle—Paul and his friends at Rome. Philemon usually gets very little serious attention from commentators. Jesus Justus is named in Colossians (4:11), but not in Philemon.

This explanation of Philemon as the letter to Laodicea at once clears up a number of problems:

1. Why was a mere personal letter to Philemon ever included in a collection of Paul's letters to churches? The answer is plain: because it was not thought of as a personal letter but as a church letter, verse 2, the Letter to the Laodiceans.

2. What has become of the letter from Laodicea, mentioned in Col. 4:16? Linked in this way from the beginning, by Paul himself, with Colossians, how could it have disappeared? It had a double chance for preservation, for both churches must have possessed copies of it. We answer: It never disappeared but, notwithstanding its brevity and meager theological content, has always been preserved with Colossians, just as one would expect.

This explains why, from the time of Marcion and the oldest known list of Paul's letters, a tradition has existed of a Letter to the Laodiceans. It also explains the strange way in which Philemon is referred to in Colossians—"the letter from Laodicea." The Colossians are to ask for Philemon and to expect to read it; their justification is Paul's own suggestion in his letter to them that they secure it and read it, lending the Laodiceans their letter in exchange.[1] Paul does not call it a Letter to the Laodiceans, or a Letter to Philemon; he leaves the matter vague, just as he does

---

[1] That the letter did not long continue to bear the name of Laodicea or Laodiceans is not strange in view of the disfavor into which the Laodicean church soon fell; cf. The Letter to Laodicea in Rev. 3:15: "Since you are tepid, and neither cold nor hot, I am going to spit you out of my mouth!"

in Philemon itself. For while the Letter to Philemon is addressed to Philemon, Apphia, Archippus, and the church that meets in Philemon's house, the real recipient is addressed in the second person singular all the way through, from verse 4 to verse 24.

This also explains the strange allusion to Archippus in Col. 4:17: "Tell Archippus, 'See that you perform the Christian service you have been assigned.'" There is something almost grim in this indirect message which the Colossians are to transmit to Archippus. He is to understand that he has a special responsibility in this matter, as the nearest Christian of influence to Philemon. It is his business to see that Philemon does the Christian thing by Onesimus. Certainly every Christian minister knows that such responsibilities sometimes come to him, and what is more obvious than that Archippus had a peculiar and very grave responsibility in the present case?

So as if in the presence of the wife and the minister of Philemon, of the Christian congregation that met in his house, and of the Christian church at Colossae, Philemon is to deal with Onesimus. There is nothing unfair or underhanded about this; Philemon, if he was the right sort, would have nothing to conceal from any of them; but if he were not the right sort, they would exercise a most salutary check on his vindictiveness or violence, and Onesimus would be saved. There was already in the social pressure of the Christian groups a safeguard that Paul, though in prison at Rome, could throw about the slave Onesimus.

About the only thing that can be alleged against these positions is the reference in Col. 4:9 to Onesimus as "of you"—"one of you," "from among you," or "one of your number." From this it has usually been inferred that Philemon was a Colossian. But that does not necessarily follow. Onesimus might have been of Colossian origin without Philemon's having lived there. Moreover Colossae, Laodicea, and Hierapolis were close together. "They are very near," says Ramsay, "Hierapolis being about six miles north, and Colossae eleven miles east, from Laodicea. . . . . Laodicea and Hierapolis . . . . are in full view of one another on opposite sites of the glen."[1] They must have been in daily, even hourly, contact. And viewed from the distance of Rome, the distinctions between them would tend to disappear. Even if Onesimus were from Laodicea, Paul writing to the immediately neighboring Colossae could easily think of him as "one of you." It is much easier to think of this phrase in this way than to dispose of the Laodicean atmosphere of Col. 4:15–17. It would, moreover, be entirely natural for Paul to seek to interest the Colossians in the fate of Onesimus by reminding them that he belonged to their district—Phrygia and the Lycus Valley.

In any case, the expression "of you," or "from you" cannot be narrowly interpreted, for Onesimus was certainly not a member of the Colossian church when he robbed his master and ran away. It is certainly used in some more inclusive sense, and who can say that the sense must be extended to the city of

[1] *Op. cit.*, p. 172.

Colossae and limited to it? Why not the general region of the cities of the Lycus Valley?

But even if 4:9 established the Colossian origin of Onesimus (cf. Rom. 9:5), it would not make Philemon a Colossian, for Archippus is definitely a third person to the Colossians and Paul (4:17); he is a townsman of Philemon and is introduced in Colossians in a connection that points unmistakably to Laodicea. There is no escaping this. Archippus is not a Colossian, and the implication of 4:15–17 is that he was a Laodicean. And he necessarily carries with him Philemon, Apphia, and the church that met in Philemon's house. It was a Laodicean church.

What was the effect of Paul's letter to Philemon? The fact that it was preserved among church letters along with Colossians shows that it reached the congregations Paul intended and that they valued it. It is altogether probable that Philemon willingly acceded to Paul's wishes and received Onesimus back into his household and into Christian fellowship.

But Paul intimated that he really wished something more. He would have liked to keep Onesimus with him. Onesimus had become useful to him, as his name, which means "helpful," suggested. He feels toward him like a father; sending him back is like sending his very heart.

I would have liked to keep him with me, to wait on me in your place, while I am in prison for the good news, but I do not wish to do anything without your consent, so that your kindness might be voluntary and not have the appearance of compulsion. . . . . Come, brother, let me make something out of you in a Christian sense! Cheer my heart as a Christian . . . . I know that you will do even more than I ask.

Dr. John Knox has recently pointed out that what Paul demands in Philemon is forgiveness and humane treatment for Onesimus; but what he earnestly desires is that Philemon will send Onesimus back to be with him. Did Philemon do both?[1]

Fifty or fifty-five years after Paul wrote this letter Ignatius, the bishop of Antioch, was being taken across Asia to Rome to suffer martyrdom there. From Smyrna he wrote a letter to the Ephesian church, in the opening chapters of which he has much to say about their bishop Onesimus. He makes a great deal of the meaning of his name and in many ways reflects acquaintance with this Letter to Philemon. We cannot be sure that Onesimus, bishop of Ephesus ca. 107–17, was the boy Onesimus whom Paul had sent back to Philemon, as the martyrologies suggest, but it is not impossible that he was; that Philemon did indeed send him back to Paul again, as Paul so much wished he would do; that he lived to become a Christian leader in his own country, Asia, and was the bishop of Ephesus when Ignatius passed through that region ca. 107–17. If it be urged, with Lightfoot, that he would be too old,[2] let it be remembered that his col-

---

[1] John Knox, *Philemon among the Letters of Paul* (Chicago, 1935), pp. 4–11.

[2] "This Onesimus seems to be a distinct person . . . . from S. Paul's convert the slave of Philemon, who, if still living, would be too old at this time, ..." (*The Apostolic Fathers*, II, 32). But cf. Lightfoot (*Colossians*, p. 314): "It is not altogether impossible therefore that the same person may

league Polycarp, bishop of Smyrna, afterward suffered martyrdom at eighty-four, and in more modern times John Voysey, at the age of one hundred and three, made way for Myles Coverdale as bishop of Exeter and resumed the office again two years later. There is not the slightest difficulty in supposing that Paul's young friend Onesimus lived to the late sixties or seventies; in 107 he would be approaching seventy. And it must be agreed that the way in which Ignatius again and again alludes to the Letter to Philemon in his Letter to the Ephesians, chapters 1–6, makes it decidedly probable, as Knox has shown, that they were one and the same. If this is true, it opens up some very interesting possibilities as to the personalities behind the collecting of Paul's letters and their first publication.

That antiquity should have kept silent about the identity of Onesimus of Ephesus with Paul's young friend, supposing they were the same individual, may be due to the fact that Onesimus appears in this connection with Paul as a thievish runaway slave—a very disreputable episode in the early life of a great churchman, which his contemporaries might well be willing to forget. On the other hand, it is at least possible that it was the interest of the runaway himself, now grown to sober middle age, that caused the letter about his youthful escapade to be included in the Pauline corpus, for the light it threw upon Paul's character

---

be intended." For the tradition making Paul's Onesimus bishop of Ephesus, Lightfoot refers to *Acta Sanct. Boll.* xvi. *Febr.* (II, 837 f., new ed.).

and in gratitude for the help he had had from the great apostle at the turning-point of his life. It may even have been he that instigated the collecting of Paul's letters, for that collection was made at Ephesus and the nucleus of it, as we shall see, was Philemon-Colossians. These are conjectures, it is true, and incapable of proof, but they are far from improbable. Certainly some Christian of the Lycus Valley churches kept these letters and carried them to Ephesus before the Pauline letters had begun to be published, and it would be hard to imagine anyone to wh m these particular letters would mean so much e boy they had saved and perhaps freed. Certainly no one owed more to Paul than he.

If he did indeed rise to be the bishop of Ephesus, his was very probably the hand that preserved just these two letters and carried them to Ephesus, there to become the nucleus of the Pauline letter collection. I am indebted to the work of Dr. John Knox for the suggestion underlying these conjectures and for establishing the use of Philemon in Ignatius' Letter to the Ephesians, chapters 1–6—a point which had escaped even Lightfoot himself. "Onesimus is the real subject of these six chapters."[1] If Onesimus were nearing twenty in A.D. 60, a very reasonable estimate, he would be in the early fifties when the Pauline corpus was made soon after A.D. 90, and sixty-five to seventy-five when Ignatius wrote his letter to the Ephesians, A.D. 107–17. Great things were done in Ephesus and Smyrna between A.D. 90 and 125—the writing of Ephesians

[1] Knox, *op. cit.*, p. 53.

and of the Revelation and the Letters and Gospel of John, the publication of the Pauline corpus and the Fourfold Gospel—and personalities like Onesimus and Polycarp were unquestionably concerned in them.

Much has been said of the taste and charm of the Letter to Philemon, of its beauty, delicacy, tact, dignity, and courtesy.[1] It has been compared with Pliny's letters to Sabinianus interceding with him on behalf of one of his freedmen who had offended him.[2] But the true picture of Philemon is a far graver one. In it we glimpse for an instant the grim facts of slavery— the deepest sore on the ancient world's life.

LITERATURE

KNOX, JOHN. *Philemon among the Letters of Paul* (Chicago, 1935).

LIGHTFOOT, J. B. *St. Paul's Epistles to the Colossians and Philemon* (3d ed.; London, 1879).

[1] Vincent, *op. cit.*, p. 168.

[2] *Letters* ix. 21, 24.

X

THE GOSPEL OF MARK

+

Occasion. The gospel is Christianity's contribution to literary types. It is without doubt the most effective literary form of religious expression that has ever been devised.[1]

As we approach the Greek gospels, we naturally turn to Greek literature to see what precedents or analogies it affords for this new literary type. The origins of Greek biography are found in Xenophon's *Cyropaedia* and his *Memorabilia of Socrates* (430–350 B.C.), and it developed somewhat luxuriantly in the Alexander romance of the later centuries before Christ. Such works no doubt created a taste for biography among the Greeks, as the works of Plutarch (*ca.* A.D. 90) show, but they seem to have had little influence upon the early gospels.

Much closer parallels to the Gospel of Mark, at least, are afforded by the Elijah and Elisha cycles of the Books of Kings: I Kings, chapter 17—II Kings, chapter 2; and I Kings 19:19, II Kings chapters 2–13. It is a striking fact that almost everything Jesus is re-

[1] In ancient manuscripts of the gospels, the collected four are entitled "Gospel," each one receiving a heading: "According to Matthew," "According to Mark," "According to Luke," and "According to John." This use of the preposition κατά is difficult, but it is probably distributive in force—"(The Part) According to Matthew," etc.

ported as doing in Mark has parallels in these cycles, which it is plain had a great influence on the writer. Indeed, the shadow of Elijah or Elisha falls on almost every page of the Gospel of Mark, and it would seem that for some reason the selective memory of the early church instinctively recorded about Jesus anything that recalled the doings of these great prophets. Of course, the idea that John was Elijah come back to earth as Forerunner of the Messenger of the Covenant, Mal. 3:1; 4:5, had a good deal to do with this. But it is hardly fair to quote these cycles as literary precedents for Mark, since they did not exist as literary units but as parts of the Books of Kings.

Our earliest Christian literature, the letters of Paul, gives us glimpses of the form in which the story of Jesus and his teaching first circulated. That form was evidently an oral tradition, not fluid but fixed, and evidently learned by all Christians when they entered the church. This is why Paul can say, "I myself received from the Lord the account that I passed on to you," I Cor. 11:23. The words "received, passed on"[1] reflect the practice of tradition—the handing-down from one to another of a fixed form of words. How congenial this would be to the Jewish mind a moment's reflection on the Tradition of the Elders will show. The Jews at this very time possessed in Hebrew, unwritten, the scribal interpretation of the Law and in Aramaic a Targum or translation of most or all of their Scriptures. It was a point of pride with them not to commit these to writing but to preserve them

---

[1] παραδιδόναι = tradere, traditio

unwritten but unaltered.[1] In such circles it would be entirely natural to treat the earliest account of Jesus' deeds and words in just this way. It is to this practice that Paul unmistakably refers, quoting from the Christian tradition our oldest account of the institution of the Lord's Supper, I Cor. 11:24, 25. It will be noted that he speaks of having previously passed this account on to the Corinthians. He speaks in a similar way in I Cor. 15:3-7 of the resurrection accounts which he had communicated to them: "I passed on to you as of first importance, the account I had received."

Acts similarly speaks of "remembering the words of the Lord Jesus," 20:35, and quotes words of Jesus that have never been found in any written gospel. Clement of Rome, in writing to the Corinthians about A.D. 95, in two places—13:1 and 46:7, 8—quotes sayings of Jesus not quite like any in our gospels, admonishing his readers in both passages to "remember the words of the Lord Jesus." Polycarp of Smyrna in his letter to the Philippians, about A.D. 107-17, does the same, introducing the quotation with the words, "Remembering what the Lord said," Phil. 2:3. It seems clear that all four are quoting an Oral Gospel.[2]

This is internal evidence. Is there any external evi-

---

[1] This attitude is clearly reflected in the story that Gamaliel the First, about A.D. 50, seeing a written copy of an Aramaic translation of Job, immediately had it destroyed. The Targum was not to be written but remembered; cf. Meyer Waxman, *History of Jewish Literature* (New York, 1930), II, p. 113.

[2] All these writers quote written documents in quite another way: I Cor. 7:1; Gal. 3:13; Acts 1:20; I Clem. 47:1, 2; Pol. Phil. 3:2.

dence, any possible reference to such a work, in our earliest Christian writings? It was, of course, the Jewish practice to preserve in oral form the sayings of the great rabbis, as the Pirqe Aboth ("The Sayings of the Fathers") shows. Conditions among the earliest Christians, who thought of Jesus as among other things a "rabbi"—Mark 9:5; 10:51; 11:21; 14:45, etc.—or a "teacher" (twelve times in Mark), favor such a way of preserving his teaching; it would, in fact, have been inevitable; and subsequent quotations seem to show its use, as we have seen. But is there anything that looks like an actual ancient mention of it by name?

In the early years of the second century there lived in Hierapolis, in Asia, a Christian bishop named Papias, who made it his business to interview any Christian of the previous generation who came near and to record these memorabilia in a book, which he called *Interpretations of the Lord's Sayings*. Though the book existed in convent libraries in Europe until the thirteenth and fourteenth centuries,[1] it seems now to have disappeared, except for a few fragments of it quoted by ancient or medieval writers. One of these was Eusebius, who in his famous *Church History*, finished in A.D. 326, quoted this sentence from Papias: "So then Matthew composed the Sayings in the Aramaic language and each one translated them as [best] he could."[2]

[1] A. Harnack, *Geschichte der altchristlichen Litteratur: Die Ueberlieferung und der Bestand* (Leipzig, 1893), p. 69.

[2] *Church History* iii. 39. 15.

It has proved impossible to apply this strange statement to the Gospel of Matthew, which demonstrably rests upon written Greek sources, some of them shared with Luke. It cannot be understood to mean one of the sources of the gospels, as was at one time supposed. If it means that Matthew wrote the *Sayings*, in Aramaic, his action was contrary to the whole Jewish procedure of his day. But Papias does not say "wrote" as he does when speaking of Mark's gospel, just before; his word here is "composed" (so Lightfoot)— a word that seems to be quite appropriate to what may may be called "oral composition."[1]

The composition of the original Oral Gospel would naturally come from some personal follower of Jesus, like Matthew. It would inevitably be in Aramaic, the language Jesus used. When the Greek mission began, it would of course be translated (still orally) into Greek, and variously translated as different missionaries found occasion to put it into Greek. As Luke puts it in his preface, 1:2, "the original eye-witnesses who became teachers of the message have handed it down to us." It would seem that it was the task of the "teachers" to teach this Oral Gospel to new converts, very much as the Jewish *Tanna'im* (teachers) taught the oral interpretation of the Law to their disciples. It is to oral instruction in this tradition that Luke refers, when he proposes to pro-

---

[1] According to the new Liddell and Scott *Dictionary*, συγγράφω means to compose a writing or speech, or draw up a contract or motion. Isocrates i. 3 speaks of "those who compose hortatory discourses [λόγους] addressed to their friends" (Norlin, *Isocrates* ["Loeb Library"], I, 7). The middle is used of "getting speeches [λόγους] composed" (Plato *Euthydemus* 272*a*).

vide for Theophilus a fuller and more exact account of the things Theophilus "has been orally taught."[1]

It seems probable that what Papias here refers to is the original Oral Gospel, and that the tradition of the church was that it was the work of Matthew. So understood, Papias' bewildering observation "and each one translated them as best he could" becomes perfectly clear and natural.

Such an identification solves a number of problems:

1. It explains Papias' statement, which has never been fitted into early Christian literary history.

2. It explains what Paul, Luke, Clement, and Polycarp were quoting from.

3. It explains why Matthew's name should later have been given to the leading written gospel; he had from the beginning been the great primitive figure behind the (oral) gospel.

4. It corroborates Luke's remark in his preface, 1:2, about the original eyewitnesses becoming teachers of the message and handing it down through oral tradition. What could be more natural, if the apostle Matthew composed the Oral Gospel they had all been taught?

5. It corresponds exactly with Palestinian Jewish attitudes toward the middle of the first century—the *oral* preservation of groups of *sayings* of great *teachers*.

6. It explains the use of the phrase "Remember the words" in Luke (Acts 20:35) and Clement (13:1; 46:7) and "Remember what the Lord said when he

[1] $\kappa\alpha\tau\eta\chi\acute\eta\theta\eta\varsigma$.

taught" in Polycarp (Phil. 2:3). Matthew's work was called "The Words" or "Oracles."

7. It corroborates the general critical dismissal of the Matthaean Logia, as not a written document.

On the whole, the mysterious Logia of Matthew would seem to have been the original Oral Gospel, reflected in Paul, Luke, Clement, and Polycarp. They are spoken of as "logoi," it is true, in Acts 20:35 and I Clem. 13:1 and 46:7, but the second Oxyrhynchus fragment of Sayings of Jesus (Oxyrhynchus Papyri 654, ca. A.D. 250) begins, "These are the . . . . Words [logoi] which Jesus . . . . spoke," so that it is altogether natural for Luke and Clement to speak of these earlier sayings of his by that name.

It is natural for us moderns to suppose that the first written gospel was simply the writing-down of this Oral Gospel, and some scholars have leaped to that conclusion. We instinctively feel that, if we had known it, we would have written it right down. This would have been a Greek way of doing; it was a Greek saying that if you found a saying of one of the philosophers and had no paper, you should write it upon your garments!

But the Jewish mind moved in exactly the opposite direction, and it was among Christians of Jewish blood that the first gospel tradition took shape. And when we compare the fragments of this Oral Gospel that we have found in Paul, Acts, Clement, and Polycarp with Mark, to our amazement not one of the fragments reappears in Mark. We may therefore conclude without hesitation that, whatever the origin of the Gospel of

Mark, it did not originate through the writing-down of the Oral Gospel. It does not contain the fragments of that gospel that have come down to us, nor any of these fragments.

The existence of this Oral Gospel in fact really renders our problem more difficult than ever. For if the early Christians had an Oral Gospel, why produce a written one? We can hardly suppose the Roman church, in which Mark evidently arose, was without the Oral Gospel; Paul and Peter had both lived and labored in Rome, and Clement's use of it in writing to the Corinthians shows that by his time (*ca.* 95) certainly, it was well known there. The Oral Gospel must have been the prevalent and dominant gospel form there. If a written gospel originated there, it must have done so under the shadow of this Oral Gospel, which it must have been designed to supplement. What situation could have brought this about? There must have been some very definite, specific occasion that, in the midst of a nonliterary Christianity and in the presence of the accepted Oral Gospel, precipitated the writing of the first written gospel.

In one of the few surviving fragments of Papias' *Interpretations*, he says:

Mark having become the interpreter of Peter, wrote down accurately everything that he remembered, without however recording in order what was either said or done by Christ. For neither did he hear the Lord speak, nor did he follow him, but afterwards, as I said, attended Peter, who adapted his instructions to the needs of his hearers, but had no design of giving a connected account of the Lord's oracles. So then Mark made no mistake while he thus wrote some things as he remembered them; for he made it his one care not to omit anything that he heard, or to set down any false statement therein.[1]

While there is much that is vague about this fragment, and we would give a good deal for its context, it seems to bring up the picture of Peter, an old man, visiting Rome in his later years and there preaching in his native Aramaic to the Greek congregation. They must have listened with rapt attention as the old apostle told of his walks and talks with Jesus in Galilee, and of the swift tragedy of betrayal and crucifixion which had followed in Judea. Then suddenly Peter is himself snatched from them and suffers martyrdom. It was one of the most famous of all martyrdoms; St Peter's marks the supposed spot on the Vatican Hill,[2] and legends like the stirring "*Domine, quo vadis?*" have gathered about it.[3] It must have filled the Roman congregation with grief. No more would they hear the old man uttering his inimitable reminiscences of Jesus, for with his death a priceless treasure of such memories perished from the earth.

But not entirely. For as the old man had preached, there had stood beside him, of course, now one, now another of them, who could understand his Aramaic speech and immediately translate it into Greek for his Roman hearers. He had used these memories only to

[1] Eusebius *Church History* iii. 39. 15.
[2] Cf. Eusebius *Church History* ii. 25. 7.
[3] *Acts of Peter*, chap. 35.

illustrate and strengthen his own preaching, and from hearing some incidents over and over a number of times and putting them into Greek, a capable and alert interpreter would come to have a very definite memory of their wording. Out of such memories, Papias means to say, one of these interpreters named Mark composed his gospel.[1]

It is certainly a fact that almost everything in Mark might have been obtained from Peter, and much of the roughness and obscurity of the book would be explained on such a theory of its origin. Papias' reflection upon its order of treatment is probably due to his greater regard for Matthew, which he knew and no

---

[1] A. H. McNeile argues that the word "interpreter" (ἑρμηνευτής) in Papias "does not imply that while St. Peter was preaching in Aramaic, St. Mark gave to his audience a Greek translation of his words sentence by sentence" (*An Introduction to the Study of the New Testament* [Oxford, 1927], p. 48). But in Gen. 42:23 (LXX) (cf. I Cor. 14:28) the word is used of immediate personal translation or interpretation. If Peter visited Rome, and the tradition that he did is overwhelming, he would require such help in addressing his Greek-speaking congregation, just as Marshal Joffre did on his visit to America, when U. S. Grant III was his usual interpreter, and as visitors to the Orient—China, India, Japan—constantly do today. Someone must have acted as Peter's interpreter on these occasions, and Mark's gospel seems clearly to have been written in Rome. McNeile's interpretation that "Peter preached in Aramaic and that St. Mark at a later time, after the Apostle's death in fact, set down in Greek for other circles of Christians all that he remembered" too much dilutes the plain meaning of Papias' words: Μᾶρκος μὲν ἑρμηνευτὴς Πέτρου γενόμενος, ὅσα ἐμνημόνευσεν, ἀκριβῶς ἔγραψεν. I Pet. 5:13 first links Peter, Mark, and Rome, doubtless in allusion to Mark's service rendered to Peter there, and what came of it. The Roman church, it must be remembered, was a Greek church from the beginning until toward the middle of the third century. Our first Roman Latin father is Novatian, *ca.* A.D. 250.

doubt preferred for its greater richness of teaching and tradition.

The chief question about Mark is its relation to these Petrine memoirs: Is it identical with them, or is it based upon them and some other source, perhaps the much discussed Matthean-Lucan source "Q," that is, *Quelle* or source? The latter position has often been assumed, the opening paragraphs of the gospel being referred to the redactor, or editor, who supposedly blended the two sources into what we know as Mark. Indeed, Bacon went so far as to say that Mark 1:1–13 was the masterpiece of the redactor.

But if we look closely and coldly at these paragraphs, we find a great deal that does not support this view.[1] The opening words, "The Beginning of the Good News of Jesus Christ," at once create a problem. Are they a title, or do they form part of the first sentence? Indeed, what is the first sentence in Mark? Is it verse 2, verses 2, 3, or verse 4? Modern interpreters offer different answers to this question. It is evident that the writer, whoever he was, was not very fortunate in his opening lines.

He is no better in his first quotation, the famous Malachi ("My Messenger") oracle, Mal. 3:1, which he attributed to Isaiah and attached to Isa. 40:3. The editorial writers who produced the gospels of Matthew and Luke made no such mistake, which is much more easily understood in a primitive document like the Petrine memoirs than in the work of a redactor.

[1] Cf. E. J. Goodspeed, "The Marcan Redactor," in Leary, *From the Pyramids to Paul* (New York, 1935), pp. 57–66.

John the Baptist is abruptly introduced, as though well known to the reader (doubtless through the Oral Gospel already mentioned). He is rather cryptically spoken of as "preaching a baptism of repentance into forgiveness of sins." His clothing and fare are described, probably in token of his resemblance to the other desert prophet Elijah, but so crisply that few readers, ancient or modern, have understood the allusion.

Jesus, too, is abruptly introduced—because already well known from the Oral Gospel used by Paul and his converts. There is no scruple about describing him as accepting a repentance baptism. The description of the heavens as split or ripped open and the Spirit plunging down like a dove to enter into him is so harsh and bold that two actual redactors—Matthew and Luke—have greatly softened it. Mark describes Jesus as taken possession of by the Spirit, but in Matthew and Luke the Spirit simply lights upon him. Mark's idea of the Spirit entering him is in fact so extreme that it has hardly ever been translated even into English, although it is probably the key to his understanding of Jesus.[1]

The Spirit's control of Jesus is described in the roughest terms: It drives or throws him into the desert. All this is greatly softened by the Matthean and Lucan redactors, who change the word to "leads" or "guides." Verse 13 is a perfect knot of riddles and has suggested to some interpreters the most grotesque ideas of primitive initiation rites and circles drawn in

[1] Cf. B. W. Bacon, *Beginnings of Gospel Story* (New York, 1909), p. 12.

the sand. But as a matter of fact it is simply a very loose reminiscence of Ps. 91:11–14; the references to "God's beloved"—"in the desert"—"among wild animals"—and "looked after by angels" are unmistakable. Yet so obscurely is it all reflected that some skilled modern interpreters have altogether missed it.[1]

It seems clear that this is not the work of any redactor; these are the traits and traces of an original source, unrevised. A redactor might be so unequal to his task that he would let some of these things stand, but certainly no redactor would have missed them all. We know how Matthew and Luke handled this very passage, and they left hardly one of these things unchanged. The passage, in short, shows just the roughness, harshness, obscurity, and difficulty that we should expect in a work written in the circumstances Papias suggests—at arm's length, from memory, after the sponsor for the stories was gone and could not be consulted. This is just the way Mark would sound if the writer were trying to put down something he had heard, just as he heard it, without dressing it up after his own ideas of taste. It is just the way some other parts of Mark do sound, such as the reference to Abiathar as high priest in 2:26, whereas I Sam. 21:1–6 tells this story of Abiathar's father, Ahimelech, who paid for his friendly deed with his life. Here, again, a redactor should have mended matters. The two stories of the feeding of the multitude, 6:41, 8:6, so manifestly variant accounts of the same event, show the absence of the redactor's hand; Luke and John

---

[1] W. C. Allen, *St. Mark* (New York, 1915), p. 57.

omitted the second, though it is true Matthew included both.

After these opening paragraphs we find ourselves
in 1:16 in the more or less immediate presence of Peter
and continue so throughout the book, except for the
story of Herod and John the Baptist, 6:14–29. The
Little Apocalypse of chapter 13 is the most extended
piece of discourse in the book and may have been taken
up into it ready-made or nearly so. But, on the whole,
it must be agreed that the Gospel of Mark comes very
near being the memoirs of Peter of which Papias
spoke, which were written down from memory soon
after the martyrdom of Peter in A.D. 64–67, by one of
his Greek-speaking interpreters in Rome.

Contents. The gospel begins, as we have seen,
with a few sentences pointing out the prophetic
oracles fulfilled in the appearance of John the Forerunner. Among John's penitents Jesus appears, seeking
baptism. With that experience there comes to him a
great sense of commission. The Spirit of God takes
possession of him and hurries him into the desert for
a mysterious ordeal of temptation. Only after John's
arrest does Jesus begin to preach. He declares that the
time has come for the reign of God to begin on earth
and calls on the people to repent and believe the good
news. Unlike John, he goes about among the villages
and cities, preaching. He calls four Capernaum fishermen to be his companions and teaches in the synagogue
there. He casts out demons and cures the sick. (The
whole gospel is cast in the ancient religious vocabulary of demon and marvel.) He turns his back upon

his sudden popularity and journeys about, his public the unchurched "people of the land" who simply could not carry out the scribal refinements of pharisaic religion, 1:1-39.

Dr. Horton has written a book on *The Cartoons of St. Mark*.[1] And Mark can be considered as a series of great pictures, boldly and simply drawn. A situation is sketched. Jesus appears in the midst of it, and says something or does something that relieves it. It has often been remarked that his words flash through these scenes like a bright sword, with a power and genius quite beyond the skill of the evangelist. We may contrast the situation in John, where it is sometimes hard to tell where Jesus leaves off and the evangelist begins, e.g., John 3:16. The distinction which these sayings of Jesus, in Mark, possess is a strong guaranty of their nearness to the actual scenes they describe.

Moving on about Galilee, Jesus cures a leper, which embarrassingly increases his fame, and then a paralytic on the Sabbath, which incenses the Pharisees. Their hostility is increased by his calling a tax collector to follow him and by his eating with such people. His disciples disregard the current fasts; he is indifferent to the refinements of the Law of the Sabbath, and finally on the Sabbath he cures a man whose hand is withered. As a result the Pharisees plot to put him to death, 1:40—3:6.

Before this peril Jesus retreats with his disciples to the seashore, 3:7. He seems to adjust his plans to the new situation by calling twelve men to be his associ-

[1] R. F. Horton, *The Cartoons of St. Mark* (New York, 1894).

ates and messengers and by resorting to parables or figures, which partly veil and yet convey his message. He stills the tempest, casts out demons, raises Jairus' daughter, and preaches at Nazareth, where his townsmen's refusal of his message fills him with surprise. He sends the Twelve out to preach repentance, cast out demons, and cure the sick. He feeds the multitudes (as Elisha had done)[1] and again saves the disciples from storm. The criticism of the scribes and Pharisees about his practice of eating with unwashed hands leads him to denounce their insincerity and sweep away the whole doctrine of clean and unclean foods, 3:7—7:23.

After thus throwing down the gauntlet to his enemies in Galilee, he again retreats, 7:24, this time to the vicinity of Tyre and Sidon. He wishes no one to know of his presence and returns by a roundabout way to the shores of the Sea of Galilee. Again he feeds the crowds, and the Pharisees confront him with a demand for a sign of his authority. He retreats a third time, 8:27, this time to the villages about Caesarea Philippi, to the north of Galilee. He asks the disciples who people say he is and who they think him to be. Peter says, "You are the Christ." Jesus warns them not to say this about him to anyone, 7:24—8:30.

Increasingly conscious of the peril confronting him, Jesus tells his disciples that he must soon be put to death but, in language evidently taken from Hos. 6:2, declares his faith that even in death God will not for-

---

[1] II Kings 4:42–44.

sake him: "He will revive us in two or three days; he will raise us up that we may live before him."

The transfiguration follows. The great painters of the Renaissance have made us think of the transfiguration as a sort of feat of levitation, but of course it was really a great spiritual experience. The disciples are beginning to think of Jesus as Messiah, which might mean any one of many things. In the transfiguration experience his closest followers learn to think of him along with Moses and Elijah—and great molders of Israel's religion. It is in that realm that his Messiahship, his anointing, lies, 8:31—9:50.

Jesus now turns sharply upon his foes, 10:1. Three times he has given ground before them; now he takes the offensive. The period of seclusion is over—the retreats, the incognito. He sets out for Judea. It is as though he had resolved that, if he must face death in his work, he would not do it obscurely in some corner of Galilee but conspicuously, dramatically, in Jerusalem, the capital, and before the Jewish people gathered for its great annual feast. Of course, Mark does not say this in so many words. We have a strange feeling in Mark that we are very close to the mind of Jesus; we are nearer to his confidence than anywhere else in the New Testament, yet very little is explicitly told about his hopes and plans.

There is indeed a stern picture of him as he goes on his way: "As they went on their way up to Jerusalem, Jesus walked ahead of them, and they were in dismay, and those who still followed were afraid." No longer affable and familiar, he is now remote and absorbed striding on alone before them, unapproachable and wrapped in his own thoughts. He has never been like this, and the sight fills them with dismay and fear. He breaks his silence only to repeat his dark forebodings of what is to happen in Jerusalem—disgrace and death, though not without resurrection too, 10:1–34.

Zebedee's sons are so oblivious of his mood that they actually ask for the leading places in his coming triumph. He reaches Jericho, then as he draws nearer Jerusalem, Bethphage and Bethany. Jesus has secretly prepared for his triumphal entry, so that he may come into the city not as a warrior Messiah but as a peaceful prophet, such as Zechariah had described. His fame has preceded him, and the pilgrims welcome him with cheers. He enters the city and visits the Temple, as if in preparation for the momentous morrow. Then, as it is late, he goes out with the Twelve to lodge in Bethany, 10:35—11:11.

The next day he throws down the gauntlet to the priests and Sadducees. He clears the Temple of buyers and sellers and denounces their abuse of it in his unforgettable way. Chesterton says that Jesus' style was gigantesque—full of camels leaping through needles and mountains being hurled into the sea. The next day the Temple authorities call upon him to give an account of himself and tell by what authority he has taken his highhanded action. He parries and at the same time answers their question with another about John's authority, which they are afraid to answer. He tells the story of the Vineyard and the Wicked Tenants, to show what he thought of them. Nothing could be more dramatic than these debates in the Temple courts, with throngs of eager pilgrims hanging on the words. Eight centuries before Amos had challenged the Hebrew priesthood, but a greater than Amos was here, 11:12—12:44.

The simple Galilean disciples wonder at the Temple's splendor: "What wonderful stones and buildings!" But to his mind they are all simply ripe for overthrow. "Do you see these great buildings? Not one stone shall be left here upon another, that shall not be torn down." The discourse on the fall of the city and the end of the age follows, 13:1–37.

Jesus' preparations for the Passover supper are made with the same secrecy that had marked his arrangements for his triumphal entry. By the story of the man with the pitcher of water, Mark clearly means to convey the sense of apprehension and precaution that colored these anxious days in Jerusalem. They have been staying outside the city in Bethany, but the Passover must be eaten, at whatever risk, in Jerusalem itself.[1] Even there at the Supper, when they are all safely gathered at table, there is foreboding and suspicion; one of the Twelve will betray him; and in the Passover bread and cup he sees the symbols of his redemptive death.

Up to the last night of his life Jesus did not give up hope that he might win his people to his message. Stopping after the Supper to pray in the garden on the Mount of Olives, he is arrested by a posse from the high priests, and after a hurried examination is tried

[1] Deut. 16:5–7.

before the Roman governor and immediately executed. The story is told with a restraint and simple power that make it one of the classics of heroic tragedy, 14:1—15:47.

The Gospel of Mark breaks off abruptly, 16:8, with glimpses of resurrection.[1] Its dilapidation must be due to its absorption in Matthew, which no doubt seemed to its first readers an improved and enlarged form of Mark. Certainly Matthew quickly replaced Mark, which probably fell into disuse and neglect. Mark twice promises a reunion of Jesus with his disciples in Galilee, 14:28; 16:7, and that is just what Matthew proceeds to record, in 28:9, 10, 16–20. As Matthew is following Mark's language very closely, phrase by phrase, in 28:1–7, it is altogether likely that he continued to use Mark in this way to the end, and as he actually gives us the very climax which Mark has twice foreshadowed, there seems to be no reasonable doubt that he derived it from Mark. That Mark was complete when Matthew used it is altogether likely; as we have seen, the loss of its conclusion is probably the result of its being replaced in popular use by the newer Gospel of Matthew.

It is reasonable to conclude that Mark originally

[1] Mark 16:9–20 is absent from the Vatican and Sinaitic manuscripts of the fourth century; from the Old Latin Bobiensis, fifth or sixth century; the Old Syriac Sinaitic manuscript, fourth or fifth century; and from some Georgian, Armenian, and Ethiopic codices. The Codex Regius, eighth century, follows Mark 16:8 with the Short Conclusion, preceded with the words φέρετε που καὶ ταῦτα—"This also is in some cases present." After the Short Conclusion it proceeds, "This also is current after 'For they were afraid,'" and gives the Long Conclusion, 16:9–20.

ended with an account of the reunion of Jesus with the disciples in Galilee.[1] Reassembled as he had ordered in their old haunts, they felt his presence once more, heard his voice again, and knew that he had come back to them never to leave them until the end.[2] It is a little surprising, and perhaps not without significance, that the gospel which began with *Arche*—the beginning—would in this case have ended with *telos*—the end.

Christian antiquity did not greatly prize the Gospel of Mark. Hippolytus described Mark as "stub-fingered," a man whose fingers were thumbs.[3] What he meant was that Mark, compared with Matthew, seemed clumsy and obscure. Augustine thought Mark a condensation of Matthew.

It was left for modern learning to perceive the extraordinary values of the Gospel of Mark. For while it has no difficulty in pointing out, as we have done, the solecisms and obscurities, even the mistakes, of the gospel and the meagerness of its account of Jesus' teaching, it fully recognizes the historical worth of the gospel, which brings us nearer to the immediate circle of Jesus' followers than any other record of him that we possess. It is as though Mark felt that he was in the presence of something too great for him to master or control, which he must simply record as faithfully

[1] Goodspeed, *New Solutions of New Testament Problems* (Chicago, 1927), pp. 116–22.

[2] As Dr. George A. Buttrick recently put it, "Their memory of Jesus had quickened to a presence" (*Life*, December 28, 1936), p. 49.

[3] κολοβοδάκτυλος (*Refutation* vii. 18).

as he might. This is why we get in Mark as in no other gospel this strange vague sense of great things close at hand—conflicts, insights, purposes, decisions. It shows us Jesus not primarily as a teacher but as a man of action. He moves through the narrative with masterful vigor, finally even facing the nation's priesthood not with mere words but with bold acts of reformation. It is not without significance that in this earliest gospel we see Jesus as a man of action.

Indeed, the Gospel of Mark possesses the quality of action to a higher degree than any of the others.[1] Matthew has made so much of Jesus' teaching that we have almost forgotten that he had another very different side. When he saw an evil, he did something about it. It was this trait of his and not his teaching that cost him his life, for it was his cleansing of the Temple that sealed his fate. It was more than the priestly authorities could brook.

The three retreats of Jesus before his foes and then his turning against them and attacking them in their stronghold give Mark a dramatic quality peculiarly its own, and its thrilling account of the betrayal, arrest, trial, and death of Jesus makes it the supreme martyrdom, for Matthew and Luke have done little but elaborate it here. From one point of view, indeed, Mark is a martyrdom, for the shadow of the cross already falls across the narrative from the beginning of the third chapter (3:6) on. It remained the pattern gospel to the end of the gospel-making age, and, in-

[1] Cf. E. W. Burch, "Tragic Action in the Second Gospel," *Journal of Religion*, XI (1931), 346–58.

formal and unambitious as Mark's narrative is, no more convincing or dramatic account has ever been written of the sublime effort of Jesus to execute the greatest task ever conceived—to set up the Kingdom of God on earth.

Problems. It is now fairly settled that the Gospel of Mark is the earliest of the gospels and did not develop out of an earlier stage as a Primitive Mark, as once supposed. Its place of composition was certainly Rome.[1] It must have been written after the Jewish War of A.D. 66–70; compare 13:14–20:

"As soon as you see the dreadful desecration standing where he has no right to stand" (the reader must take note of this), "then those who are in Judea must fly to the hills; a man on the roof of his house must not go down or go into the house to get anything out of it, and a man in the field must not turn back to get his coat. . . . . There will be such misery in those days as there has never been since the beginning of God's creation until now, and never will be again."

This is an unmistakable reflection of the horrors of the siege of Jerusalem; Josephus himself declared that no other city ever suffered such miseries (*Wars* v. 10. 5); certainly it would be difficult to imagine anything worse than what he describes (*Wars* v. 12—vi. 9). Josephus says that eleven hundred thousand people perished in the siege, and whatever may have been the correct figure, this shows what was thought in the first century about the matter. Such stories about the

---

[1] B. W. Bacon, *Is Mark a Roman Gospel?* (Cambridge, 1919).

fall of Jerusalem are evidently back of Mark, chapter 13.

We cannot therefore regard the date of the death of Peter (A.D. 64? 67?) as the *terminus a quo* for the book. Certainly as we have it, including the Little Apocalypse of chapter 13, Mark was written after A.D. 70, but not very long after, since Matthew soon made it the basis of his own gospel.

But was chapter 13 an original part of the book? This brings us to our most serious Marcan problem— Mark's use of sources. Efforts have been made to show that he made use, for example, of the hypothetical "Q" (the supposed second common source of Matthew and Luke). They rest primarily on the occurrence in Mark of a few small but striking items which appear also in the common non-Marcan portions of Matthew and Luke. Believing that a probability of literary relationship is thus created, some scholars proceed to build up a body of common material of more dubious resemblance. The mistake in this procedure lies in its tacit assumption that *the ultimate documents of the Synoptic Gospels must have been mutually exclusive*, which is manifestly the reverse of probable.

The written sources of the gospels rested not so much upon the fixed Oral Tradition, which was of very definite content and limits, as upon such elements of Jesus' life and teaching as had found their way into Christian preaching and suffered modification and amplification under the stress of Christian experience. This is the sort of thing that underlies what Papias says of the oral materials out of which Mark was written.

As a matter of fact, Mark shows few traces of the use of written sources. As we have seen, the evangelist is not a redactor. The Little Apocalypse of chapter 13 comes nearest to being a written source; it has been identified with the Christian apocalypse which Eusebius says was given to the Christians in Jerusalem on the eve of the siege and led them to make their escape from the doomed city to Pella (*Church History* iii. 5. 3).

Eusebius says that "the people of the church in Jerusalem had been commanded by a revelation, vouchsafed by approved men there before the war, to leave the city and to dwell in a certain town of Perea called Pella." This certainly sounds very much like Mark 13:14, though it must be admitted there is no mention of Pella in Mark. Moreover, the revelation mentioned by Eusebius was in anticipation of the siege; the Little Apocalypse of Mark looks back upon it. Further, a "revelation" does not necessarily suggest a written apocalypse; compare Gal. 2:2; I Cor. 14:26; II Cor. 12:1. It remains true that the warning to flee from Jerusalem is contained in Mark, chapter 13, and is reported in a more specific form in Eusebius, but a documentary dependence of Mark upon such a work can hardly be maintained.

The fall of Jerusalem is understood in chapter 13 to mark a definite stage in the progress of the apocalyptic program but not the end of it, for before the end the good news must first be preached to all the heathen,

13:10. The persecuted Christians can find that much comfort in it, 13:7, 8, 10, 13. A whole series of matters incident to the siege and destruction of the city appears in the chapter: the desecration of the Holy City, 13:14; the escape before the siege, 13:14–16; the dreadful misery, 13:19. The chapter as a whole reflects the horrors of persecution, 13:9–13; the siege and fall of Jerusalem, 13:14–20; and the apocalyptic hope, 13:21–27, followed by the warning to be on the watch, 13:28–37. Even such a memory would, in any case, be modified by the evangelist to suit its function in his gospel, where it carries the persecution and martyr interest to its peak, 13:11–13.

For the martyrdom of Peter, which we have seen probably gave the impulse to the writing of Mark, did not stand alone. It was but one, though the most notable, of a series of martyrdoms that ravaged the Roman church. Peter's memories culminated in the great account of Jesus' own martyrdom, and in a time when the horrors of persecution were fresh in the Christian mind, Jesus' passion would loom as a supreme model for his followers.[1] Such a narrative of his sufferings would nerve the Roman Christians against the renewal of such persecutions as they had recently suffered; certainly in August of A.D. 64, as Tacitus records.

We may therefore think of the Gospel of Mark as first undertaken under the impulse to preserve the martyred Peter's memories of Jesus, especially of his martyrdom, for a Roman public just emerging from

[1] D. W. Riddle, *The Martyrs* (Chicago, 1931), chap. viii.

a persecution and likely at any time to have to face another one; and completed and published, doubtless with the aid of other Roman memories of Peter's preaching, soon after the fall of Jerusalem in A.D. 70.[1]

Wellhausen's stimulating suggestions about Mark have recently been revived and summarized by Lightfoot.[2] They are: that Mark consists of little sections which at first had a separate existence; that the book has been subjected to revision; and that it reflects contemporary church beliefs and conditions. The recognition of the little sections, drawn from contemporary preaching, accords very well with the view of the origin of Mark that has been outlined above. The revision theory is less probable: It is possible that Mark, if first put forth after the death of Peter, sustained some later addition after the fall of Jerusalem; it may possibly have been supplemented by the introduction of the Little Apocalypse, not long after the main body of it was first written down. But anything like a revision or a series of revisions is made very improbable by the nature of the book itself. That Peter's preaching should have developed, keeping pace with the developing church life, is likely enough; he must have preached almost thirty-five years. It is not

[1] We must not suppose that all available material on the subject was drawn upon, however, since the long current account of the Last Supper (reported from the Oral Gospel in I Cor. 11:24, 25) has not colored the account of the same event in Mark 14:22–25, and the Oral Gospel's account of the resurrection appearances, I Cor. 15:4–6, seems to have been quite different from that of Mark, as nearly as we can determine it.

[2] R. H. Lightfoot, *History and Interpretation in the Gospels* (New York, 1935), p. 23.

necessary to suppose that his preaching underwent no development during this time or that Mark was a colorless or mechanical interpreter. That Mark should have put his own stamp upon the gospel in writing it is not in the least improbable; modern oriental interpreters frequently adjust the addresses, which they stand by to translate, to their own views and those of the public before them.

The longest continuous narrative in Mark is the account of the trial and death of Jesus, 14:1—16:8, and this fact is sometimes alleged to mean that Mark found that account already substantially formed. No doubt it was a matter which had been told over and over again in Christian preaching before Mark wrote it down. But did he have it before him in written form, that is, did he owe it to a written source? Here, as in the Little Apocalypse, the question of Mark's sources—that is, written sources as distinguished from oral information—becomes acute.

Now it is at once apparent that these particulars—anointing, Passover, Last Supper, agony, betrayal, arrest, examination, denial, trial, crucifixion, resurrection—did not select or record themselves. They may perhaps be said to fall naturally into a certain order, though Luke has departed from Mark's order in some considerable details. Mark's order may have been orally communicated by Mark's informant, or it may have been created by him as the most natural sequence for the several items; they do not seem capable of any more reasonable arrangement.

There is no serious reason for supposing that anyone

has previously put them in written form; that would have been a most unnatural thing for Jewish hands to do, in view of the first-century Jewish aversion to written composition. And Christian eschatological expectation would have left no room for such a proceeding in ordinary circumstances; what point could there be in writing down an account of Jesus' Passion, when he might at any time reappear on the clouds of heaven? The effort to push written accounts of the Passion into the first generation after Jesus' death loses sight of the prevailing Christian mood in that period as Paul reflects it, I Cor. 7:29–31. It is remarkable enough that we possess written accounts as early as Mark. The first Christians were not the kind of people that write books—they lived in a first-century Jewish atmosphere definitely averse to literary composition, even to taking notes—and they cherished an apocalyptic expectation that promised neither time nor reason for such efforts. It is therefore a mistake to postulate written documents before those of which we have certain knowledge, and even these call for very definite and pressing situations to explain their appearance.

To push back the Passion narrative of Mark to an earlier document, therefore, does not make the problem easier; it makes it more difficult. It leaves us with the further problem, which cannot be avoided, of accounting for the composition of the earlier document. What pressing situation called it forth? Why did it have to be written? And all the time we must honestly remember that the farther back the writing-down of it is pushed, the more difficult it becomes to explain.

Of course, the incidents of those last momentous days and those hours of grim, dreadful tragedy would be burned into the memories of those who shared them, and of them Peter is the one most likely to have told and retold them most unforgettably. First, because he was apparently the most outspoken and energetic of the group and, second, because his own defection is so emphasized, 14:27–31, 66–72. The Passion narrative of chapters 14–15 is almost wholly free from the miraculous; the darkness, 15:33, and the rending of the Temple veil, 15:38, are the only items that even suggest any interruption of the natural order. It would in fact be difficult to write a more objective piece of sheer, stark tragedy than these seven tremendous pages. Their greatness lies in their Spartan restraint and their terrible, unsparing simplicity. One feels that the writer is so profoundly moved that he cannot for an instant relax his hold upon his feelings or they will sweep him away. And if they show great story-telling power, it is just the power that has characterized the most of the Gospel of Mark from its beginning.

Nor is the bulk of Mark such as to demand a labored sourcing of its contents. It is a little book—really only a pamphlet—of some forty pages, which can be read aloud in an hour. Built up it no doubt was, but primarily from memories of Peter's preaching, enriched with such matters as the fate of John, 6:17–29, and possibly the core of the Little Apocalypse, chapter 13.

But there is no sufficient reason to suppose that even these came to the evangelist's hands in written form.

The undoubted want of cohesion[1] which has been detected in Mark is just what one would expect if the book had the origin suggested by Papias. Peter would ordinarily tell incidents in Jesus' work to illustrate or enforce some point he was making in his own preaching, just as Papias says; these materials, scattered through Peter's discourses, Mark afterward assembles from his memory of Peter's sermons. It is very natural, therefore, for each of the detached items or units into which Mark, chapters 1–12, so easily falls should seem to deal with some problem of early Christian thought or life; it was for that that Peter meant them.[2] It is also probable that Mark colored his material with his own theological views and gave the work a stamp of his own, almost as positively as Matthew and Luke did in writing their gospels.[3]

The association of Peter, Mark, and Rome, reflected in the famous fragment of Papias, really appears much earlier, in I Pet. 5:13: "Your sister-church in Babylon, chosen like you, and Mark my son wish to be remembered to you." We shall see that I Peter was written by the Roman church late in the first century, and in these words it clearly connects Peter, Mark, and Rome—the "Babylon" seated on seven hills of Rev. 17:5, 9. This combination, Peter-Mark-Rome, at once

[1] McNeile, *An Introduction to the Study of the New Testament* (Oxford, 1927), pp. 50 and 51.

[2] F. C. Grant, *The Growth of the Gospels* (New York, 1933), p. 105.

[3] C. H. Dodd, *The Gospel in the New Testament* (London, 1926), pp. 13–16.

suggests the traditional origin of the Gospel of Mark and was probably meant by the writer of I Peter to do so. It comes as near to a direct reference to the posthumous Petrine Gospel of Mark as anyone writing under the name of Peter could very well come; the writer of II Peter, long after, manifestly overdoes it when he makes the reference to the gospel explicit: "I will also take care that after I am gone you will be able at any time to call these things to mind," 1:15.

As to the original conclusion of Mark, in view of Mark's repeated promise of a Galilean reunion— "After I am raised to life again, I will go back to Galilee before you," 14:28, and "He is going before you to Galilee; you will see him there, just as he told you," 16:7—combined with the continuity of the account of a Galilean reappearance in Matthew with Matthew's faithful use of Marcan material, Matt. 28:1–10, 16–20, it seems plain that Mark ended with an account of a Galilean reappearance, which may be reconstructed on the basis of Matthew's form of it, as follows:

And Jesus met them and said, "Good morning!" And they went up to him and clasped his feet and bowed to the ground before him. Jesus said to them, "You need not be afraid. Go and tell my brothers to go to Galilee and they will see me there." And they went with great joy and ran to tell his disciples.

And the eleven disciples went to Galilee, to the mountain to which Jesus had directed them. There they saw him and bowed down before him. And Jesus came up to them and said, "Go and preach the good news to all the heathen. I will always be with you, to the end."

LITERATURE

BACON, B. W. *The Beginnings of Gospel Story* (New York, 1909).

————. *The Gospel of Mark: Its Composition and Date* (New Haven, 1925).

————. *Is Mark a Roman Gospel?* (Cambridge, 1919).

GOULD, E. P. *The Gospel According to St. Mark* (New York, 1913).

GRANT, F. C. *The Growth of the Gospels* (New York, 1933).

LIGHTFOOT, R. H. *History and Interpretation in the Gospels* (New York, 1935).

MENZIES, A. *The Earliest Gospel* (London, 1901).

MONTEFIORE, C. G. *The Synoptic Gospels*, Vol. I (2d ed.; London, 1927).

STREETER, B. H. *The Four Gospels* (New York, 1925).

XI

THE GOSPEL OF MATTHEW

+

Occasion. In presenting the Christian gospel to the Greek world, Christian leaders in the first century were more and more embarrassed by the fact that the Jewish people, among whom the new faith had arisen, did not in any large numbers accept it. Christianity seems to have failed in its first campaign. Its first field was obviously the Jewish people among whom it had arisen; Jesus was their Messiah, foretold by their prophets. But his own people had refused him. What did it mean? The prophets had been full of pictures of the redeemed nation. The coming of the Messiah was to release a new program of spiritual glory for Israel. In the cherished messianic drama his appearance was to be the cue for the nation to take the stage. But the nation had not responded. The Christians joyfully accepted the Jewish scriptures as their Bible, but the prophetic program seemed to be breaking down.

Yet Christianity was not failing. It was winning an amazing success, but in the Greek, not in the Jewish, world. Christianity was, in fact, rapidly becoming a Greek religion. But this success of Christianity in the Greek world only increased the difficulty of the problem. It was nothing like what the prophets had said would happen when the Messiah came.

Paul had seen this difficulty and grappled with it in Romans, chapters 9–11. He cherished the hope that eventually the Jewish people would turn and accept their own Messiah. But in the years that had since passed matters had gone steadily the other way.

An event had now happened that revolutionized Christian thinking on the subject and put into the hand of the evangelist the key to the problem. Jerusalem had fallen. It was a disaster that overturned a good deal of thinking, Jewish and Christian, and had to be reckoned with. Josephus tells terrible stories of carnage, famine, cannibalism, and suicide when rival Jewish groups fought one another in the city and the Roman legions pressed in to destroy the survivors.[1] It might well seem that all the righteous blood shed from the foundation of the world had come upon their heads, Matt. 23:35.

This fearful event put the Jewish rejection of Jesus into a new perspective. For here, within a generation of their refusal of him, they were destroyed, and their cultus and national existence extinguished. To the evangelist the lesson was obvious. Jesus *was* the Messiah of Jewish expectation. He had offered himself to the nation, but it had rejected him and in so doing condemned itself and sealed its own fate. It had now been rejected in its turn and punished, and the Kingdom of Heaven, which might have been its inheritance, had been given to the Greeks who saw its value. These others from the larger Greek world are

[1] Josephus *Wars* v. 12–vi. 9.

therefore the true heirs of the Kingdom and the Scriptures.

To present this philosophy of history, the evangelist plans a book. It is to be a life of the Messiah, from his ancestry and birth to his resurrection, and it is to articulate Christianity with Jewish prophecy and show that it does fulfil the great hopes of the prophets. This is why Matthew especially emphasizes the fulfilment of prophecy, sometimes in trivial and even verbal details: "I called my son from Egypt"; "He shall be called a Nazarene." The book is also to present Jesus as a teacher and so to form an ethical statement of Christianity, comparing its morality with that of scribal Judaism.

For such an interpretative sketch of Jesus in his larger relations the author had various materials at his command. There was first the gospel we know as Mark, and this he made the basis of his book. There were already other brief written accounts dealing with portions of Jesus' work and teaching, and by combination with these and with materials current in the traditional preaching of the church, Mark could be built up into a gospel which should be a vehicle for the new interpretation of Jesus in his relation to the Jews, to the Greeks, and to the Jewish scriptures. This is what the writer seeks to do, keeping himself studiously in the background, from which he emerges just for an instant now and then to point out some fulfilment of Scripture, with the words, "This happened to fulfil what was said by the prophet," 1:22; 2:15, 17, 23; 4:14; 8:17; 21:4; compare also 2:5; 26:31, 54, 56. It has been suggested by Dr. J. Rendel Harris and others that Matthew was making use in these passages of a collection of testimonies or Old Testament texts regarded as fulfilled in Christ and his work;[1] but it seems more probable that the literary use of this sort of thing had its beginning with Matthew and grew into the kind of collection Dr. Harris has so well described. The finding of ten or a dozen Old Testament texts which might be thought of as fulfilled in the gospel history is no large achievement that would require the use of a book of such texts to explain. Moreover, such a book, if it already existed, must certainly have contained Isaiah's words about being reckoned with the transgressors, 53:12 (the crucified thieves), and with the rich in his death, 53:9 (Joseph's tomb), and Hosea's reference to resurrection the third day, Hos. 6:2, none of which is pointed out in Matthew.

Contents. The Gospel of Matthew is biography with a purpose. Jesus, though legally descended from Abraham through David, is really the child of the holy Spirit—a very Jewish way of saying that he is both sinless and the Son of God. It was the Jewish practice to cast their beliefs in story form, instead of in propositions, like the Greeks. Think of the first clause of the Apostles' Creed, "I believe in God the Father Almighty, Maker of Heaven and Earth," side by side with the first words of Genesis.

In the genealogy, 1:1–17, the generations are grouped into three fourteens, so that Jesus would begin the seventh seven—a symbol of his supreme sig-

[1] *Testimonies* (Cambridge, 1916).

nificance, reminding us of the use of sevens in the Revelation: 1:4; 2:1; 3:1; 4:5; 5:1; 8:2, 6; 10:3, 4, etc. The four women named in the genealogy— Tamar, Rahab, Ruth, and Uriah's wife—are mentioned perhaps as a kind of apologetic for the Nativity in advance of the narrative, as much as to say, "If anyone stumbles at what he may think an irregularity in the immediate ancestry of Jesus, look at the ancestry of David and the kings of Judah."

The generations seem arbitrarily compressed by the omission of three from the second series—Ahaziah, Joash, and Amaziah being left out with reigns totaling seventy years, II Kings 8:25; 12:1; 14:2. This may be due to the similarity of the names of Ahaziah and Azariah, which may have led Matthew or his source to skip from Ahaziah to Azariah, combined with the attractiveness the series of three fourteens would have for Matthew. Matthew was not always accurate in his use of the Old Testament, as is shown by his reference of a passage in Zech. 11:13 to Jeremiah the prophet, 27:9, and his confusion of the martyred priest Zechariah, 23:35, with the prophet Zechariah, the son of Berechiah, and with the "son of Baruch" in Josephus.[1]

---

[1] It would seem that Zechariah the son of Jehoiada is meant, for his murder "in the court of the house of the Lord" is the last one recorded in the Jewish scriptures, in which the Books of Chronicles stood last. The vast sweep intended would be from the murder of Abel, recorded at the beginning of the scriptures, Gen. 4:8, to that of Zechariah, recorded at the very end of them, II Chron. 24:21. Zechariah the son of Berechiah was the prophet Zechariah, Zech. 1:1, of whose death nothing is known. But it is a curious fact that Josephus (*Wars* iv. 5. 4) records the murder of a Zechariah the son of Baruch "in the middle of the Temple," in the course of the

The narratives that had grown up about the infancy
of Jesus (ignored by Mark) describe every movement
of the infant Messiah as divinely directed, usually
through the dreams of his father Joseph. Mary is
steadily mute and passive, a lay figure in the drama,
in strong contrast to the Mary of Luke's story, Luke
1:26—2:20. The homage of the astrologers meant to
the ancient mind, as Ignatius said forty years later,
that with the coming of Christ magic was over-
thrown.[1] Astrology it must be remembered commanded the attention of some of the ablest men of the
first century, like Tiberius, who, before he became
emperor, seems to have spent years at Rhodes in the
study of it.[2]

We must not overlook the fact that with the infancy interest in Matthew a new concern for childhood
appears. The measures taken by Herod to destroy the
infant Messiah leads to the Slaughter of the Innocents
at Bethlehem, 2:16–18. It was an age of callous in-
difference to childhood. A personal letter from a hus-
band in Alexandria to his wife in Oxyrhynchus, written in 1 B.C., instructs her that, if her child when it is
born is a boy, she is to let it live, if a girl, it is to be
exposed,[3] either to die or to be picked and reared as

---

excesses that preceded the siege. This recent event probably influenced the
confusion of names in Matthew's reference to the death of Zechariah.
Matthew's Greek suggests the form "Barachiah" for the father's name.

[1] Eph. 19:3.

[2] F. Cumont, *The Oriental Religions in Roman Paganism* (Chicago, 1911),
p. 180; Suetonius *Tiberius* 11.

[3] G. Milligan, *Selections from the Greek Papyri* (Cambridge, 1910), p. 32.

a slave.[1] Justin Martyr speaks of the ancient practice of exposing undesired children (*Apology* xxvii. 1). Nor is the infancy interest of Matthew confined to the infant Messiah: "Beware of feeling scornful of one single little child, for I tell you that in heaven their angels have continual access to my Father in heaven," 18:10. "It is the will of my Father in heaven that not a single one of these children be lost," 18:14.[2]

Jesus is divinely addressed as Messiah at his baptism and is victorious in the temptation conflict. He proceeds to declare his message in a series of six great sermons, most of them dealing with some aspect of the Kingdom of God or, as Matthew prefers to call it, the Kingdom of Heaven. The first of these is the Sermon on the Mount.

The approach to the sermon is carefully built up by the evangelist. Jesus has already achieved a wide reputation as a healer, exorcist, and preacher. Great crowds followed him about. When he saw the crowds, he went up on the mountain, as Moses had done. We must not soften Matthew's "mountain" to "hillside," for he uses the stronger word advisedly to remind us of another who went up on a mountain, Exod. 19:20, and came down with the Tables of the Law. What can the new lawgiver offer to equal that? Matthew's answer is the Sermon on the Mount. "There he seated himself," he goes on—the sign that Jesus was about to teach, for the oriental teacher taught seated, Luke

---

[1] Cf. Hermas, *The Shepherd: Vis.* i. 1. 1, "He who brought me up sold me to a certain Rhoda, in Rome."

[2] Cf. also Matt. 19:14, but it is paralleled in Mark and Luke.

4:20. It was the signal for the disciples to throng about to hear him. So "when his disciples had come up to him, he opened his lips to teach them."

The Sermon on the Mount deals with the Standards of Uprightness in the Kingdom of Heaven. It develops into a great statement, probably never surpassed, of the ethical ideals of Christianity. It begins with a commanding series of beatitudes and includes the Lord's Prayer, 6:9–13, and the Golden Rule, 7:12. This masterly body of teaching shows at once why Matthew immediately and permanently overshadowed Mark. Luke also has beatitudes and a Lord's Prayer, but these formulations of his have never rivaled Matthew's and are generally forgotten. Few people are aware that Luke contains a Lord's Prayer, and no one ever thinks of using it in public or private worship.

It would be easy to rhapsodize over the Sermon on the Mount; so many people say, "I have no theology; my religion is the Sermon on the Mount." It would be hard to find a nobler religion, but the rest of the New Testament has its religious values too. We must recognize the part the author of the gospel had in building up this sermon, for it is really his work, as anyone can see who will compare it section by section with the parallels in Mark and Luke. However much the evangelist owed to his sources, the arrangement and organization of the sermon at least are his work.

The end of the sermon, as of most of the six sermons in Matthew, is marked by a formal statement: "When Jesus had finished this discourse, the crowds were astounded at his teaching, for he taught them like one who had authority, and not like their scribes." The sermon is followed by a series of incidents, gathered chiefly from Mark, designed to show that Jesus really possessed such authority, for his wonders showed it. Then the evangelist returns to his series of sermons, for his plan is to interweave sermon with incident. In fact, Matthew is doing two things in his book; by the six sermons he is exhibiting Jesus as a supreme teacher; and he is at the same time showing how he offered himself and the Kingdom to the Jewish people and was refused by them, to their own destruction.

The second sermon, chapter 10, deals with the Proclamation of the Kingdom—how it is to be preached. It is prefaced by the calling of the Twelve, and in many particulars reflects what was felt to be the proper missionary approach at the time when the gospel was written. Certainly not a little of the experience of the young church is reflected in its words. The end of the sermon is emphasized by the formal statement, "When Jesus had finished giving his twelve disciples these instructions, he went on from there to teach and preach in their towns."

After a number of short narratives, chapters 11, 12, mostly drawn from Mark, the third sermon is introduced, 13:1–52. It deals with the Growth and Worth of the Kingdom and consists of a series of parables— the Sower, the Weeds, the Mustard Seed. The disciples now recognize Jesus as the Messiah. He welcomes Peter's confession but foretells his own death.

In a fourth discourse, chapter 18, Jesus speaks of

Life in the Kingdom, telling the parables of the Ninety-nine Sheep and the Unforgiving Debtor. He sets out for Jerusalem, well aware of his danger in going there, enters the city in messianic fashion, as Matthew is careful to point out, and proceeds to clear the Temple of money-makers. Challenged by the authorities, he responds with the Marcan parable of the Wicked Tenants, the point of which Matthew under-scores by inserting the words. "That, I tell you, is why the Kingdom of God will be taken away from you, and given to a people that will produce its proper fruit. Whoever falls on that stone will be shattered, but whoever it falls upon will be pulverized!" To Matthew's readers the meaning was only too plain. The cornerstone, which had been rejected by the Jewish people, had fallen upon them, and they had been pulverized. Matthew did not overestimate the blow that had befallen them. Nineteen centuries have passed, and their national existence and cultus have never been revived.

This sentence marks the turning-point in the action of the Gospel of Matthew. Jesus had confined his efforts to the Jews; "I am sent only to the lost sheep of Israel's house," he had said to the Canaanite woman, 15:24. He had sent the Twelve not to the heathen or to the Samaritans but to the lost sheep of Israel's house, 10:5, 6. Now he turns from them. In a fifth discourse he denounces the people's religious leaders for their hypocrisy and pretense, chapter 23. Their superior religious privilege—prophets, wise men, and scribes—they had steadily refused, 23:34, and in consequence there was coming upon that age all the blood guilt of history. "All the righteous blood shed on the earth, from the blood of Abel the upright to the blood of Zechariah, Barachiah's son, whom you murdered between the sanctuary and the altar! I tell you, all this will come upon this age."

All that Jesus says in the gospels could have been uttered in two or three hours. Out of all that he uttered, the selective memory of the church preserved what its experience underscored. Of course, the reason Matthew wrote this terrific sentence was that he had heard of its fulfilment. He could hardly refer more unmistakably to the terrible scenes attending the fall of Jerusalem in A.D. 70, which Josephus so graphically describes (*Wars* v. 12—vi. 9). It is idle in the presence of such a picture to say that Matthew does not show any knowledge of the fall of Jerusalem, and on the other hand it cannot have been very long after that event that he wrote so feelingly about it:

O Jerusalem! Jerusalem! murdering the prophets, and stoning those who are sent to her, how often I have longed to gather your children around me, as a hen gathers her brood under her wings, but you refused! Now I leave you to yourselves. For I tell you, you will never see me again until you say, "Blessed be he who comes in the Lord's name!"

This great invective, built up by Matthew from a number of sources, is almost immediately followed by a final discourse, the sixth, foretelling the fall of Jerusalem and the end of the age, chapters 24, 25. It can hardly be thought of as forming one sermon with chapter 23, for Matthew is careful to describe Jesus as leaving the Temple, 24:1, and climbing the Mount of Olives, 24:3, on the other side of the Kedron ravine. The sermon continues with three parables, ending with the Last Judgment. This tremendous apocalyptic picture also carries the ethical teaching of the gospel to its highest climax—"In so far as you failed to do it for one of these people who are humblest, you failed to do it for me." There is an emotional power about this parable that is not surpassed in the gospel, or anywhere else, as anyone who has had occasion to read it in public will agree. One might suppose that a gospel which gave so much in its first great broadside, the Sermon on the Mount, might end in anticlimax, as far as moral teaching was concerned, but this is far from true. And it is principally for this supreme moral note that the parable is recorded.

The drama of betrayal, arrest, trial, and crucifixion is played through in Matthew very much as in Mark, though with some additions designed to emphasize the guilt of the nation for Jesus' death; "His blood be on us and our children" was their terrible cry, 27:25. These words must have taken on an awful significance for a generation with the scenes attending the fall of Jerusalem fresh in their minds. Matthew records them for an age in sharp conflict with the synagogue, but he can hardly have dreamed of the long-enduring bitterness against the Jews his words would engender.

After his death Jesus reappears to some women and then to the eleven disciples at the mountain rendezvous they had agreed upon in Galilee. They are now to go not to the lost sheep of Israel's house, but to all the heathen, and he is to stay with them, an enduring presence, until the age ends. So the curtain falls on the Gospel of Matthew, with Jesus restored to his disciples, never again to be taken from them. This is very significant for the doctrine of resurrection that Matthew held.

The Gospel of Matthew accomplished a number of things of great value and importance. It interpreted the Gospel of Mark. It substituted Jesus the Teacher for Jesus the Man of Action. It solved the writer's problem as to the apparent failure of the program of the prophets. It united his several sources into one. It rescued the Old Testament for Christianity, and it produced an ethical statement of Christianity that has never been surpassed.

It did all this with great religious and literary tact, although it is not literary in its Greek style. The gospels are, as Renan said, the first books written in colloquial Greek, and many of us will be inclined to agree with his judgment that the Gospel of Matthew is the most important book in the world.[1]

Problems. In writing his gospel the evangelist made use of a variety of sources. There was in the first place the gospel we know as Mark, which formed the basis of the book. It is not difficult to find fifteen-sixteenths of Mark reproduced in Matthew. Indeed, Matthew is from one point of view simply a revised and enlarged Gospel of Mark. Of course it is much more than that; but it is certainly that. And it must

[1] Ernest Renan, *Les Évangiles et la seconde génération Chrétienne* (Paris, 1912), pp. 212–13.

be remembered that this missing sixteenth is not a single block that Matthew turned away from but is made up of tiny fractions, a verse here and a phrase there, the longest being the story of the poor widow dropping her two coppers into the Temple treasury, Mark 12:41–44—a passage of only seventy-five words.

It is easy to see how Matthew, with his disposition to organize and assemble his material, should have omitted this, for it would hardly fit in with his teaching against public giving. We may say there is really no fundamental conflict between them, and yet we would not want to record them together, no matter how much we prize them both. In fact, there is hardly a detail given by Mark which Matthew has omitted which we cannot understand his omitting. The demonic recognitions of Jesus, the difficulty Jesus sometimes seems to have in effecting a cure, Mark 8:23–25, his apparent use of means in healing, Mark 7:33; 8:23—these may have deterred Matthew from using some accounts when he had what he may well have considered better ones with which to fill his gospel.

This Marcan material, which can be seen displayed in any Greek or English harmony of the gospels,[1] Matthew somewhat rearranged, yet in using it he followed the order of Mark's phrases to an extraordinary degree. We can form a very fair idea of the way in which Matthew used his sources by the way he used Mark, and while he rearranged blocks and items of material with some freedom, in detail he was singularly

---

Burton and Goodspeed, *Harmony of the Synoptic Gospels* (New York, 1917); *Harmony of the Synoptic Gospels in Greek* (Chicago, 1920).

faithful to the source he was using. Certainly that is the way he used Mark, and it seems reasonable to suppose that was the way in which he used his other sources.

To most moderns it seems an act of sheer plagiarism to use another man's book so freely and say nothing about it. But we must always remember that both Matthew and Mark were anonymous; neither writer gave his name to his gospel or claimed it as his own; both were probably well aware that their gospels were in a sense social products, to which other minds had contributed. Matthew's was certainly organized and refined by one person, peculiarly alive to the needs and possibilities of the situation. Yet he so carefully concealed himself behind his work that his name has disappeared, and we call him Matthew only because since early in the second century his work has been known by that name.

The question arises: What other sources had Matthew for the writing of his gospel? It is plain that one, at least, of these other sources was used by Luke also, since many things absent from Mark are present in both Luke and Matthew and in the same form of words. Luke is especially instructive here, for his method, unlike Matthew's, was to use his sources en bloc, not minutely interwoven. So it comes about that there are in Luke considerable areas where Mark has not been used at all; we may call them Mark-free areas. Since these alternate with solid extracts from Mark, which were evidently taken directly from that gospel with slight verbal changes, it seems very probable that the non-Marcan passages were likewise taken from other written sources, which Matthew also used in his own peculiar way.

The longest of these Mark-free areas in Luke is 9:51—18:14. Then, after an excerpt from Mark, 19:1–28 is again Mark-free. These may be called the Perean Section,[1] since their scene is laid in Perea. They probably formed a separate document or documents; certainly they were used by Matthew.

Another of these Mark-free areas in Luke is 6:20—8:3, which may be called the Galilean Section, as its action takes place in Galilee. But with it we may naturally group scattered passages such as 3:7–18; 4:2–13, wanting in Mark and yet used also by Matthew. Whether these two sections, the Galilean and the Perean, were separate or are to be thought of as one (the so-called "Q" or "Quelle") has been much discussed; they are different in certain definite respects, and Luke in his preface, 1:1–4, leads us to expect him to show the use of a number of sources: "Many writers have undertaken to compose accounts, ..." It is clear that Luke and Matthew used the material of these sections, in addition to Mark. There is no substantial reason for supposing that they were combined into one document, and Luke's statement, 1:1, is definitely against it. They had reached written form probably somewhere in the Greek world.

Papias of Hierapolis, in one of the fragments from

[1] Cf. D. R. Wickes, *The Sources of Luke's Perean Section* (Chicago, 1912), and E. W. Parsons, *A Historical Examination of Some Non-Marcan Elements in Luke* (Chicago, 1914).

his *Interpretations of Sayings of the Lord* preserved in Eusebius, says, "Matthew composed the Sayings in the Aramaic language and each one translated them as he was able."[1] This cannot possibly mean our Gospel of Matthew, for the identities of Greek expression between it and Mark and Luke cannot be reconciled with the idea that it is a translation; the Greek relationship between the three must have come through Greek and could not have survived independent translation, which always breeds variation in abundance.

This supposed Aramaic document mentioned by Papias used to be reckoned the second source of Matthew and Luke, from which they obtained their greater richness in Jesus' teaching. But their common discourse material shows so much identity of Greek language that this view has been given up. The non-Marcan materials of Matthew and Luke came to them from Greek sources; there can be no possible doubt of that, as an hour's examination of the non-Marcan parallels in Matthew and Luke will show.[2]

We can only conclude that Papias is here speaking not of a written document at all, but of the Oral Gospel used by Paul, Luke (Acts 20:35), Clement, and Polycarp, which would of course be composed in the Aramaic language and be variously translated into Greek by the pioneers of the Greek mission. His remark may therefore be dismissed as of no significance for the sources of Matthew.

[1] *Church History* iii. 39. 16.

[2] Burton and Goodspeed, *Harmony of the Synoptic Gospels in Greek* (Chicago, 1920), esp. pp. 162–231.

Yet Matthew probably had other sources, chiefly traditions of sayings of Jesus, current in more or less developed forms in Christian preaching, which he wrought into fuller and more finished forms, e.g., in the finely rounded parables of chapter 25. These may have been combined into a document or they may have existed separately. They had been reduced to writing somewhere in Greek Christian circles, probably about Antioch. They would be of that "formless," that is, unorganized, type of sayings collection natural enough in the oral stage in Jewish Christian groups, since it was in this way that the Jews were wont to gather and transmit (of course orally) the sayings of the rabbis.[1]

While there are touches in the Revelation of John that seem to show the influence of Matthew, the most striking early reflections of it are to be found in Ignatius of Antioch, who makes unmistakable use of it in Ephesians, chapter 19 (the virginity of Mary, the star, and the end of magic, suggested by the Adoration of the Magi), Smyrnaeans, chapter 1, etc. Streeter traces some fifteen reminiscences of Matthew in Ignatius' letters.[2] As Ignatius was bishop of Antioch in Syria, it seems probable that it was there the gospel was written. Antioch was, in Harnack's phrase, the first great fulcrum of Christianity.[3] It was there it had

[1] F. C. Grant, *The Growth of the Gospels* (New York, 1933), p. 163; R. R. Brewer, "The Source of the Matthaean Logia" (unpublished dissertation; Chicago, 1929), "University of Chicago Abstracts of Theses, Humanistic Series," viii, 481.

[2] *The Four Gospels* (New York, 1925), p. 505.

[3] Harnack, *Mission and Expansion of Christianity* (2d ed.; New York, 1908), II, 184.

first addressed itself directly to Greeks, Acts 11:20. It was the mother of the Greek mission. All this makes it a natural place for the composition of such a considered Greek gospel as Matthew. Moreover, Matthew is not much influenced by the work of Paul, as Western churches were likely to have been; it views Jesus as the giver of a new and better Law. Its emphasis upon Peter, 10:2; 14:29; 16:17–19, etc., fits well in Antioch, as does the presence of its infancy material, chapters 1, 2. In Antioch, with its numbers of Jews and Christians, the fall of the neighboring city of Jerusalem would be keenly felt. There, too, the comparison of Jesus' ethical teachings with those of scribal Judaism would be very natural.

The date of Matthew is fairly fixed by its use of Mark and its evidently intense interest in the fall of Jerusalem, A.D. 70. The place the fall of Jerusalem plays in the writer's thought makes it likely that he wrote not long after that event and before its influence upon Christian thinking had subsided. This consideration finds some striking corroborations in the gospel:

1. In his discourse on the fall of the city and the end of the age, Jesus says that, immediately after the misery of the fall of the city, the messianic advent will occur. A book containing such a statement can hardly have been written very long after A.D. 70. This is all the more striking as the word "immediately" is absent from Mark 13:24 which is the basis for the passage in Matthew.

2. In 16:28 Jesus says to the disciples, "Some of you

who stand here will certainly live to see the Son of Man come to reign!"

3. In sending out the Twelve Jesus says, "You will not have gone through all the towns of Israel before the Son of Man arrives," 10:23.

4. Jesus answers the high priest, "You will soon see the Son of Man seated at the right hand of the Almighty and coming upon the clouds of the sky!" 26:64. The words translated "soon" are not in the parallel passage in Mark 14:62, which is Matthew's source here.

These facts point toward a date only a few years after A.D. 70, perhaps not long before or after the year 80. To date Matthew about 100, as some have done, is not only greatly hindered by these facts but rendered practically impossible by Matthew's evident non-acquaintance with the published letters of Paul, which came into circulation very soon after A.D. 90, since they are reflected in Ephesians, Revelation, Hebrews, I Clement, and I Peter.[1] The apparent use of Matthew in the Revelation is also incompatible with this late date.[2]

---

[1] E. J. Goodspeed, *New Solutions of New Testament Problems* (Chicago, 1927), chaps. ii–iv.

[2] The influence of the Gospel of Matthew upon the Revelation has been affirmed by Dr. R. H. Charles (*The Revelation of St. John* [London, 1920], I, lxxxiv f.); by Provost Streeter (*The Four Gospels* [New York, 1925], p. 469); and by Dr. Lloyd V. Moore (*The Use of Gospel Material in Pre-Catholic Christian Literature* [unpublished dissertation; Chicago, 1929], pp. 97–113). Rev. 1:3 reflects Matt. 28:18; Rev. 1:16 resembles Matt. 17:2; Rev. 3:3 reflects Matt. 24:42–44, and 25:13; Rev. 3:5 reflects Matt. 10:32, perhaps combined with Luke 12:8; Rev. 13:10 repeats the substance of Matt. 26:52; and Rev. 19:9 reflects Matt. 22:1–14. Other minor resemblances are noted

While the author of Matthew was probably a Christian of Jewish blood, 1:1–17, the traditional view that Matthew was written for Jews cannot be maintained. The gospel steadily depreciates the practices and ethics of Judaism. It lays the responsibility for the death of Jesus at the door of the Jewish people with terrible solemnity. It gives the impression that the church and the synagogue are growing more and more hostile. It nowhere has the appearance of seeking to win or to conciliate Jews. Its purpose is rather to explain their refusal of the gospel and to establish the Jewish scriptures as a possession of the church. The upshot of its action is that, whereas Jesus had confined his efforts to the Jewish people, now that they have refused him (21:43; 27:1, 22, 23), his apostles are to carry his message to all the heathen, 28:19. This would be a strange approach to a Jewish public. The attitude of the Gospel of Matthew is rather that the Jewish mission is definitely and finally over. It is the Greek mission that is now before the church.

Great as is the author's devotion to the Greek mission, he does seem to be of Jewish blood. The long genealogy, mostly derivable from Genesis, Ruth, and I Chronicles, chapter 3, shows a Jewish interest; the conviction that every detail of the Law must be observed; the view of Jesus as a new Moses with a new and nobler Law; his fashion of gathering Jesus' sayings into extended discourses; his interest in Christianity as

by Dr. Moore. On the whole, these make it very probable that Matthew was used by the writer of the Revelation and was therefore not unknown in the circle of Ephesus about A.D. 90 or soon after.

fulfilling Jewish prophecy—these and other traits in his gospel make it probable that he came of Jewish stock.

At the same time other items just as definite tend to show that he was not of Palestine but of the Dispersion. His view of the new faith is indeed very different from Paul's—almost as far from it as possible. But he writes in Greek for Greeks; he despairs of converting the Jews; they have lost their golden opportunity and have paid the penalty; he repeatedly departs from the king lists of the Books of Kings and the genealogical lists in I Chronicles, chapter 3; he ascribes to Jeremiah (Matt. 27:9) an oracle of Zechariah, 11:13; he makes use of the Septuagint Greek version. On the whole, he seems to have been—like Paul, Barnabas, and Stephen—a Hellenist, a Jew from the Greek world. He was certainly one of the greatest of those early Christians in whom the new faith had awakened such undreamed-of powers.

LITERATURE

BACON, B. W. *Studies in Matthew* (New York, 1930).

McNEILE, A. H. *The Gospel According to St. Matthew* (London, 1915).

XII

THE WORK OF LUKE

+

Occasion. The commanding feature of the Christian story, from the work of Paul onward, is the swift spread of the Christian movement over the Greek world. That movement first emerges into the clear light of history with the letters of Paul, written in Greek to Greek churches, and, as Harnack once remarked, Christianity remained a Greek movement almost to the end of the second century. Paul's letters and the earliest gospels were written by Christian Jews, it is true, but they were written in Greek. It was inevitable that the Greeks would soon seize the pen and begin to produce their own Christian literature. The first of them to do this was Luke.

No finding of modern New Testament study is more assured than that Luke and Acts are not two books, written at different times, but two volumes of a single work, conceived and executed as a unit. This distinction may not seem significant, but it is, as a matter of fact, of the utmost importance. It is one thing to write a pamphlet or a book; it implies a certain degree of reflection, research, and organization. It is a very different thing to plan a book in two volumes, each in some degree a unit in itself but even more an integral part of a larger whole. Further, to recognize that Luke and

Acts form two volumes of a single work enables us, so to speak, to gather all the light that each one of them has to throw on authorship, purpose, sources, date, interest, etc., and focus it upon both of them.

What are the grounds for this opinion? In the first place, the preface of Luke's gospel is, upon closer scrutiny seen to be really the preface of the larger work. There is nothing in it to limit it to the gospel; it definitely aims at recording the development of the Christian movement from the very beginning.

This idea is supported, in the second place, by a glance at the opening lines of Acts, which simply pick up the thread laid down in the earlier preface in the briefest fashion.

Third, these opening sentences of Luke and Acts are very much like the opening sentences of Josephus in his *Against Apion*, books i and ii. These latter afford close parallels to the two much-discussed opening paragraphs in Luke-Acts—that at the beginning of book ii referring to and resuming from that at the beginning of book i. The parallel is in fact so close as to lead some to think Luke must have seen this work of Josephus. But this is unnecessary; it is enough that this was the literary fashion of those times.

A fourth point is that the Gospel of Luke does not reach the goal it sets itself—the impartation of the Spirit to the disciples. The gospel tells them, 24:49, "I will send down upon you what my Father has promised. Wait here in the city until you are clothed with power from on high." The fulfilment of this promise does not come until the second chapter of

Acts. It is hard to believe that Luke would think his story was told, with such a forecast left hanging in the air unfulfilled. But of course this is simply the art of the continued story—to foreshadow in one instalment something of great importance that is to be related in the next. By these verses Luke links book ii to book i in unmistakable fashion.

Of course, all this would be much clearer if the Acts had not been anciently separated from the Gospel of Luke when the gospel was gathered into the great quartet of gospels early in the second century. It is the fact that, as we first know these books, John comes between Luke and Acts that obscures their continuity and actually hides it from us.

Sixty years after the death of Christ the success of the Christian movement in the Greek West awakened some Christians to the fact that it was no narrow local affair but was fast swinging into the great race with the ethnic, mystery, and philosophical religions for the mastery of the ancient world. The Greek mission was a success, and some record must be made of its beginnings before it was too late.

The first great element in the record was naturally the work of Jesus himself, and this claimed the first volume. For this there was also a special need, since written narratives about it were so numerous and conflicting, while the Oral Gospel would naturally undergo alteration and improvement as it was handed on among Greek groups, less schooled to faithfulness to the letter than were Jews. This is the picture so comprehensively sketched in Luke's first lines—a marvelously compact account of situation, purpose, dedication, sources, and method.

Here, at last, is a writer conscious of the great outside world-organization, who tries to fix his narrative, when he can, against the background of imperial chronology. "In the fifteenth year of the emperor Tiberius" was once thought an eccentricity on Luke's part, but is really just the way in which papyrus documents in the first century are regularly dated. To Luke we owe our only definite information about dates in the gospel story.

Jesus' work was among the Jews of Palestine, but the narrative is not without hints of the writer's broader view of him and his mission. The genealogy does not stop with Abraham but pursues Jesus' lineage back through the antediluvians to Adam, the son of God, 3:23–38. The hero of one of the most notable parables is a Good Samaritan, 10:30–37; and of the ten lepers cured, only one came back to thank Jesus, and he was a Samaritan, 17:16—foreshadowings of the future Samaritan mission, Acts 8:4–25. Salvation is to be preached to all the heathen in Jesus' name, Luke 24:47. And yet the wonder is that the evangelist has so far succeeded in keeping his wider outlook and his knowledge and consciousness of the great developments that lay just ahead from coloring his gospel picture.

Contents. The infancy narratives, 1:5—2:52, offer an interesting contrast to those of Matthew. They describe the foretelling of the birth and work of John in ways often reminiscent of the narrative of I Samuel, chapters 1 and 2. Luke's angels are no mere dream visitants, as in Matt. 1:20; 2:13, 19, but appear in broad daylight or at least in waking hours, Luke 1:11, 26; 2:9; Acts 12:7–10. The women are not mute and passive in Luke's story but become the leading figures in it, breaking forth, like Samuel's mother Hannah, into inspired song. These songs and hymns in Luke, chapters 1 and 2, are the beginnings of Christian hymnology, and at once suggest the time of the Revelation with its great choruses and antiphonies. Here the stream of Jewish psalmody is seen entering its new Christian channel.

It is not without significance that Luke does not begin his gospel in Galilee or even at Bethlehem, but chooses a scene in Jerusalem and actually in the very heart of the Temple there. We remember that his narrative ends in Rome, the center of the ancient world. The holy Spirit is already, from the beginning, appealed to by the evangelist as the explanation of all that is wonderful in his story: the birth of Jesus, the psalms of Elizabeth and Zechariah, the clairvoyance of Symeon, 1:35, 42, 67; 2:27. While still a boy of twelve, long before his baptism, Jesus is conscious of his divine sonship, and thinks of the Temple as his Father's house.

The more historical body of the gospel opens with an elaborate effort to date the work of John the Baptist in the usual ancient way, by regnal years of the Roman emperors. So common was this method that Greek papyrus documents dated in this way have been published from every single year of the first century.

It is important here as reflecting the writer's interest in relating the Christian story to its historical background in the great world. It is plain that we are in the presence of an intelligent and cultivated man, acquainted with the literary habits of his day (preface, dedication, sources) and concerned about dates and reigns.

Luke's genealogy differs from Matthew's not only in not following the royal line of descent from David down, but in pushing the ancestry back beyond Abraham to Adam, the son of God, 3:23–38. Jesus announces himself as Messiah in the synagogue at Nazareth, quoting Isaiah, chapter 61, in what has been called the "frontispiece" of the Gospel of Luke. Luke has taken some pains to make this the beginning of his account of Jesus' ministry, for he has transposed a section of Mark, 6:1–5, to bring this about.[1] Jesus goes to Capernaum and Galilee; calls four disciples; appoints the Twelve, naming them apostles; and preaches the Sermon on the Plain, 6:17–49. He and his apostles move about Galilee together, then he sends them out in pairs, in the midst of growing opposition. At last he moves toward Jerusalem, 9:51. "It is not right for a prophet to die outside Jerusalem," 13:33. On the way he utters the striking parables of the Good Samaritan, the Prodigal Son, and the Pharisee and the Tax Collector, chapters 10, 15, 18. In Jerusalem the drama of denunciation, betrayal, and death is portrayed, but this time with fuller resurrec-

[1] His only other substantial disturbance of Mark's order is in 5:1–11, where he makes Mark 1:16–20 follow Mark 1:39.

tion accounts, much more material in character and culminating in the Ascension—the necessary sequel of Luke's doctrine of material resurrection if Jesus was to take his place at God's right hand. This concrete strain in Luke pervades both volumes; angels are for him visible, audible, and tangible, Luke 1:11, 28; Acts 12:7; the coming of the Spirit on the disciples in the Acts and Paul's conversion, both essentially spiritual experiences, are attended with striking physical manifestations, as was the coming of the Spirit upon Jesus at his baptism when "the holy Spirit came down upon him in the material shape of a dove," 3:22. The first volume closes, not like Matthew with reunion in Galilee and the Great Commission, but with the disciples gathered in Jerusalem awaiting the power from on high that is to clothe them, 24:49, 52—a strong hint that there is more to come.

Renan calls it the most literary of the gospels and the most beautiful book in the world, but of course it must not be viewed as a book at all but only as the first volume of one, and its interests—social, humanitarian, universal, educational, literary, and apologetic —are simply those of the larger work of which it is a part.

As we enter volume two, the writer's larger purpose becomes more clear. He proposes to sketch the beginnings of Christianity, especially of Greek Christianity, into which the Christian movement had developed. The thread of the narrative is no mere biography but the providential fashion in which the gospel had groped its way out of Judaism into widening circles—Roman and Ethiopian, proselyte and Samaritan—until at length, in Antioch, the apostles began to preach to Greeks with no Jewish preparation and then to the whole Mediterranean world. No man plans it, not even the apostles. It happens involuntarily but inevitably, in an almost casual way, by human contacts.

Philip, trudging southward, falls in with the traveling car of an Ethiopian proselyte and enters into conversation with him over a passage of Isaiah which the man (quaintly enough) was reading aloud—to himself! The Ethiopian is converted and goes joyfully on his way, while Philip hurries on his. They have simply brushed against each other on their travels, but the Christian faith has been imparted by the casual contact.

Peter is the chief figure at first in Jerusalem, but it is Paul who soon leads the missionary campaign westward from Antioch. With him the gospel presently passes out of Asia, the continent of its origin, into Europe, the continent of its destiny. A man of Macedonia in a dream calls Paul to help them. So at length the gospel is planted in Rome, the center and capital of the world.

Old chapter and verse divisions, sometimes worse than meaningless, 21:40, have blocked and obscured the swiftly running current of the Acts with its rapid, exciting action, which ought by all means to be read, as it was intended to be read, at a single sitting. Where within eighty pages will be found such a varied series of exciting events—trials, riots, persecutions, escapes, martyrdoms, voyages, shipwrecks, rescues—set in that amazing panorama of the ancient world—Jerusalem, Antioch, Philippi, Corinth, Athens, Ephesus, Rome? And with such scenery and settings—temples, courts, prisons, deserts, ships, seas, barracks, theaters? Has any opera such variety? A bewildering range of scenes and actions passes before the eye of the historian. And in them all he sees the providential hand that has made and guided this great movement for the salvation of mankind.

The narrative which began in Jerusalem culminates in Rome, where Christianity has already been mysteriously established. The style, which is full of strange variety in the opening chapters of the Acts, settles into the writer's own manner when Paul takes the center of the stage—a strong hint that the author is here on his own ground.

Acts may appear at first little more than a storybook of the early Christian movement, but this means only that the writer has skilfully concealed his didactic and left the intrinsic interest of his materials to carry the reader on. Each story has a point of its own, but the whole has a larger meaning of its own too, which the writer has not spoiled by elaborating but has left to the intelligence of his readers. And he has told his story to the end, for with Christianity established in Rome accounts of its further extension to obscure places in Gaul or Spain would be sheer anticlimax. There is an obvious propriety in a narrative which, beginning in Jerusalem, the historic seat of the old religion, ends in Rome, the center of its field, which was to be the world, Luke 24:47; compare Matt. 13:38.

Modern historians realize that history is not just a record of wars and dynasties but has to do with new ideas, currents of thought, and attitudes of mind. The rise of Christianity seemed a matter of no consequence to the ancient classical historians. But Luke saw something of its importance, and we cannot be too grateful that he wrote of it as he did. In this respect he was a sounder historian than they. There are, of course, a hundred questions we wish he had answered, but he had his goal in view and kept to it. To have added an obituary of Paul at the end of the Acts, just because Paul was dead, Acts 20:25, 38, would have seemed to compare his martyrdom with that of Jesus and have made it necessary to report Peter's death too. It would also have changed the book's direction at the very end, for it is not a biography of Peter and Paul but an account of the progress of the Greek mission up to its establishment in the capital of the world.

Problems. *Two volumes.* Some have thought that Luke meant to write a third volume, because he refers to what we call the Gospel of Luke as his "first." But the Greeks were just as much accustomed to speak of the first of two as the first as we are. None of us ever speaks of "the former volume" of a two-volume work; we always say "the first volume" or "Volume I." And what Luke could have reserved for such a volume, unless it be the martyrdoms above mentioned, it is difficult to see. These scholars forget Luke's manifest fondness for great cities as starting and stopping points in his narratives. He did not need to begin either volume in Jerusalem; Matthew did not begin or end his gospel there, nor did Mark, if as we have seen his conclusion was like Matthew's. But Luke begins both volumes in Jerusalem and ends the first one there. Where better could the whole work end than in Rome?

If anyone has any doubt that Luke and Acts are two volumes of a single work, and that this is what their opening lines are meant to convey, a glance at the opening lines of Josephus' *Against Apion*, books i and ii, will dispel them. They are as follows:

In my history of our Antiquities, most excellent Epaphroditus, I have, I think, made sufficiently clear to any who may peruse that work the extreme antiquity of our Jewish race, the purity of the original stock and the manner in which it established itself in the country which we occupy today. . . . . Since, however, I observe that a considerable number of persons, ... discredit the statements in my history concerning our antiquity, ... I consider it my duty to devote a brief treatise to all these points, in order at once to convict our detractors of malignity and deliberate falsehood, to correct the ignorance of others, and to instruct all who desire to know the truth concerning the antiquity of our race.

Book ii begins in this way:

In the first volume of this work, my most esteemed Epaphroditus, I demonstrated the antiquity of our race, corroborating my statements by the writings of the Phoenicians, Chaldaeans, and Egyptians. . . . . I also challenged the statements of Manetho, Chaeremon and some others.

I shall now proceed to refute the rest of the authors who have attacked us.[1]

The resemblance to Luke's opening lines in his two "books" or volumes (*logoi*) is clear. Luke followed the literary fashion of his day in these opening sentences, dealing in them, like Josephus, with occasion, dedication, and purpose.

Date. We have seen that the idea of writing such a work as Luke-Acts on the beginnings of the Christian movement could hardly have occurred to anyone until the Greek mission was a marked success and a great future had begun to open before the Christian faith. And wherever we test the book, it gives unmistakable signs of lateness of date, such as:

1. Its literary form—carefully organized into two volumes, each with its own distinct sphere and field and yet integrated with the other so as to be practically inseparable.

2. Its literary features: preface, dedication, account of sources, purpose, and method.

3. Its infancy interest, pushed back to the birth of John. One is reminded that in the Book of James[2] (the Protevangelium), half a century or more later, this infancy interest is pushed still farther back to the nativity of the Virgin herself.

4. Its resurrection interest, including a whole series of appearances, visits, eatings, penetration of locked doors, protracted through forty days. This is in

[1] Thackeray's translation; cf. H. J. Cadbury, in Jackson and Lake, *Beginnings of Christianity* (London, 1922), II, 491–92.

[2] M. R. James, *The Apocryphal New Testament* (Oxford, 1924), p. 38.

marked contrast to Matthew's (which was probably also Mark's) account and is much nearer to the second-century representations of Jesus' long post-resurrection conversations with the apostles, e.g., the Epistle of the Apostles, *ca.* A.D. 150.[1]

5. Its doctrine of the holy Spirit, which pervades both volumes. The holy Spirit is to come over Mary, 1:35; it fills Elizabeth, 1:42, and Zechariah, 1:67. It came down upon Jesus, 3:22; he was full of the holy Spirit, 4:1. It is on almost every page of the Acts, the whole narrative of which seems to float upon a sea of it. Luke evidently has a definite and developed doctrine of the holy Spirit, which was the fruit of no little religious reflection.

6. The interest in punitive miracle, a feature conspicuous in the Elijah-Elisha cycles of Kings but wholly wanting from Mark and Matthew. It marks the opening scene of Luke (Zechariah is struck dumb) and plays a prominent part in the Acts: Ananias and Sapphira are struck dead, 5:5, 10; Elymas is struck blind, 13:11; compare 12:23. In this trait we are on our way to the fondness for punitive miracle in the infancy gospels of the second century, which also found it edifying, e.g., the Gospel of Thomas.[2]

7. The passing of the Jewish controversy; this interest, so acute in Paul's day, has become a dead issue when Luke is written.

8. The interest in Christian psalmody. Luke preserves hymn after hymn, 1:42, 46, 68; 2:14, 29—the

[1] M. R. James, *The Apocryphal New Testament* (Oxford, 1924), p. 485.

[2] *Ibid.*, p. 49.

Magnificat, the Benedictus, the Gloria in Excelsis, the Nunc Dimittis. Nowhere else do we find any such early interest in Christian poesy, except in Eph. 5:14 and in the arias, choruses, and antiphonies of the Revelation. Already that liturgical endowment, which Walter Pater once said was one of the special gifts of the early church,[1] was beginning to appear.

9. Church organization; the Twelve appear in the Acts as a sort of college of apostles, stationed in Jerusalem, watching over the progress of the Christian mission. With them are associated the elders, 15:2, 6, 22; 16:4, etc. Paul is represented as appointing elders in each church, 14:23, so the presbyteral organization is recognized as established, though Paul himself in his list of types of Christian leadership in I Cor. 12:28 says nothing about elders. The office of deacon is also traced back to the earliest days of the church and given added dignity and luster by the story of Stephen, chapters 6, 7. Luke's account of Ananias and Sapphira shows an interest in church funds when he wrote the Acts, and the story of Dorcas sewing for the poor, 9:39, also points to a considerable degree of organization. The point made here is not as to the fact of such embezzlement or charitable doings in the church, but of the writer's interest in recording them. Here belongs also the emphasis upon baptism as a condition of church membership, forgiveness, and salvation that is so characteristic of the Acts, 2:38; 8:12, 36; 9:18; 10:47; 16:15, 33.

10. The Speaking with Tongues; this was simply

[1] *Marius the Epicurean*, p. 277.

ecstatic utterance with Paul, I Corinthians, chapters 12–14, but in the Acts it has come to be a miraculous endowment with the power to speak foreign languages, Acts 2:4–11.

11. Paul is dead; that he is still living when the curtain falls upon the Acts in 28:30, 31, is outweighed by his farewell to the Ephesian elders, 20:25, with its solemn declaration that none of them would ever see his face again, underscored by its repetition in 20:38: "they were especially saddened at his saying that they would never see his face again." Such presentiments are remembered and recorded only when they have proved true.

12. Paul has risen to hero stature. He is not only dead; he has become a hallowed memory. He is no longer a man struggling and grappling with difficulties, as in his letters; he has become a heroic figure and towers above priests, officers, governors, and kings. This is simply the retrospect of history. Lincoln rose in a generation into a heroic figure, very different from the man his contemporaries knew. The manner of his death no doubt contributed to this, but Paul's death too made its contribution to the reverence in which he came to be held, for he was probably the first of the Roman martyrs. Time has to play its part in the development of these attitudes. The success of the Greek mission naturally drew attention to the figure of the leader of that movement.

13. The emergence of the sects; men of their own number were appearing and teaching perversions of

the truth in order to draw the disciples away after them, 20:30. Apart from this reference to them in Acts, the first we hear of the sects is in Eph. 4:14; compare 4:3–6, and in the Revelation, where the mysterious sect of the Nicolaitans is mentioned with abhorrence, 2:6, 15. Early in the second century the Docetists appear (cf. I, II John, Ignatius), then the Marcionites and Gnostics, and then the Montanists. Here, again, Acts seems to belong to the time of Ephesians and the Revelation.

14. Nonacquaintance with Paul's collected letters. The letters of Paul would have been of great value to the writer of the Acts; if he had known them, he could not have helped making use of them along with the numerous sources he mentions in his preface. It is next to impossible, if one knows Paul's letters, not to reveal the fact when writing about his life and work. In fact, they are ideal materials for such a task. But the Acts nowhere betrays any knowledge of them.

15. The situation presupposed by the conception of such a work—the wide success achieved by the Greek mission.

Luke-Acts might be still more definitely dated if it could be shown that Luke made use in it of the *Antiquities* of Josephus, which appeared in A.D. 93. The chief points of resemblance are the Theudas-Judas passage, *Ant.* xx. 5. 1, 2 (cf. Acts 5:36, 37), and the Lysanias reference, *Ant.* xx. 7. 1 (cf. Luke 3:1, 2), but, in both, matters are so very differently understood and stated in the Acts that it seems more probable that the two accounts are not immediately related to each other.[1] If Luke did use Josephus, he put the Judas of the time of Quirinius' census after the Theudas of the times of Fadus, forty years later, and represented Lysanias as still tetrarch of Abilene sixty-five years after his death. Even the best of modern critical writers do not always escape just such errors, but it would be strange for Luke to do this if he really had Josephus.

It is not too much to say that, wherever we sound the book of Acts, the result is the same; it reveals itself as a work of the last decade of the first century. Even two or three of the considerations just listed would make such a date highly probable, but taken altogether they are overwhelming. Such points are too often dismissed as "difficulties" or dealt with atomistically—one at a time—the others being momentarily put aside. But it is their cumulative effect that is so significant. They are, as a matter of fact, clues to the solution of the problem of the date of the two volumes, and they may fairly be said to demonstrate that Acts (and Luke of course with it), was written about A.D. 90, about the time of Ephesians and Revelation but probably before the regulations of Domitian had brought the church acutely into collision with the empire over the matter of emperor worship.

Scholars have been too much absorbed with the subject matter of Acts and sought to base a date upon it, whereas their real concern in seeking to determine the

---

[1] Cf. A. H. McNeile, *Introduction to the Study of the New Testament* (Oxford 1927), pp. 34, 35.

date of the work is not so much with subject matter
as with the use made of it and the contemporary interests reflected by the writer, which must be scrupulously distinguished.

Author. The literary problem of Luke-Acts is how,
at the late date at which the work was evidently
written, the writer could have obtained the body of
primitive material embodied in the Acts. This is a
very real and difficult problem. The primitive material has led some very able scholars to lose sight of
the main facts of date, purpose, and occasion that we
have just surveyed and to affirm a date soon after A.D.
60.[1] But this we have seen to be impossible, in view
of all the prevailing traits of the work. The whole
color of the book—the very occasion for writing it—
belongs a generation later. But how at that time
could the writer have obtained his material?

Now it is a mistake to suppose that a writer gathers
literary material only for an immediate purpose.
People with a literary bent are constantly gathering
materials, though they may have no idea of how they
will use them. Anyone who writes at all will agree
to this. Most modern writers frequently use, for a new
project, material they have had for years and have
perhaps already made use of in other ways—lectures,
speeches, letters—or have simply kept in reserve in
their notebooks, through a feeling that some day it
would be useful. Sometimes it is the possession of such

[1] A. Harnack, *The Date of the Acts and of the Synoptic Gospels,* trans. J. R.
Wilkinson (London, 1911), pp. 91, 124.

materials that, as some new situation arises, suggests the book that may be written.

This is the familiar experience and even practice of everyone who writes or preaches. Yet it must be stated, for obliviousness of it has seriously affected research in the origin of Luke-Acts. Such literary methods are not novel; they were familiar to ancients like Xenophon—and Luke, the great story-teller of the New Testament. Such minds are like magnets; they constantly draw to themselves and retain things they see the value of, long before they see how best they can use them.

It is illuminating to remember how Greek historical writing began in those very Ionian cities from which Luke is supposed to have come. Travel-loving Greeks from them went out to the East and visited Babylon and Egypt, saw the sights, heard what the priests had to say of their ancient glories, and returned to tell the stay-at-home Greeks the story. Such travel narratives were called *logoi*, "accounts," and one of these logographers was Hecataeus of Miletus. Another did it so surpassingly well that his work was the beginning of history; his name was Herodotus.[1]

Why was it necessary for these outsiders to be the describers of those wonders of oriental travel? Why did not their contemporaries in Babylon and Egypt do it? Why are not the ballads and legends of the Kentucky mountaineers written down by the mountaineers? Why did not the Ojibways record their

---

[1] W. C. Wright, *A Short History of Greek Literature* (New York, 1907), chap. ix.

legends and traditions, instead of leaving that work to an outsider like Schoolcraft? For two reasons: one, they did not have the gift and, another, they did not have the public. It was the visitor of insight and literary ways who saw what could be made of it and knew how to do it, and knew where there was a public that would be interested in it.

Now imagine Luke, a Greek from those same Ionian cities, traveling with Paul to Palestine, Acts 20:6; 21:7, 15, 17, etc., and remaining there more than two years, though he may have come and gone more or less during that time. Still he is again with Paul when Paul is sent west for trial, 27:1, and the likelihood is that he stayed in Palestine all that time. There, with the Greek bent for taking notes, what treasures of early Christian song and story he could accumulate![1]—Not to write Luke-Acts with—no one had thought of such a thing—but because he was the kind of man who could write Luke-Acts—the literary type of man, the Christian successor of Hecataeus and Herodotus, a logographer like them. These materials he would use in his preaching through the years: stories of Peter, Stephen, Philip, Paul. Then, long after, when the movement had proved its greatness and the idea of writing its history came to him and he began to look about for materials, beside his written sources for the gospel, he had his own memories of these old stories gathered in Palestine thirty years be-

[1] "Luke during the two years he was at Caesarea in the company of Paul made good use of his opportunities of collecting information and made copious notes" (B. H. Streeter, *The Four Gospels* [New York, 1925], p. 218).

fore and often retold by himself in his preaching, and these, with his own knowledge of Paul and his travels, gave him the materials for the Acts volume. After all, the early part, not about Paul, is of no great bulk; only a dozen chapters—thirty pages.

So we may reasonably think of Luke as the Christian logographer. It is interesting to note that he calls his first volume a *logos*, Acts 1:1. Certainly his work has functioned just as did that of Herodotus, for it was the beginning of Christian history. It has sometimes been assumed that a companion of Paul could not have lived to write of him as late as A.D. 90, but I think most of the writers who say this are themselves older than Luke would have needed to be when he wrote Luke-Acts. Luke joins Paul's party bound for Palestine not earlier than A.D. 55. He was probably a young man, for such men find it easier to leave home and move about the world with their chosen leaders than middle-aged men with families and responsibilities. Suppose he was twenty-five or thirty years old. By A.D. 90 he would be sixty or sixty-five, not too infirm we may suppose to have written a book of one hundred and sixty columns of Greek.

But suppose we abandon the effort to identify the author, and content ourselves with describing him in terms of his own writing. He was a Greek, a companion of Paul on his journeys, 16:11, 15, etc.; with him in Palestine, 21:17, 18; with him on his voyage to Rome, 27:1; 28:14; who late in life was moved to write the story of Christian beginnings. Why should we feel obliged, or even justified, in seeking some other name for this adventurous man than that of Paul's dear doctor, Luke? (Col. 4:14). He is mentioned only once in the first hundred years of Christian literature (that is, before the Pastorals) and is a wholly obscure and colorless figure—except as the writer of Luke-Acts, which at once transforms him into the most voluminous contributor to the New Testament and the writer of one-fourth of its contents. Tradition calls the man who thought of this and executed it "Luke," and I can find no serious objection to this. It is one thing to have lost the name of the Jewish author of Matthew, but his gospel was anonymous, while Luke's work is dedicated to Theophilus and so can hardly have been anonymous. Moreover, it was more like the Greeks to claim their literary productions and write under their own names. The literature of Western Asia, as Edouard Meyer once observed, was prevailingly anonymous; the Hebrew literary prophets stand out as striking exceptions.

We-sections. Further, in the Acts the first person of Luke 1:2, 3 is resumed from time to time in the accounts of Paul's movements, and the natural implication is that the author himself is with the apostle on these journeys.[1] Modern learning has named these portions of Acts the We-sections and has sometimes sought to account for them in other ways; such as that the editor of the Acts in these places is drawing upon a diary of one of Paul's traveling companions, which had fallen into his hands. There are a number of critical difficulties with this view. For one thing,

[1] 16:10–18; 20:5–16; 21:1–18; 27:1—28:16.

no evidence has been offered that the ancients kept diaries; the supposed parallels in Xenophon's travel notes—so many days, so many stages, so many parasangs—is not a case in point, but quite the contrary. There we have Xenophon, a literary man, making his own travel notes and later using them himself, exactly as Luke seems to have done.

And, further, what a marvel it would be for such a diary, kept supposedly by one of Paul's travel companions, to have survived for thirty or forty years and then fallen into the hands of the man who had conceived the idea of writing the history of those travels! And above all, how strange it is that, in using it, he should have forgotten that it was not his own work and mistakenly copied the first persons unaltered in it in seventy-seven instances, when he should of course have changed every one of them to the third person! We must here remember that this author of Luke-Acts is no stranger to us, for we have seen him carefully using the Gospel of Mark and other sources in his gospel and making no such crude blunders as this.

On the whole, it is safe to say that the idea that the We-sections were drawn by the author from somebody else's diary must be given up, simply because it involves such a series of improbabilities, none of which has been grappled with, much less answered, by its advocates. The We-sections thus resume their normal place as the most important guide to the authorship of the book, showing conclusively that it was written by a companion of Paul.

Against this, however, is urged that the writer cannot have been a follower and companion of Paul, for he is not a good Paulinist and the picture he gives of Paul's attitude to Jewish ritual is hopelessly out of keeping with Paul's own account of it in Galatians and elsewhere. But with the lapse of time the Jewish question had ceased to be important in the early church; it had become a dead issue. The passage of time has precisely the same effect upon modern writers who deal with events in which they have participated; it would be easy to illustrate this. The mistake we have been making about the Acts is that we have dated it too early; in a document contemporary with Paul such a picture of his attitude toward Judaism is indeed inconceivable in one of his followers or in any-one else. But the Acts was not written in Paul's day, as we have seen. Changing issues in a living move-ment would lead any writer, whether a companion of Paul or not, to changed interests and emphases.

That Luke is not a good Paulinist is another point raised against the tradition that he wrote the Acts. But here, again, we are in danger of being artificial and doctrinaire. A great Old Testament scholar in his teaching constantly and characteristically used the phrase "idealized history." But his leading pupil and successor never used that expression; his pupils never heard it or heard of it. Some might argue that the younger man could never have known the older, much less have been his disciple. But as a matter of fact he studied under him, occupied his study with him for years as his literary secretary, became his colleague and assistant, and finally his successor. If this can happen in the twentieth century, why should it not in the first? The truth is, we have been too stringent in our ideas of what was possible or impossible in the relations of these ancient persons. Moreover, it must be admitted that Paul himself was not always a perfectly sound Paulinist; compare Gal. 3:28 and I Cor. 14:34, 35.

Surely it is in the highest degree artificial to turn away from the natural interpretation of the We-narratives and regard them with suspicion and distrust as though the writing of Luke-Acts were a crime, the perpetrator of which had taken great pains to cover his tracks and conceal his identity. The objections usually urged against the Lucan authorship of Luke-Acts fade out when the true date of the work is perceived. They are all sufficiently explained by the lapse of a generation.

Sources. The material of Luke's story has been so skilfully divided into two equal parts each about the maximum convenient length for an ancient papyrus roll that the first volume, or *logos*, has just the proportions of a gospel and since A.D. 125, at least, has circulated with those of Matthew, Mark, and John. The preface introduces us to a time when the old familiar Oral Gospel had undergone local modifications in the Greek world, Luke 1:2, while narratives of varying scope had come into existence under its shadow, 1:1, as we have seen Mark doing. Luke refers frankly to these sources, which he says came from many hands, and this remark of his is usually regarded as a pardonable hyperbole.

The more we explore this first volume critically, however, the more sources it seems to resolve into. There is, of course, first and foremost the Gospel of Mark, which Luke has used less fully than Matthew but a good deal more faithfully. Perhaps three-fifths of Mark can be identified in Luke. But every section of Mark that Luke has taken over except two stands in exactly the Marcan order; that is, wherever Mark is used, the sequence of sections is just what it was in Mark. This makes Luke the joy of the harmonist, just as Matthew is his despair. A glance at the pages of any gospel harmony, Greek or English, will illustrate this procedure of Luke's.

Luke has made one considerable omission of Marcan material, 6:47—8:26. For some of it he had parallels elsewhere, Luke 11:29; 12:1. Some of it may have been distasteful to him, 7:24–37; 8:22–26. Some of it he probably rightly dismissed as a duplication of other Marcan material, 8:1–10. The walking on the sea, 6:45–56, may have seemed to him a duplication of the stilling of the storm, 4:35–41, which he had already used. The explanation of Jewish ceremonial customs, 7:2–4, he might well regard as superfluous, as Matthew did. This leaves very little of the section which Luke would have required, and it must be remembered that each of his two volumes contains about as much as a convenient Greek papyrus roll could hold. This seems a more natural explanation of the absence of this section of Mark from Luke's gospel than to suppose that Mark is already so dilapidated through neglect that Luke's copy has in it a gap of such size, except at one end of the roll it formed.

We have already spoken of the presence in Luke of two bodies of non-Marcan material: one Galilean, comprising 3:7–18; 4:2–13; 5:1–11; 6:20—8:3, and one Perean, 9:51—18:14, plus 19:1–28, which may be regarded as two distinct sources or less probably as two pieces of a single source. In either case this material was much of it known to Matthew, perhaps in a less developed form.

It has in recent years been established that Luke also possessed a Passion narrative,[1] from which he took over such passages peculiar to his gospel as 19:37, 39, 41–44; 22:15–17, 27–32, 35–38; 23:5–10, 12–15, 27–31, etc. His infancy narratives, chapters 1 and 2, are peculiar to him and may represent another written source or have come to him orally during his visit to Palestine, Acts 21:3 f.

How far the oral tradition entered into Luke's work it is difficult to say, but with this assortment of documents there is not much room left for its use. He makes one unmistakable allusion to it, Acts 20:35. It was clearly Mark that supplied his framework. But the statement of his preface that many writers had undertaken to compose accounts of the Christian movement, 1:1, would seem to be fairly justified by the array of written sources he evidently did make use of. He may have known of others that he did not use and probably assumed the existence of still others un-

---

[1] Alfred M. Perry, *The Sources of Luke's Passion Narrative* (Chicago, 1920).

known to him, although his claim to have investigated it all carefully from the beginning, 1:3, shows that he did not proceed without making careful search for worth-while material.

It was the sheer variety and multiplicity of these reports of the life and work of Jesus, oral and written, that impelled him to seek to organize and unite them, so that cultivated adherents of Christianity like Theophilus might indeed be reliably informed about the things they had been orally taught, 1:4. This is the testimony of the preface, and this is the testimony of the gospel itself, objectively examined.[1] The theory that Acts 1:1—15:35 was written in Aramaic in Palestine about A.D. 50, and first seen by Luke in Rome about A.D. 62, two years after he had written his gospel, is incompatible with the amazing array of coincidences of information or predilection shown in the two works. I have noted thirty-five of these in *New Solutions of New Testament Problems* (Chicago, 1927), pages 82–84.

Dr. Riddle has urged the apologetic tone of Acts as pointing to the middle years of Domitian.[2] That is without doubt its period, and there is certainly in it a strong strain of Christian apologetic, that is, against civil persecution by the state; all Paul's trials recorded in the Acts tend to show him innocent and acquit him. But any connection with Paul's final trial is negatived

---

[1] Cf. E. D. Burton, *Principles of Literary Criticism and Their Application to the Synoptic Problem* (Chicago, 1904), pp. 52–53.

[2] D. W. Riddle, "The Occasion of Luke-Acts," *Journal of Religion*, X (1930), 545–62.

by all the considerations we have reviewed above, bearing upon its date. Paul is certainly dead when Acts is written and has been dead a long time. The idea formerly advanced that Acts is a brief for Paul's trial also loses sight of the all-important fact that Acts is not a separate, independent work but the second volume of a larger work, as we have seen.

The place of the writing of Acts can hardly have been Rome, as Streeter urges: "Everything," he says "points to Rome as the church for which the Acts was written."[1] Certainly not everything. The Acts has more to say of Paul's work in Ephesus than of what he did in any other city he evangelized, 18:19-21, 24—20:1. Furthermore, it is a striking feature of the Acts that, when Paul made his last voyage about the Aegean, the only church to which Acts records his making a formal farewell was Ephesus; 20:17-38. It was at Ephesus, as we shall see, that Paul's letters were collected and published soon after the appearance of Luke-Acts. The literary history of this period of Christianity centered in Asia and about Ephesus. If Rome had recently produced Acts or Luke-Acts, Hebrews a little later could hardly have rebuked the Roman church for having failed to teach the churches, 5:12. The peculiar interest Luke has in the church at Ephesus makes it probable that it was there that the Acts, and hence Luke-Acts, were written. Of course, his name has long been conspicuously associated with that site—"Ayasalook," *Hagios Loukas*—but such as-

[1] Streeter, *The Four Gospels* (New York, 1925), p. 531.

sociations are of little confirmatory significance unless they can be pushed back at least to the second century.[1]

LITERATURE

CADBURY, HENRY J. *The Making of Luke-Acts* (New York, 1927).

FOAKES-JACKSON, F. J. *The Acts of the Apostles*, "The Moffatt New Testament Commentary" (New York, 1931).

FOAKES-JACKSON, F. J., and LAKE, K. *The Beginnings of Christianity*, Part I: "The Acts of the Apostles," Vols. I–V (New York, 1920–33).

PLUMMER, ALFRED. *The Gospel According to St. Luke* (4th ed.; New York, 1901).

[1] Eusebius' connection of Luke with Antioch, *Church History* iii. 4. 7 ("he was of Antiochian parentage"), even if true has no bearing upon the place of the writing of Luke-Acts.

XIII

THE FIRST COLLECTION OF
PAUL'S LETTERS

✠

The Pauline corpus. Luke-Acts stands forth as a great missionary record. It is the story of the Greek mission. It carries the reader straight up to the martyrdom of Paul but with great restraint stops short of narrating it, while unmistakably forecasting it in the underscored presentiments of his farewell to the Ephesian elders, Acts 20:25, 38; 21:13. It must have greatly revived and stimulated interest in the figure of Paul, which was already beginning to disappear into the past, as all figures inevitably tend to do. But with all his interest in Paul and admiration for him, Luke has no acquaintance with his letters.

It is sometimes maintained that, if he had been with Paul, he must have known the letters he wrote. But this is to forget that writing letters was the least of the activities of the living Paul. They were simply incidents in his busy life of effort and movement. Paul's conversation, his preaching, and his journeys would be much more outstanding features of his in the eyes of his personal companions and associates. Nor were the letters we possess written during the periods when Acts represents Luke as being with Paul. Moreover, Paul's letters were all addressed to immediate local situations, and with the passing of each of these the interest of the letter concerned with it naturally evaporated. This is the explanation of the fact that the gospel literature we have thus far surveyed—Mark, Matthew, and Luke-Acts—shows no influence of Paul's letters.

But from this point on the situation is reversed. Every Christian document shows acquaintance with Paul's letters—the Revelation, Hebrews, I Clement, I Peter, the letters of Ignatius and Polycarp, the Gospel of John. This is, in fact, the key to the later literature of the New Testament; it is all written in the presence of the collected Pauline letters. Over against the total nonacquaintance of the earlier evangelists the difference is positively glaring. Before the publication of Luke-Acts nobody knew them; after the appearance of Luke-Acts everybody knows them.

And not just one or two of them, or three or four. Almost the first book to show acquaintance with them is the Revelation of John, written by the prophet of Ephesus in exile on Patmos. His book is so swayed by the newly published corpus of Paul's letter to seven churches that he actually begins his book with a corpus of letters to seven churches. If any literary resemblance could be more striking and massive than this, it is difficult to imagine what it would be. Yet students of the Revelation have been so engrossed in its apocalyptic atmosphere that this obvious fact about it, which strikes one in the face on the first page, has actually escaped their attention.

But it is most unnatural for an apocalypse to begin

with a letter, still less with a corpus of letters—seven letters, in fact—and these letters addressed to Christian churches. Can this possibly be dismissed as coincidence? Not when we observe the further fact that the Revelation corpus is not a real collection of letters that have been sent to their several readers; the collection is avowedly a literary device, and all the letters go to all the churches. It is no actual collection of letters once sent and later collected that meets us in Revelation, chapters 1–3. The letters are written as a collection and made to form the portal of the Apocalypse, and the whole work is sent to all the churches in the list.

We cannot suppose that this artificial corpus of letters preceded the actual gathering-together of Paul's letters scattered among seven churches. It is clear that the real collection of letters to seven churches must have preceded the artificial one, which was simply an imitation of it. Indeed, if the Revelation had been discovered yesterday, instead of having been familiar to us all from childhood, this fact would have been at once apparent and would have been everywhere recognized. The portal of the Revelation was suggested by the recent appearance of a collection of Paul's letters to seven churches. Even the salutation of 1:4, "Blessing to you and peace," is the characteristic Pauline letter salutation, unknown elsewhere in the New Testament and strange to Greek epistolary practice.

It is important to observe the extent to which the letters of Paul are reflected in the literature immediately following Luke-Acts, and perhaps the accompanying tabular view will make this clear.

	Rev.	Heb.	I Clem.	I Pet.	John	Ign.	Poly.	Jas.	Mar-cion	Pas-torals	II Pet.
Eph	X	X	X	X	X	X	X	X	X	X	X
Rom.........	X	X	X	X	X	X	X	X	X	X	X
I Cor........	X	X	X	X		X	X	X	X	X	X
II Cor........	X		X	X		X		X	X	X	X
Gal..........	X	X	X	X	X		X	X		X	X
Phil..........	X	X	X	X		X	X	X	X	X	X
Col..........	X	X	X			X	X		X	X	X
I Thess.......	X	X	X		X	X	X	X	X	X	X
II Thess......	X				X	X		X		X	X
Philem........	X	X				X	X			X	X

This table owes much to the one prepared by Dr. A. E. Barnett in his elaborate study, "The Use of the Letters of Paul in Pre-Catholic Christian Literature" (p. 612).[1] The conservative character of his results is shown by the fact that he lists as reasonably certain the use of only five Pauline letters in II Peter, and yet that epistle speaks of "all his letters," regards them as Scripture, and laments the heretical (Marcionite) misuse of them, so that its author quite certainly possessed all ten. McNeile quotes Turner as saying that the Epistle of Polycarp is "crowded with indubitable echoes of at least eight" of Paul's letters, but this includes I and II Timothy, which Turner thought were quoted; the others are Romans, I and II Corinthians, Ephesians, II Thessalonians, and Philippians.[2]

[1] *University of Chicago Abstracts of Theses*, "Humanistic Series," IX, 509.

[2] *Introduction to the Study of the New Testament* (Oxford, 1927), p. 315.

It is customary to explain these facts by the supposition that different collections of Paul's letters existed in different hands. But this loses sight of four important considerations:

First, few people who possess all Paul's letters make use of all of them in a single letter or group of letters—II Thessalonians and Philemon, for example. It would be manifestly wrong to infer from the fact that you or I do not quote these writings that we did not possess them but used a collection of Paul's letters from which they were absent.

Second, the theory makes it necessary to suppose that there were four or five different collections of Paul's letters in circulation about the close of the first century.

Third, the Revelation, the earliest book to reflect them, reflects a collection of letters to seven churches, preceded by a general letter to all seven; which makes it extremely likely that the writer had all ten of the letters in the collection known at Ephesus, for it consisted of a general letter and letters to seven churches.

Fourth, Ephesians, which was from the beginning in the collection (for it was used in I Clement, as Bishop Lightfoot long ago saw), shows unmistakable acquaintance with all nine of the accepted letters—Romans, I and II Corinthians, Galatians, I and II Thessalonians, Philippians, Colossians, Philemon. The table appended to my *Meaning of Ephesians* will, I think, satisfy the reader of this fact.[1] When this is

---

[1] In opposition to this it has been argued that Ephesians was simply using the customary paraenetic language of its day; but if that is true, why

once recognized, all the subsequent uses of the Pauline letters fall into natural relations. We have only one collection of Pauline letters to postulate and explain. The whole matter of the uses of Paul's letters in the Christian writings about the end of the first century and the beginning of the second is cleared up.

It is natural to ask what situation could have precipitated the making of such a collection. It is usually the death of a great man that arouses interest in his work and leads to the publication of his collected letters. But it cannot have been Paul's martyrdom that led to the collecting and publishing of his letters, for in that case the collection would have been in circulation before the writing of any of the gospels, and their nonacquaintance with it would be unaccountable.

The next event that drew marked attention to the figure and work of Paul was the appearance of Luke-Acts with its impressive picture of him and his work for the Greek mission. It was the most imposing Christian literary work that had thus far appeared and must have notably revived interest in Paul as the apostle to the Greeks, the founder of the Greek mission, the martyr to that cause, Acts 20:25, 38. The Pauline interest forms an unmistakable crescendo in the Acts from his introduction in 7:58 to the end. To

---

does it stand alone in this? It is the only work of pre-Catholic Christian literature for which such a showing of Pauline parallels (*The Meaning of Ephesians*, pp. 85–112) can be made. The same thing was later crudely done on a smaller scale in the spurious Laodiceans, a jumble of Pauline expressions with no coherent sense.

suppose that this ringing glorification of Paul could have had no effect upon early Christian literature is hardly reasonable. We should expect it to have some effect and to have it at once, for in ancient as in modern times a book's best chance of influence is immediately upon its publication, when the public for which it was written and out of which it grew is still alive, and the situation which called it forth is still acute. What could possibly have been added to what Acts says about Paul, except to assemble his letters? But how could anyone have thought of this unless he already knew of some letters of Paul? There is nothing whatever in the Acts to suggest that Paul ever wrote any letters of any particular moment any more than anyone else.

Yet Paul himself had given a hint for the bringing-together of two of his letters when he instructed the Colossians to send his letter to them on to the Laodiceans, and to read the letter that was coming from there, Col. 4:16. These two letters must have been preserved together, either at Colossae or at Laodicea or in both churches. Suppose a man who had been in one or the other of those churches, or who had visited those places and seen those letters, read the glowing account of Paul in the Acts, the most telling and unforgettable account of him that has ever been written. The Book of Acts unrolls before him a whole series of Paul's movements of which he has been unaware. The thought occurs to him: Perhaps some of those churches—Rome, Corinth, Galatia, Thessalonica, Philippi—may have received letters from Paul and may even still possess them. It is a curious and striking fact that the Acts would have guided an Asian collector of Pauline letters to all these churches, but it would never have guided a Roman or Corinthian collector to Colossae or Laodicea, for those places are not mentioned in the Acts. It is therefore extremely probable that Colossians-Laodiceans (=Col.-Philem.) formed the nucleus of the Pauline collection, and doubly so when we remember that Paul himself had been instrumental in getting those two letters together.

A series of considerations thus arises pointing to some Asian center of Christianity, such as Ephesus, as the place where the Pauline corpus was probably first assembled:

1. Colossians-Philemon seems to have been the nucleus of it, for Acts would never have guided the collector to the churches at Colossae and Laodicea, while it would have guided anyone already possessed of Colossians-Philemon to all the other Christian centers represented in the corpus by letters. But Colossians and Philemon were letters written to churches in Asia.

2. The use of so much material from Colossians in Ephesians is most naturally explained if the writer of Ephesians had long known Colossians and pored over it, as he must have done when it was the only considerable Pauline letter he possessed. Almost three-fifths of Colossians is paralleled in Ephesians.

3. Ephesus had become the leading Christian center by A.D. 90, being, as Harnack put it, the second ful-

crum of Christianity after Antioch. It was the home of the writer of the Revelation, in which the Pauline corpus finds its first literary reflection after Ephesians, Revelation, chapters 1–3.

4. Ephesus a few years later witnessed (and probably stimulated) the writing and collecting of the letters of Ignatius, another collection of letters conditioned by the Pauline corpus.

5. At about the same time Ephesus witnessed the writing of the Gospel of John, a work strongly influenced by the Pauline corpus.

6. It also produced the Johannine letter-corpus for missionary and apologetic purposes, I, II, and III John.

7. It also in all probability produced the fourfold gospel collection, *ca.* A.D. 120, to promote the circulation and influence of the new Gospel of John.

8. The fact that the collectors of the letters had Phoebe's letter of introduction (Rom., chap. 16) points to Ephesus, where as we have seen she was probably going, and where the letter might be preserved as a souvenir of Paul and unobtrusively worked into the collection when it was afterward made. It would be difficult to explain its presence anywhere else.

9. It is a perplexing fact that Ignatius writes to the Ephesians, chapter 13, that Paul in every letter "mentions them" or "calls them to mind."[1] He certainly does not "mention" them in anything like every

---

[1] μνημονεύει.

letter. But if the Ephesian church had published the Pauline letters, the difficulty disappears. For in Ignatius' day every letter of Paul would bring to the reader's mind the Ephesians as the collectors and publishers of his letters. The Ephesians would understand the gracious allusion.

Not only did the publication of the Pauline corpus so revive interest in the letter as an important form for Christian instruction, and thus call forth a shower of church letters —Revelation, Hebrews, I Clement, I Peter, Ignatius, Polycarp, etc.—but it led to the production and circulation of other corpuses of letters.

The ancients were familiar with published letter collections. There was the Plato letter collection of thirteen letters. There were the letters of Aristotle and Epicurus. The letters of Apollonius of Tyana were soon after collected and circulated. In Latin there were the letters of Cicero, from the middle of the first century before Christ, and early in the second century A.D. Pliny published his own letters, dedicating the collection to his friend Septicius who, he said, had often urged him to collect and publish his letters: "Frequenter hortatus es ut epistulas, si quas accuratius scripsissem, colligerem publicaremque," i. 1.

It is striking that, after the Pauline corpus, there followed in Christian circles the letter corpus of the Revelation, chapters 1–3 (letters to seven churches, preceded by a general letter to all seven); the Ignatian corpus of seven letters, six to churches and one to an individual, A.D. 107–17; the Johannine corpus—for the organization of that collection, with one general letter, one church letter, and one personal letter, at once suggests that it was written as a unit, and the brevity and comparative slightness of II and III John make it most unlikely that they would have been preserved and circulated by themselves; and the Pastoral corpus, written as a corpus and circulated as part of the enlarged Pauline corpus into which it was at once incorporated. For all these corpuses the Pauline is the great precedent and model, and to all of them it is in a sense the key.

We must therefore no longer treat the several units of these various corpuses atomistically; they must be studied as corpuses if they are to be historically understood, for they originated not as separate units but as full-fledged collections. This is recognized in the case of the Revelation corpus, and it must be recognized in the case of the Johannine and the Pastoral corpuses as well.

In one other respect the collection and publication of the Pauline corpus are of great significance for subsequent Christian literature. It was the beginning of the *publication* of Christian letters, and Christian letters were thereafter often written for publication. That is, the publication of Paul's letters with the new encyclical "Ephesians" at their head led directly to the Christian *epistle*—Hebrews, I Peter, I John, James (originally a sermon but published as an encyclical epistle), etc.

In all these ways the Pauline corpus has important significance for New Testament Introduction. A new

literary atmosphere now pervades the Christian movement. From this time on all its writing is done in
the presence of the Pauline corpus.

LITERATURE

GOODSPEED, EDGAR J. *New Solutions of New Testament Problems*
(Chicago, 1927).

———. "The Place of Ephesians in the First Pauline Collection," *Anglican Theological Review*, XII (1930), 189–212.

———. *New Chapters in New Testament Study* (New York,
1937), chapters i–iii.

XIV

THE EPISTLE TO THE EPHESIANS

+

Occasion. Jülicher long ago perceived that on most accounts the natural explanation of the purpose and aim of Ephesians was to serve as an introduction to a collection of Pauline letters. I had come to that position independently and find great satisfaction in his interest in it. It was in fact only what he considered its excessive use of Colossians that prevented him from adopting that explanation and led him to declare the problem of the origin of Ephesians still unsolved. But of course the extreme use of Colossians in Ephesians simply means that the writer of Ephesians has known Colossians longest and so must be an Asian Christian. This is the explanation of that excessive influence: The collector of the letters, aware from his possession of Colossians-Laodiceans that Paul was a powerful writer of letters, informed by the Acts of his relations with other churches, and stimulated by its heroic picture of Paul, collects all the Pauline letters he can find with its aid and writes Ephesians as a general introduction, to introduce the collected letters to the churches. In doing so he makes use of all the Pauline letters he has found, but of course he has known Colossians longest and is most pervaded by its language; hence its stamp is most deeply imprinted on

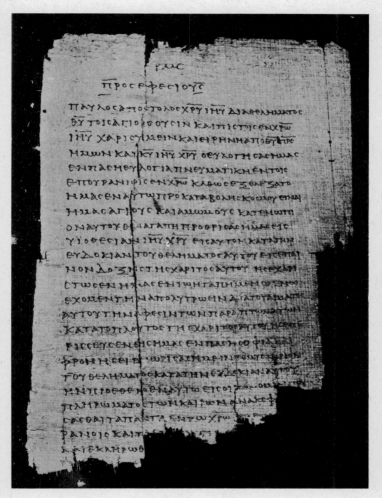

ΡΜϹ

ΠΡΟϹΕΦΕϹΙΟΥϹ

ΠΑΥΛΟϹΑΠΟϹΤΟΛΟϹΧΡΥΙΗΥ ΔΙΑΘΕΛΗΜΑΤΟϹ
ΘΥ ΤΟΙϹΑΓΙΟΙϹΟΥϹΙΝ ΚΑΙΠΙϹΤΥΕΝΧΡΩ
ΙΗΥ ΧΑΡΙϹΥΜΕΙΝΚΑΙΕΙΡΗΝΗΑΠΟΘΥΠΡΟ
ΗΜΩΝ ΚΑΙΚΥΙΗΥ ΧΡΥ ΘΕΥΧΟΤΗϹΩϹΗΜΑϹ
ΕΝΠΑϹΗΕΥΛΟΓΙΑΠΝΕΥΜΑΤΙΚΗΕΝΤΟΙϹ
ΕΠΟΥΡΑΝΙΟΙϹΕΝΧΡΩ ΚΑΘΩϹΕΞΕΛΕΞΑΤΟ
ΗΜΑϹΕΝΑΥΤΩΠΡΟΚΑΤΑΒΟΛΗϹΚΟϹΜΟΥΕΙΝΑΙ
ΗΜΑϹΑΓΙΟΥϹ ΚΑΙΑΜΩΜΟΥϹ ΚΑΤΕΝΩΠΙ
ΟΝΑΥΤΟΥΘΕΝΑΓΑΠΗΠΡΟΟΡΙϹΑϹΗΜΑϹΕΙϹ
ΥΙΟΘΕϹΙΑΝ ΙΗΥΧΡΥ ΕΙϹΑΥΤΟΝ ΚΑΤΑΤΗΝ
ΕΥΔΟΚΙΑΝ ΤΟΥΘΕΛΗΜΑΤΟϹΑΥΤΟΥΕΙϹΕΠΑΙ
ΝΟΝΔΟΞΗϹΤΗϹΧΑΡΙΤΟϹΑΥΤΟΥ ΗϹΕΧΑΡΙ
ΤΩϹΕΝ ΗΜΑϹΕΝΤΩΗΓΑΠΗΜΕΝΟϹ
ΕΧΟΜΕΝΤΗΝ ΑΠΟΛΥΤΡΩϹΙΝ ΔΙΑΤΟΥΑΙΜΑ
ΑΥΤΟΥΤΗΝΑΦΕϹΙΝΤΩΝΠΑΡΑΠΤΩΜΑΤΩΝ
ΚΑΤΑΤΟΠΛΟΥΤΟϹΤΗϹΧΑΡΙΤΟϹΑΥΤΟΥ ΗϹ
ΠΕΡΙϹϹΕΥϹΕΝΕΙϹΗΜΑϹΕΝΠΑϹΗϹΟΦΙΑΚΑΙ
ΦΡΟΝΗϹΕΙ ΓΝΩΡΙϹΑϹΗΜΙΝΤΟΜΥϹΤΗΡΙΟΝ
ΤΟΥΘΕΛΗΜΑΤΟϹΚΑΤΑΤΗΝΕΥΔΟΚΙΑΝΑΥΤΟΥ
ΗΝΠΡΟΕΘΕΤΟΕΝΑΥΤΩΕΙϹΟΙ
ΠΛΗΡΩΜΑΤΟϹΤΩΝΚΑΙΡΩΝΑΝΑΚΕΦΑ
ΛΑΙΩϹΑΙΤΑΠΑΝΤΑ ΕΝΤΩΧΡΩ
ΡΑΝΙΟΙϹΚΑΙΤΑ
ΕΝ ΩΚΑΙ ΕΚΛΗΡΩΘΗ

THE UNIVERSITY OF MICHIGAN PAPYRUS, EPHESIANS 1:1–11

Ephesians. The degree of Colossian influence on Ephesians is simply a sign of the Asian origin of the collection.

Jülicher also remarked that no specific historical situation had been proposed in which a Paulus redivivus might be supposed to have written Ephesians.[1] Here is such a situation. The collector of the Pauline letters, aware that each of them was addressed to a special situation long since passed, but confident that together they would form an inestimable treasure to the churches, writes as an introduction to them a general letter to all Christians, Eph. 1:1, commending Paul to them in words largely Paul's own, as the champion and martyr of the Greek mission and as a Christian writer of inspired power, 3:1–5. This will explain the whole tangle of problems that beset Ephesians: its strange way of weaving Pauline phrases into a different style, liturgical and reverberating; its pseudonymity; its encyclical character, which presupposes knowledge on the writer's part of Paul as a letter writer par excellence; its laudation of Paul as the inspired interpreter of the secret of the Christ, 3:1–5; above all, its otherwise mysterious allusion to what Paul had previously written, which they are about to read, 3:4, 5, and the writer's confidence as to the impression it will make on them: "As you read that, you will be able to understand the insight I have into the secret of the Christ." As Chrysostom (and Calvin)

[1] *Einleitung in das Neue Testament* (5th ed.), pp. 127, 128. "It is not yet settled," wrote Johannes Weiss in his *Urchristentum*, p. 534, "whether the author of the letter to the Ephesians is not the very collector of the Pauline corpus."

saw it is to be a subsequent reading of something previously written.

Ephesians seems to begin just where the Acts left off: Jesus the Christ has made Paul a prisoner for the sake of the heathen, "if at least you have heard how I dealt with the mercy of God that was given me for you." These sentences sound very reminiscent of the Acts, which had shown how Paul had worked among the heathen and how he had at last been made a prisoner for their sakes. How else can we so naturally explain the fact that Ephesians thinks of Paul, not as at large, as a missionary, or dead, as a martyr, but as in prison, just where the Acts left him?

The elements of the problem are certainly perplexing. Here is Ephesians—an encyclical, not a church letter; not by Paul, but taking it for granted that he was a great writer of letters to churches, otherwise an encyclical from him would have no propriety; yet among the very earliest of Paul's letters to be reflected in early Christian literature, for it was unmistakably used by Clement of Rome in A.D. 95, side by side with Romans and I and II Corinthians.

Gradually the answer emerges. Ephesians was in the first published collection of Paul's letters, but, being an encyclical, it could not have stood in the middle or at the end; it must have stood at the beginning, and hence have served as an introduction to the collection. But how can we test such a possibility? We can look at the letter-corpus in Revelation, which may possibly be expected to reflect such an arrangement in the original Pauline corpus, if it existed.

We open the Revelation, and behold! here is just such a general letter to all the seven churches, chapter 1, introducing the letter collection, Ephesians–Laodiceans, that follows, chapters 2, 3. It is like getting in direct touch with the first century, asking it a question that has perhaps never been asked of it before; and the Revelation gives us our answer.

We may therefore regard Ephesians as an introduction to the collected letters of Paul, probably written by the collector of them. This position finds a curious corroboration in the observation of Dr. John Knox that Marcion's list of Paul's letters[1] was evidently arranged, except for Galatians, from the longest to the shortest, Corinthians being treated as one and Thessalonians as one; except that, in Marcion's arrangement, Ephesians (his Laodiceans) follows Thessalonians, when it should in point of length precede it. But if Ephesians and Galatians have been simply transposed by Marcion, to give his preferred Galatians the leading place, this would be explained.

This may help us to understand Marcion's action in putting his preferred Galatians first (it did not mean displacing any massive letter like Romans or Corinthians but simply a letter of about equal bulk with Galatians) and, further, his naming Ephesians "Laodiceans," for when he found it at the head of the letters it probably had no name of its own, and his transposition of it made it necessary for him to provide one. He may also have begun the practice of

[1] John Knox, *Philemon among the Letters of Paul* (Chicago, 1936), pp. 41, 42.

naming the original Laodiceans "Philemon," when he transferred that name to what we know as Ephesians, perhaps because of Col. 4:16.

If we arrange the letters in the order of length, as given in the ancient stichometries,[1] but put Ephesians first, as, by hypothesis, Introduction, we have:

Suppose Marcion simply transposed Ephesians with Galatians; it would produce his well-known order (the stichoi numbers, it will be seen, no longer control the main arrangement):

Ephesians	312	Galatians		293
Corinthians	1460	Corinthians		1460
Romans	920	Romans		920
Thessalonians	299	Thessalonians		299
Galatians	293	"Laodiceans"–Eph.		312
Colossians	208	Colossians		208
Philippians	208	Philippians		208
Philemon	38	Philemon		38

Marcion thus seems to have transposed Galatians (from fifth place) with Ephesians (from first place), regardless of the fact that this slightly disturbs the earlier order of length. This confirms the position that Ephesians had previously stood first in the corpus. How else can we explain the strange position of Ephesians (his Laodiceans) in Marcion's list?

Contents. Ephesians is a great rhapsody on the worth of the Christian salvation. Like Hebrews it belongs to an age when men needed to reflect on the worth of their faith. The situation lying back of it is

[1] J. Rendel Harris, *Stichometry* (London, 1893), pp. 38 ff.

twofold: the sects are beginning to appear, and the Pauline letters have been discovered and collected. To introduce this collection to Christians everywhere, to remind apathetic Christians of the great values of their faith, and to check the rising tide of sect and schism Ephesians is written.

It is cast in that half-liturgical style so characteristic of the last decade of the first century; we see it in the canticles of Luke-Acts, in Revelation, Hebrews, I Peter, I Clement. The first and second chapters constitute a summary of Pauline Christianity in the form of a jubilate over the blessedness of the Christian salvation. Ephesians is like the overture of an opera, foreshadowing the melodies that are to follow. All these great aspects of Christian truth the reader was to find more fully dealt with in the letters themselves, which of course followed Ephesians.

Second-generation Christianity needed to be reminded of the great religious values it had inherited, as the Revelation and Hebrews show. Ephesians opens with a jubilant summary of Pauline thought, 1:3–14. The writer sets forth the supreme worth of Christianity, which his contemporaries were in danger of forgetting, 1:15–23. The Christian experience is nothing less than a new life through the mercy of God, 2:1–10. The death of Christ has opened to the Greeks a way to God, 2:11–22.

Paul in his writings has declared the Greeks' full rights in Christianity, 3:1–13, as they will see when they read his letters. In a prayerful appeal the writer sets forth the grandeur of the Christian's experience of Christ's love, and an exultant doxology marks the conclusion of the main part of the epistle, 3:14–21.

Christians must be united against the sects, 4:1–16. There is but one body, one Spirit, one hope, one Lord, one faith, one baptism, one God and Father of all. We must not be blown about and swung around by every wind of doctrine through the trickery of men, with their ingenuity in inventing error. Christians must live the new, upright life of purity, patience, integrity, and forbearance, 4:17—5:2. They must give up their old sins and live in the new light, 5:3–21. The marriage relation is made the symbol of the union of Christ with the church, 5:22–33. Children, parents, slaves, and masters have their special duties as Christians, 6:1–9. They must all put on the Christian armor and carry on the Christian warfare, 6:10–20. The farewell, 6:21–24, mentions Tychicus, Paul's well-known messenger of Col. 4:7, Acts 20:4. This is a part of the Pauline disguise, like Timothy in Hebrews 13:23 and Silvanus and Mark in I Pet. 5:12, 13.

Problems. The leading question about Ephesians is, of course, its authenticity: Is it the work of Paul, as it expressly claims to be? In favor of this position is, first, this express claim of the letter itself, which certainly has great weight; second, the universal acceptance of it as Paul's from ancient until modern times; and, third, the wealth of Pauline phraseology contained in it—there is hardly a line in the whole letter that does not show some resemblance to one or another of the nine genuine letters, Romans–Philemon.

The letter claims to be the work of Paul both directly, 1:1; 3:1, and indirectly, 4:1; 6:20, 21, etc. It is in the oldest list of Paul's letters that has come down to us, that of Marcion, *ca.* A.D. 140, where it appears under the title of "Laodiceans." Its wealth of Pauline phraseology is fully exhibited in my *Meaning of Ephesians* (pp. 82–165) where a detailed Greek table of parallels with Colossians and all the other genuine letters is given. The fullest consideration must be given these facts.

But these claims, though once widely accepted, are by no means conclusive, and the more closely one scrutinizes the letter, the more dubious they become. It must be remembered that pseudonymity was a common practice in antiquity and is not unknown today. Some years ago the *Atlantic Monthly* published "The Letter of Kallikrates" which purported to be from a Corinthian Christian of the first century to Paul, in answer to I Corinthians.[1] It was, in reality, written by a twentieth-century Scottish minister who sought by this transparent device to reach a wider public with his message. Few classical scholars would now maintain the authenticity of all thirteen of the letters of Plato, and few New Testament scholars of the present day hold I and II Peter or I and II Timothy and Titus to be genuine apostolic writings.

But when it is further perceived that the purpose of Ephesians is to serve as introduction to the collected letters of Paul and that it is made up almost entirely of materials taken from them, its pseudonymity be-

[1] March, 1928.

comes at once intelligible. What else could the writer have done? If he had put his own name to the letter, modern scholars would have declared him a plagiarist. His proceeding is not so different from that of Basil and Gregory when they put together the *Philocalia* and called it the work of Origen. They did, indeed, make it up of selections from Origen, and so they ascribed the work to him. Yet Origen did not really write the *Philocalia*, and it would be hard to say just who did.

In his recent revision of Jülicher's *Einleitung in das neue Testament* ([7th ed., 1931], p. 142), Fascher says the idea that Ephesians was written to serve as introduction to the collected letters of Paul is ruled out by the fact that it does not sufficiently emphasize the characteristic Pauline ideas of faith and "justification." But, as a matter of fact, the word "faith" occurs ninety-eight times in the nine genuine Pauline letters, or about once per page, which is precisely the average maintained by it in Ephesians—eight occurrences in eight pages. "Justification" occurs forty-nine times in the nine genuine letters (thirty-three of them in Romans) or about once in two pages, and three times in Ephesians, or once in two and a half pages, which is doing very well, considering that the word does not occur at all in Colossians. These figures sufficiently answer Fascher's objection. But more than this, as Dr. A. Haire Forster points out, it is precisely in Ephesians, and not in Romans, that Paul's great doctrine reaches its classical formulation: "It is by his mercy that you have been saved through faith;

it is not by your own action, it is the gift of God," 2:8. So far from neglecting this aspect of Paul, Ephesians has given it its finest expression. Fascher is unconsciously comparing Ephesians with Romans, not with the Pauline literature as a whole. But it was not written as an introduction to Romans but to the whole collection of nine letters, in which not Romans but Corinthians stood first. The attitude of Ephesians to faith and "justification" is quite as favorable to the theory that it was written as an introduction to the Pauline corpus as it is to the idea that it was written by the apostle Paul.

Many things in the epistle itself conflict with its express claim of Pauline authorship:

1. In the first place, Ephesians is unlike any of the Pauline letters known to us in that it reflects no definite historical situation which it is intended to meet. In all the efforts to interpret the letter from the Pauline point of view, no such situation has been successfully or convincingly developed. Yet Paul's letters have an unfailing way of revealing with great clearness the conditions under which they were written and the purpose in the apostle's mind. Considered as a letter of Paul's, Ephesians is in this respect altogether baffling.

2. The writer's admiration and regard for Paul are so great as to give scholars who maintain that Paul wrote the letter great embarrassment. The representation of Paul's unique insight into Christian truth, 3:1-12, is very different from Paul's own attitude in I and II Corinthians, for example.

3. With this goes also the writer's veneration for the holy apostles and prophets as the foundations of the church, 2:20, and the mediums of revelation, 3:5. Paul thought of Christ as the foundation of the church and said there could be no other, I Cor. 3:11. The Gospel of Matthew is usually understood as speaking of the apostle Peter (or perhaps his messianic faith) as the rock on which the church was to be built, Matt. 16:18. The expression "holy prophets" recalls Luke 1:70, and the conception of the apostles as the foundation of the church reminds us of the heavenly city in the Revelation, the wall of which had twelve foundation stones, and on them were the twelve names of the Lamb's twelve apostles, 21:14; compare also Rev. 18:20. The grouping of holy apostles and prophets is hardly the way in which Paul, as we know him through his letters, would have expressed himself. In fact, it points to an attitude to the apostles more like that of Matthew, Revelation, and Luke-Acts than of Paul.

4. The church, in Ephesians, is always the church universal, never the individual local church; for that Ephesians seems to use *patria*,[1] the equivalent of *familia*, 3:15. But Paul uses "church" (*ecclesia*) in both senses, Gal. 1:2; I Cor. 16:19.

5. The church has become Greek; for the whole body of Christians addressed in 1:1 were once physically heathen, 2:2, 11. There is no room for any Jewish Christianity in the picture.

6. The writer himself had been in the same condi-

[1] πατριά.

tion, 2:3, and hence is a gentile Christian. Paul scrupulously distinguished between the sins of the Jews and the grosser ones of the heathen, Romans, chapters 1, 2. It is these grosser ones which the writer now confesses for himself and his readers. Both he and they are Greek; compare II Cor. 11:22; Gal. 2:15; Phil. 3:4.

7. The encyclical form of the letter (that is, with no place name in 1:1), well known from the text of the great fourth-century manuscripts Vaticanus and Sinaiticus, and recently confirmed by the Ann Arbor–Chester Beatty papyrus, *ca*. A.D. 200, clearly implies a conception of Paul as a notable letter-writer. No one would put out an encyclical letter in the name of a man who had written no letters to speak of. But this writing of an encyclical implies that the letters of Paul have been collected, so that the writer can think of him as a notable letter-writer.

8. The sects are already beginning to appear, as in the Acts 20:30 and the Revelation, 2:6, 15. Christians "must not be babies any longer, blown about and swung around by every wind of doctrine, through the trickery of men with their ingenuity in inventing error," 4:14. This is the meaning of the insistence on unity in 4:3–6.

9. While so much of the language is Paul's own, it is used in other senses than Paul's. The "secret" of Col. 1:27 is Christ in the believer; in Ephesians the "secret" is the enfranchisement of the heathen as of equal rights with the Jews in the Christian salvation, 3:6. The "principalities and dominions" that the

Colossians were tempted to worship (Col. 1:16; 2:10) have in Ephesians become the spiritual enemies with whom the Christian soldier has to grapple, 1:21; 6:12.

10. The style is reverberating and liturgical, not at all the direct, rapid, Pauline give-and-take. For example, the Spirit, or the Spirit of God, or the holy Spirit, becomes "the holy Spirit of God," 4:30.

11. The novel element in the vocabulary, that is, the words used in Ephesians but not found in the nine genuine letters, is mostly akin to works like Luke-Acts, I Clement, I Peter, and Hebrews, written toward the close of the century.

12. The interest in hymnology, illustrated by the quotation of a Christian hymn, 5:14, points to the time when that interest had begun to be active in the early church, as in the canticles of Luke, 1:42, 46, 68; 2:14, 29, and the arias, choruses, and antiphonies of the Revelation.

13. The Descent into Hades, 4:9, 10, is an extraordinary thing to have to fit into the Pauline theology and is generally passed over in silence by those who seek to reconstruct Paul's thought. The instinct that leads them to do this is entirely right, for it is almost impossible to suppose such a view had any place in Paul's thinking. In fact, he virtually excludes it by what he says in Romans, 10:6, 7. The Descent into Hades is a natural sequel to Luke's doctrine of the Ascension, reflected in Eph. 4:9. To suppose Paul, who has no Ascension doctrine, should yet have had the sequel to it, in the *Descensus ad Inferos*, is putting the cart before the horse.

14. This brings us to the use of the Acts in Ephesians. The writer of Ephesians not only thinks of Paul as where the Acts left him, a prisoner for the Greek mission, but in several instances reflects the language of Luke-Acts, while the *Descensus* doctrine of Ephesians seems to be an inference from the Ascension doctrine of Luke.

15. The reference to the breaking-down of the barrier that kept the heathen out of the Court of the Men of Israel in the Temple, 2:14, while of course figurative, is certainly more natural after the Temple had been destroyed in A.D. 70 than before.

16. The jubilant review of the blessings of the Pauline salvation, with which the letter begins, is more natural in a reader of Paul's letters than in Paul himself. Paul's way was to take one of these and dwell upon it. But in chapter 1 they fairly tumble over one another, with no full treatment of any of them. This is entirely natural if the collected letters of Paul, with full treatments of all the matters so tumultuously surveyed in chapter 1, followed Ephesians.

17. The injunction in Ephesians 6:4 to bring their children up with Christian training and instruction is out of keeping with Paul's attitude; all he had to say to parents in Colossians (written supposedly at the same time as Ephesians, if the latter is by Paul) was "Do not irritate your children," 3:21.

18. Ephesians as a whole is a generalization of Paulinism much more like a later Paulinist than like Paul himself. Someone has observed that it reads like

a commentary on Paul. Even Romans is less of a generalization of the Pauline positions than Ephesians.

19. The writer of Ephesians is far more of an ecclesiastic than Paul. He finds in the church a great spiritual fellowship, built upon the apostles and prophets, 2:20–22, the medium of God's revelation, 3:10, and the avenue of man's praise, 3:21. It is the bride of Christ, 5:25–32, compare Rev. 21:9, 10.

20. Ephesians shows the literary influence of every one of the nine genuine letters. Over and over again it reveals acquaintance with each one of them. Every Pauline letter displays something in common with one or more of the others, of course. But Ephesians shows knowledge of all the other nine—a state of things which cannot be matched or even approached in any other letter.[1] To some this seems proof that Paul himself wrote Ephesians. But elsewhere Paul never repeats himself to any such extent as this. Moreover, the writer uses these Pauline materials to build up something very different from Paul.

21. Not only are all nine letters used in Ephesians, but the remarkable thing is that they fully supply all the material that it contains. They satisfy it. The writer of Ephesians has used them and nothing else, except a little of Luke-Acts and some Septuagint texts. But that Paul's knowledge of his own mind should have been confined to what he had said in the nine letters which are all that we possess from him is out

---

[1] A. E. Barnett, "The Use of the Letters of Paul in Pre-Catholic Christian Literature," *University of Chicago Abstracts of Theses* ("Humanistic Series"), IX (1934), 509.

of the question. Paul had an extraordinarily fertile and active mind, and he had much more to say than is preserved in the hundred pages of the nine letters. The only possible explanation of the fact is that the writer of Ephesians knows the mind of Paul *only* through these nine letters; he has no independent access to it. This is a point that has never been dealt with by the adherents of the Pauline authorship, to which, of course, it is fatal. It requires no corroboration from the twenty points, small and great, listed above. It reveals the author of Ephesians as dependent for his knowledge of the mind of Paul upon the nine letters which we know and proves beyond all doubt that he was not Paul.

Such points are usually regarded as difficulties with the Pauline authorship by those scholars who still cling to it, but of course they are not difficulties; rightly regarded they are helpful and invaluable clues to the solution of the problem of the authorship of Ephesians. As a matter of fact, these points are of the greatest assistance to us in solving the problem, and it is the solving of the problem that matters, not supporting any traditional position, however cherished.

Not only are these facts thought of as difficulties, but they are dealt with one at a time, as though everything else could be harmonized if the one difficulty before us at the moment could be somehow whittled away. But this again is far from true. To treat them singly really assumes that the particular difficulty being dealt with stands alone, whereas it is, in fact, but one of a long series. It is the cumulative effect of all these clues taken together that makes them significant.

The final test of any historical setting for an ancient document is, of course, the way in which the interpretation of it responds to the situation proposed. The interpretation of Ephesians does not respond at all to any situation that has been sought for it in the work of Paul; the examination of any commentary written from that point of view will reveal this. One candid commentator has recently said that, so understood, Ephesians shows us Paul writing "for his own satisfaction." Interpreted from the point of view here presented, however, every part of the epistle turns out to be full of pertinence and timely vigor. In particular, the neglected paragraph 3:1–12, which some would call a transition, some a digression, regains its full significance as pointing the reader to the assembled Pauline letters, which Ephesians seeks to introduce to the church general.

Professor Scott asks, "Can we believe that in the church of Paul's day there was an unknown teacher of this supreme excellence?"[1] This seems a dangerous approach to the matter, for there was in the first century an unknown great enough to write the Gospel of Matthew, and another capable of the Epistle to the Hebrews, and another who could write I Peter, and soon after another who could write the Gospel of John, and yet none of these authors can we name with certainty. Early Christian literature was largely the

[1] E. F. Scott, *The Literature of the New Testament* (New York, 1932), p. 180.

work of great Unknowns. Surely we shall not ascribe all these works to Paul because we do not know of anyone else great enough to have produced them.

But if a name and an identity be demanded for the author of Ephesians, the name of Onesimus of Ephesus comes at once to the mind. The Pauline corpus came into being in the days when Onesimus and Polycarp seem to have been active in Christian work in Asia— Polycarp in Smyrna and Onesimus in Ephesus. Onesimus may have been the Laodicean Christian who brought Colossians-Philemon to Ephesus; who so likely to have cherished and pored over them as he? He may have been the collector of the Pauline corpus, of which he thus had the nucleus. And he may have been the writer of the great preface which we know as Ephesians, building thus a splendid monument to his great friend and teacher, who had saved him from slavery and paganism and opened before him a new life. One would like to think so.[1]

LITERATURE

ABBOTT, T. K. *Epistles to the Ephesians and to the Colossians* (New York, 1909).

BOWEN, C. R. *Studies in the New Testament* (Chicago, 1936), pp. 110-38.

GOODSPEED, E. J. *The Meaning of Ephesians* (Chicago, 1933).

————. *New Solutions of New Testament Problems* (Chicago, 1927).

[1] Jülicher remarks that many points in Ephesians suggest that a disciple of the apostle wrote it (*Introduction* [1904] p. 147), and Easton feels that it must be the work of a personal follower of Paul (*Anglican Theological Review*, XVI [1934], 30.)

XV

THE REVELATION OF JOHN

+

Occasion. It was the glory of the Roman Empire that it brought peace to a troubled world. Under its sway the regions of Asia Minor and the East enjoyed tranquillity and security to an extent and for a length of time unknown before and probably since. This was the *pax Romana*. The provincial, under Roman sway, found himself in a position to conduct his business, provide for his family, send his letters, and make his journeys in security, thanks to the strong hand of Rome.

The Eastern world was deeply grateful for this peace and attempted a gesture of gratitude to the great figure across the sea to whom it owed it. And so emperor worship began.

The early emperors permitted it without encouraging it. It is a mistake to say with Rabbi Browne in *This Believing World* that, from Augustus on, they demanded it.[1] Suetonius says that Tiberius forbade temples to be built or *flamens* or priests appointed for him,[2] and a letter of Claudius, written to the Alex-

[1] Lewis Browne, *This Believing World* (New York, 1926), p. 108.

[2] *Tiberius* 26; cf. Tacitus *Annals* iv. 37, 38. In a letter to the ephors and the city of Gythion in Laconia, preserved in an inscription there (Rostovtzeff, "L'Empereur Tibère et le culte impérial," *Revue historique*, CLXIII [1930], 1–26), Tiberius declined divine honors.

andrians upon his accession in A.D. 41, says in reply to their proposal of temples and a priesthood for him in Alexandria:

I deprecate the appointment of a high priest to me, and the erection of temples, for I do not wish to be offensive to my contemporaries and I hold that sacred fanes and the like have by all ages been attributed to the immortal gods as peculiar honors.[1]

Later political lawyers, however, saw in the worship of the emperor a way of insuring the loyalty of the miscellaneous and heterogeneous peoples under Roman sway that now girdled the Mediterranean, making it, as Varro said, a Roman lake. They worshiped different gods but might all be asked to add this minor deity to their pantheons, as a way of expressing allegiance to Rome. So by Domitian's time emperor worship was indeed required. The force of the empire was now put behind the practice, and it was demanded of all. The Arch of Titus, built in Domitian's day in honor of his deceased brother, is erected "To the deified Titus, son of the deified Vespasianus"—names of blasphemy to any Christian mind. Yet these men were dead; it was for the living emperor that divine honors were now demanded.

It had always been a dangerous thing to be a Christian. Roman authority definitely designated those religions that might be practiced in the empire and Christianity was not one of them. Christian leaders, from Jesus on, had suffered death—Stephen, James, Paul, Peter—and the early church had had to resort to

[1] H. I. Bell, *Jews and Christians in Egypt* (London, 1924), p. 28.

various ways of disguising itself to survive at all. At first it appeared as a sect of Judaism, a tolerated religion (*religio licita*); then as fraternal clubs, like the modern Misericordias in Italy. Christians had always been conscious of living on the edge of a volcano, for persecution might at any time break out against them. It is hardly too much to say that anyone might denounce them at any time as adherents of an unlicensed religion.

But now the danger had become acute. With the demand of emperor worship, the church and the empire were at war. For the church and the imperial cultus, the worship of the emperor, were in direct collision. The prospect was a fearful one. No power of the ancient world had been able to stand against the Roman Empire; it had swept them all aside. And against it what chance had the little scattered groups of Christians, not yet even organized into a Catholic church?

Why not then, like practical men and women, meet the situation with a little compromise? A slight mental reservation was all that was needed. Why not burn the pinch of incense, make the affirmation "Caesar is a god," bow before his image, and go one's way? Surely that was better than giving up one's self, one's family, and in fact the whole church of Christ to a cruel destruction.

It was at this point in the progress of events that the prophet John of Ephesus stood forth with his ringing message of "No compromise!" He saw that a

Christianity that had to alter its principles in order to be preserved was not worth preserving.

He casts his message in the old Jewish apocalyptic type, thus veiling his meaning from matter-of-fact Roman minds by picturing empires and monarchs under the form of beasts and monsters. The art of the apocalyptic literature—the Book of Daniel, the Book of Enoch, and the like—was the art of the grotesque, symbolizing dynasties, reigns, and forces by weird creatures of fancy grouped in mystic numbers, especially in sevens.[1]

So commanding is this feature of the book that learning has almost completely ignored other traits no less important: the influence of the collected letters of Paul and of Greek dramatic art. The portal of the Revelation is formed by something entirely foreign to the apocalyptic type—a corpus of letters to Christian churches, seven in number, preceded by a general message, chapter 1, to all seven. It is impossible any longer to ignore the fact that this is a commanding testimony of the most massive kind to the existence and influence of the published Pauline collection.[2]

The elaborate system of solos, antiphonies, choruses, and orchestration—harps, trumpets, earthquakes, thunders, mighty waters, and hail—points just as un-

[1] C. C. McCown, "Hebrew and Egyptian Apocalyptic Literature," *Harvard Theological Review*, XVIII (1925), 357 f.

[2] If more minute evidence is desired, the use of Paul's characteristic epistolary formula χάρις ὑμῖν καὶ εἰρήνη appears here, Rev. 1:4, and nowhere else outside of Ephesians and the letters of Paul; cf. E. J. Goodspeed, *New Solutions of New Testament Problems* (Chicago, 1927), chap. iii.

mistakably to the influence of the contemporary Greek drama, with its chorus of twenty-four.[1] The whole structure of the Revelation is highly dramatic.

The symbolic forms of the old apocalyptic vocabulary at once obscure the writer's meaning from outsiders and heighten his appeal for his Christian public. He has no need to conceal his identity under the name of some ancient worthy of the dim past, like Daniel or Enoch. The old Jewish view that the prophetic period ended with Ezra had made that necessary in the second and first centuries before Christ. But the early Christians believed that the time had come when the Spirit was poured forth upon all mankind, when their sons and daughters became prophets, Acts 2:17, 18; 21:9. A Christian prophet could therefore speak out in his own person like the prophets of old: "I, John, your brother and companion . . . . found myself on the island called Patmos, for uttering God's message, and testifying to Jesus," 1:9.

Contents. His task is to stiffen the churches of the Roman province of Asia against the danger of weakening before the rising persecution. The portal of his Apocalypse is, strangely enough, a group of letters, or rather one general letter to the seven churches, with individual messages for each of the seven. In all these letters there is the same note—instead of being overcome by the persecution, the Christians must overcome.

The seven churches to which the Revelation is to be carried are scattered a few miles, perhaps a day's

[1] R. R. Brewer, "The Influence of Greek Drama on the Apocalypse of John," *Anglican Theological Review*, XVIII (1936), 74–92.

journey, from one another in the province of Asia. The letters to them form the prelude to the three visions which make up the body of the book.

As we approach these, we must think of the Revelation as of some stupendous super-opera, with three awful acts, each with its scenes of dreadful woe or bewildering beauty, with its solos, its choruses, and its antiphonies, and with its prodigious orchestration, for its accompaniments are not only harps and trumpets but the mighty peals of thunder, the crashing earthquakes, and the sound of great floods of water. In fact, it is only dramatically that the Revelation can be understood.

The first vision, chapters 4–11, is that of the Roll of Destiny. Caught up like Isaiah into the very presence of God, the prophet sees him on his throne, with all the heavenly court about him. In his hand is a scroll so packed with meaning that it is written not only within but on the back as well, but it is tightly sealed with seven seals. No one can open it; and yet it seems that it must be opened, for it contains God's plan for the redemption of the world, which has only to be opened to be realized. At last a lamb appears that is able to do this. Though the lamb is alive, it has been slain, for the prophet's idea is that Jesus by his death has released God's program for the world's salvation.

As one seal after another is broken, the most woeful portents appear in heaven: the angel of invasion, the angel of war, the angel of famine,[1] and the angel of

---

[1] Famine prices are given for wheat and barley, 6:6; the added warning about oil and wine probably refers to Domitian's regulations "ordering the

death. Other portents follow the breaking of the other seals. At the breaking of the fifth, the martyrs underneath the altar cry for relief. At the sixth, there is a terrific earthquake. The slaves of God are marked on their foreheads, and a mighty army of martyrs praise God for their deliverance, for God will wipe every tear from their eyes.

When the seventh seal is broken, seven angels with trumpets stand forth to blow, and at each blast some new disaster happens. The reader is to see that he is not to be disturbed by news of war or famine or pestilence; these are only the minor accompaniment to the progress of God's program for the world's redemption. Before the seventh trumpet blows, the seven thunders lift up their voices to utter things that must not be recorded; but when it blows, marking the climax of the vision, for the three sevens are passed, loud voices are heard in heaven saying, "The sovereignty of the world has passed into the possession of our Lord and of his Christ, and he will reign forever and ever."

The "sovereignty of the world" belonged to Rome. No one disputed that. It had maintained that sovereignty against all comers for centuries. No kings or coalition of kings had been able to challenge it. But now above the imperator (the *autokrator*) stood the Omnipotent, the *Pantokrator*, 11:17, who had at last assumed his rightful power and begun to reign. The act closes with a tremendous coda—the vision of the

---

vines in the provinces to be cut down, nowhere permitting more than one half of them to remain" (Suetonius *Domitian* 7).

temple interior—and with a mighty crash of music, rumblings, peals of thunder, an earthquake, and a great storm of hail, the full cosmic orchestra marks the end.

The second vision, 12:1—19:10, is the Dragon War. The victory of the Kingdom of God is assured, but it has yet to be won. There is war in heaven, Michael the archangel leading the heavenly host against Satan. Satan is cast down to the earth, where the war is renewed. The Dragon takes vengeance on the church and her children. The prophet takes his stand on the seashore and sees coming up from the west out of the sea an animal symbolizing the empire with its worldwide dominion and its enmity for the church.

Then down from the land, from the province of Asia, comes another animal, representing the local priesthood of the imperial cultus. It compels people to worship the first animal. Without its mark or name no one can do business, buy, or sell; perhaps referring to the use of the oath by the fortune of the emperor to attest contracts and other legal documents. As every letter of the Greek and Aramaic alphabets was also a number, any name might be represented by adding up the numerical values of all its letters, though this would of course convey the name only to those who already knew it. The number 666 in Aramaic letters could mean Nero Caesar, and probably veils a still deeper allusion to Domitian, whom the church was indeed finding a second Nero, a Nero come to life again.

In contrast with the animal of Rome and his worshipers the prophet now catches a glimpse of the hosts of ransomed saints singing their new song before the throne, with the names not of the emperor but of the Lamb and his Father written on their foreheads. An angel flying in mid-air proclaims the fall of Rome, which he conceals under the name of Babylon because it played the role of persecutor to the Christian church as Babylon had done to the Jewish.

The seven bowls of the wrath of God are poured out upon the world, each outpouring being attended by dreadful disasters. As the seventh angel empties his bowl upon the air, a loud voice from the throne declares that all is over, there is a terrific earthquake, and Babylon falls.

An angel takes the prophet away to see the fallen city. He beholds her as an adulterous woman, covered with jewels, drunk with the blood of the martyrs, and seated on a scarlet animal with seven heads and ten horns. The seven heads are seven hills, on which the woman sits. They are also seven kings: five have fallen (the five Julian emperors, from Augustus to Nero), one is reigning (Vespasian), the other has not yet come (Titus), and when he does his stay must be brief.

How does the prophet know that the seventh king's reign would be so brief? Obviously because it had been brief. Titus reigned less than two years. But this would bring us to the times of Domitian, which is just what the whole setting of the book demands. The eighth king, who is also one of the seven, is evidently

Domitian, who as a persecutor of the church seemed to imaginative Christians another Nero.[1]

Then in a colossal spectacle, chapter 18, the burning of the fallen city is described. Around her at a safe distance, like so many choruses of mourners, are gathered four groups—the kings, the merchants, the dealers, and the navigators, who had grown rich through her luxury and extravagance. "What city was like the great city?" they cry, "for in a single hour she has been destroyed."

"After that I heard what sounded like the loud shout of a great multitude in heaven saying, 'Praise the Lord.' " The choruses of elders and of animals about the throne respond. A voice from the throne itself replies. The full ensemble with the full orchestra thunders back the tremendous climax: "Praise the Lord; for the Lord our God, the Almighty, now reigns." So ends the second vision, like the first, with the ultimate triumph of the Kingdom of God.

The third vision is the New Jerusalem, 19:11—22:5. The armies of heaven on white horses stream forth after their champion—the Word of God, Faithful and True. The animal and his vassal kings speedily fall before them, and Satan is hurled into the abyss. He is released after a thousand years to make one last effort against God's people. It fails, and the stupendous spectacle of the judgment passes before the prophet's eye. Upon a great white throne sits One from whose presence earth and sky fled so far that they could not

[1] Juvenal calls Domitian Nero (*Satires* iv. 37, 38), as does Martial (*Epigrams* xi. 33).

be found. The books were opened, and the sea gave up its dead.

From these lurid scenes the prophet turns to the brighter future—the new heaven and the new earth. God's dwelling is with men . . . . and he will wipe every tear from their eyes. The New Jerusalem, the Holy City, comes down out of heaven to be the bride of the Lamb. It is a place of unspeakable splendor, dazzling with gold and pearls. A river of living water issues from the throne of God and of the Lamb and runs through the city. On both sides of it grows the tree of life, and its leaves are a cure for the heathen. His people will fill the city, and there they will reign forever and ever.

The Revelation is a great document of Christian faith. To the harassed and fearful Christians of Asia all this brought comfort and courage in their dreadful situation. It reminded them that the empire was not all powerful as it claimed and seemed to be, but that God was above it and would yet bring his kingdom in on earth. It revived their waning hope in the ultimate triumph of the will of God.

Problems. Within these main divisions, it is true, there are strange sections—digressions, interludes— that seem to reflect older situations and Jewish atmospheres. The problem of the interpreter is to find out how they are meant to bear upon the persecution situation addressed in the book, rather than to trace each of them to its source in the history of ancient apocalypticism. Certainly they do not suffice to show that the Apocalypse was generally based upon an earlier Jewish apocalypse now lost; and as in the case of Shakespeare and his sources, we are more concerned with the use John of Ephesus made of his materials than with where he may have first come across them.

The Revelation was written in Asia, in the circle of Ephesus, probably in part at least on the island of Patmos, in the later years of Domitian,[1] when his embittered character was making it more and more difficult for so many of his subjects, as Pliny[2] relates. It was in consequence of his harsh treatment of members of his own family that he was finally assassinated by Stephanus, the freedman of Domitian's banished and widowed niece, Domitilla, in revenge for her wrongs, A.D. 96.

It was to be read publicly in each of the seven churches, for a blessing is pronounced, 1:3, upon him who reads it and upon those who hear it read. It was probably not intended for permanent church use, but its great claims as the work of a Christian prophet, writing at the dictation of Christ himself, and its undoubted spiritual power, especially in the times of persecution which were all too frequent, preserved and finally, though only after much controversy,[3] canonized it in the New Testament.

[1] This is also the testimony of antiquity. Irenaeus says of the Revelation, "It was seen not long ago but almost in our generation, toward the end of the reign of Domitian" (*Refutation of Gnosticism* v. 30. 3). This judgment is twice quoted by Eusebius (*Church History* iii. 18. 3; v. 8. 6).

[2] *Letters* i. 12; ix. 13, etc.; cf. also Suetonius *Domitian* 10, 11, 17.

[3] Eusebius, *Church History* vii. 25.

LITERATURE

BREWER, R. R. "The Influence of Greek Drama upon the Apocalypse of John," *Anglican Theological Review*, XVIII (1936), 74–92.

CASE, S. J. *The Revelation of John* (Chicago, 1919).

CHARLES, R. H. *The Revelation of St. John* (2 vols.; New York, 1920).

XVI
THE EPISTLE TO THE HEBREWS
+

Occasion. Of all the early churches none surpasses in interest or significance the one at Rome. Our first glimpse of it is when Paul writes the Letter to the Romans, about A.D. 56. The Acts gives us an account of Paul's arrival there and his stay there as a prisoner for two years, somewhere about A.D. 60. Then comes Nero's attack upon the church, in August of 64, so tellingly described in Tacitus. There follows the writing of the Gospel of Mark, about 70. And then the writing of what, ever since the time of Tertullian at least, has been known as the Letter to the Hebrews.[1]

Forty years had now passed since Paul had written Romans. The Roman church was in its second generation. Roman Christians had grown up in the faith. It had been familiar to them from childhood. Most of them had never known any other. They came of Christian parents and had never thought of being anything but Christians. But the primitive apocalyptic expectations had waned. The great distinctive values of Christianity had grown dim. The early enthusiasm had evaporated. Christianity was coming to be an old story. Apathy was pervading the church.

Upon a church thus spiritually decayed the blow of

[1] "Barnabae titulus ad Hebraeos," *De pudicitia* 20.

253

Domitian's attack fell, as it had fallen on Ephesus and the neighboring churches of Asia. The demand of emperor worship as a test of loyalty to the empire found a church cooled in its zeal, like Ephesus, to which John had written in the name of Christ, "You do not love me as you did at first."[1]

The Roman church had a great tradition. It had had its baptism of fire in that terrible August of 64 when Nero tried to lay upon it the blame for burning the city. Tacitus in his *Annals* (xv. 44) describes what happened:

First those were seized who confessed that they were Christians. Next, on their information, a vast multitude were convicted, not so much on the charge of burning the city, as of hating the human race. And in their deaths they were also made the subject of sport, for they were covered with the hides of wild beasts and worried to death by dogs, or nailed to crosses or set fire to and when day declined burned to serve for nocturnal lights. Nero offered his own gardens for the spectacle.[2]

Those terrible days are reflected in Hebrews in very similar words:

You must remember those early days when after you had received the light, you had to go through a great struggle with persecution, sometimes being actually exposed as a public spectacle to insults and violence, and sometimes showing yourselves ready to share the lot of those in that condition. For you showed sympathy for those who were in prison, and you put up with it cheerfully when your property was taken from you, for you knew that you had in

[1] Rev. 2:4*b*.   [2] Translation in "Harper's Classical Library."

yourselves a greater possession that was lasting. You must not lose your courage, for it will be richly rewarded, but you will need endurance if you are to carry out God's will and receive the blessing he has promised [10:32–36].

The Roman Christians had done a great work and shown their love for the cause by giving help to their persecuted fellow-Christians, 6:10. But now, with their zeal declining, they were confronted by this fresh attack under Domitian, and to the danger of apathy was added that of apostasy.

Two things were pressingly demanded. They must be shown the immense value of the religion they had come to take as a matter of course, and they must be told how awful the consequences of renouncing it would be. Apathy must be cured and apostasy prevented. But since, sometimes, people unequal to their present tasks can be stirred to meet them only by being called upon to do something still more exacting, so now the Roman church is stingingly reminded that, old as it is among the churches, it is not leading and instructing the others as it should do. From the length of their Christian experience they ought to be teaching the others, but as it is, they actually need someone to teach them over again the very elements of Christian truth, 5:12.

It was to accomplish these ends that Hebrews was written. To counteract the prevalent apathy of the Roman Christians, it compared Christianity point by point with the next greatest religion, Judaism, showing how at every point the new faith far surpassed it. To prevent apostasy, it showed the dreadful, even irreparable, consequences of such a course, for which there could be no repentance or forgiveness. (This terrible doctrine was to have important consequences in Christian history.) And to rouse the Roman church from its lethargy, it was called upon to accept the great role that belonged to it and become the teacher of the churches, 5:12.

The writer of Hebrews had for his model the Pauline letter-type, which had just clearly emerged before the churches in the published collection of Paul's letters. His letter is about two-thirds the length of Paul's letter to Rome, written almost forty years before. Like Paul, the new writer varies instruction with entreaty, only much more frequently than Paul had done. Barnett finds it reasonably likely that Hebrews used eight of the ten letters of the primary Pauline canon—all except II Thessalonians and Philemon.[1] Its clearest use of them is in the great catalogue of the heroes of faith, where Paul's characteristic doctrine of faith is glorified somewhat in the manner Paul himself used in dealing with love in I Corinthians, chapter 13, only much more elaborately and rhetorically. Hebrews is, in fact, the most elegant rhetoric in the New Testament. Indeed, its atmosphere is for the most part really that of a sermon: "My time would fail me if I told of Gideon, Barak, Sampson, Jephthah, David, Samuel, and the prophets," 11:32. "Listen patiently to this appeal"—the same expression as that

[1] A. E. Barnett, "The Use of the Letters of Paul in Pre-Catholic Christian Literature" (unpublished dissertation; Chicago, 1932), p. 612; *Abstracts of Theses* ("Humanistic Series"), IX (1934), 509.

used of the synagogue address or sermon in Acts 13:15. And yet the writer goes on, "For I have written you but briefly," 13:22. He evidently means in comparison with Paul's great letters to the Romans and Corinthians, each of which is considerably longer. Hebrews is both letter and sermon and naturally enough, since it was intended to be read in Christian meetings as a sermon. Read in that way, it would take forty-five or fifty minutes—a rather long sermon, yet not so long as Romans or I or II Corinthians.

To modern ears Hebrews does not sound at all like Paul, but the ancients viewed it very differently. The great Alexandrian fathers from Pantaenus to Origen considered it Paul's, and the recently published papyrus manuscript of Paul's letters, dating from about A.D. 200 (Gerstinger, Wilcken) to 250 (Kenyon, Sanders), already has Hebrews standing second among the Pauline letters, following Romans and preceding I Corinthians.[1]

Whether Hebrews was originally pseudepigraphical and actually claimed the name of Paul is an interesting question. Its early acceptance as among the Pauline letters would strongly suggest that it did, and the reference to Timothy quite in the Pauline manner, 13:23, makes this rather probable.

If we are right in thinking it is strongly influenced by the published Pauline corpus, we may date it with some definiteness in the eventful period just before or

[1] H. A. Sanders, *A Third Century Papyrus Codex of the Epistles of Paul* (Ann Arbor, 1935), Pl. I; F. G. Kenyon, *The Chester Beatty Biblical Papyri*, Fasc. III, Suppl. (London, 1936), p. viii.

about A.D. 95, for Hebrews was copiously used, as even Eusebius observed (*Church History* iii. 38. 1), in the Letter of Clement of Rome to the Corinthians, written probably before the death of Domitian in A.D. 96.

Of its name we can say only that it reflects an ancient mistaken editorial inference from the very large part Judaism plays in its argument, from which as early as the end of the second century it was imagined that it must have been addressed to a Jewish public, seeking to win it to the Christian faith, or to Christian Jews, seeking to confirm them in it. But the writer's Judaism is not actual and objective, but literary and academic, manifestly gained from the reading of the Septuagint Greek version of the Jewish scriptures, and his polished Greek style would be a strange vehicle for a message to Aramaic-speaking Jews or Christians of Jewish blood. Before his mind is always the Tabernacle in the Wilderness, never the Temple in Jerusalem. The picture he gives of the church he is addressing does not at all fit Jerusalem; though as we have seen it is strikingly appropriate to Rome. To say that the church at Jerusalem had not taught the churches would be at variance with all the familiar facts, 5:12. The Jerusalem church ceased to exist in the Jewish War of A.D. 66–70, and to seek to push Hebrews back into the period before that war would be fantastic.

Moreover, it is at Rome that the letter is first reflected—in I Clement, a letter written to Corinth in the name of the Roman church. It reflects Hebrews a score of times, especially in chapter 36, and indeed much of its plan is copied from that of Hebrews. This is altogether natural if, as seems probable, I Clement was written in response to the demand of Hebrews that the Roman church begin to instruct the other churches.

The letter as we have it is anonymous, and of its author little can be said. We cannot even be sure he was of Jewish blood. If he knew Hebrew at all, he preferred to use the Septuagint Greek version of the Jewish scriptures, as in Ps. 40:6—"You have provided a body for me" instead of "You have opened my ears." He is very familiar with the Greek Bible, but so was Clement of Rome, his contemporary. While the Alexandrians identified him with Paul (perhaps in part because of his mention of Timothy, 13:23), Tertullian called him Barnabas (*De pudicitia* 20), and the western church did not accept his letter as Paul's or as Scripture until the middle of the fourth century (Hilary of Poitiers, †A.D. 367). The words, "The brothers from Italy wish to be remembered to you," 13:24, suggest that the letter was written to an Italian—that is, Roman—congregation from outside of Italy, but of course this latter is not certain.

Contents. Hebrews opens with a bold contrast between the new revelation and the old. The revealer of the new religion is no mere prophet or angel like those of the old but the Son of God, in whom the writer sees the divine wisdom personified. As such he becomes the agent of creation, the reflection of the glory of God, and the sustainer of the universe, chapter 1. The Book of Wisdom (about A.D. 40) has strongly influenced him here. A warning follows against being indifferent to such a salvation, 2:1–4. Resuming his first subject, the writer proceeds to interpret the sufferings of Christ as a preparation for his high priestly task, 2:5–18.

The argument showing the superiority of Christ, the Son, to Moses, the servant, of God, 3:1–6, is followed by another warning against repeating the error of the Israelites, who, though they followed Moses out of Egypt, were refused permission to enter the promised rest, 3:7—4:13.

Returning to the priesthood of Christ, the writer urges his readers to hold fast to their religion, 4:14–16. Christ is a true high priest by virtue both of his divine appointment and of his human experience, 5:1–10. An extended exhortation, 5:11—6:20, laments the readers' backwardness, warns against apostasy, and proclaims the Melchizedek priesthood of Jesus. This, he explains, 7:1–28, is an older order, far superior to that of Aaron in its permanence, efficacy, and dignity.

Hebrews is pervaded by the a fortiori argument: Good as the old covenant was, the new everywhere excels it. The new high priest performs a service immeasurably better than that of the old Aaronic priests, 8:1—10:39. That was but a shadow; his is the reality. His priesthood carries with it the new and better covenant foretold in Jer. 31:31–34, Heb. 8:1–13. His is a better sanctuary, a better sacrifice, and a better ministry, 9:1–28. In place of the old, futile, daily butcherings, which never had any real spiritual value, he has once for all offered himself in a sacrifice of eternal efficacy, 10:1–18. A fresh warning against apostasy follows, 10:19–31: "It is a fearful thing to fall into the hands of the living God!" Stirring reminders of their former heroism recall the steadfastness of the Roman church in the Neronian persecution of A.D. 64. They must not lose that courage now, 10:32–39.

In a brilliant passage, reminiscent of the glowing account of Israel's heroes in Ecclessiasticus, chapters 44–50, the writer shows that the Jewish saints had not lived to see the fulfilment of their hopes, but all died "in faith, without having received what has been promised them." Faith was the power through which they had done their heroic work and gained God's approval, 11:1–40. This great survey of the heroes of faith is followed by an exhortation to follow their great example and particularly that of Christ, their leader and example in faith, and to accept the trials of life as a spiritual discipline, 12:1–13. They should be warned by the fate of Esau against moral failure with its terrible penalty, 12:14–17.

In a final, sweeping comparison the old revelation, with all its repellent, material aspects, is contrasted with the new—heavenly, ideal, and eternal, 12:18–29. Theirs is a kingdom that cannot be shaken. Varied exhortations—to hospitality, charity, morality—with personal matters and farewells complete the letter, 13:1–25. The Christians must be hospitable and charitable. They must keep the marriage relation sacred and be free from avarice. The memory of their martyred leaders (Paul and Peter, as Clement of Rome clearly saw, obeying this command to remember them in his chap. 5) should nerve them to imitate their faith. They are warned against the sects, 13:9; Jesus is their great sin-offering. They must be loyal to their Christian leaders. (This point really became the text of I Clement.)

Problems. Much of the difficulty felt by scholars in explaining Hebrews is due to failure to perceive its indebtedness to the published Pauline letters. Though written in imitation of the Pauline letter-type established by that collection, it was not simply a private letter to a church but probably from the beginning was given a wide circulation; in fact, it was published. The fact that it was addressed to the Roman Christians would not interfere with this circulation at a time when Paul's letters to individual churches were being accepted as having a message for all Christians everywhere. Its address to Rome was hardly more than a dedication; it was meant for the churches. Its great warnings against apathy and apostasy would have immense value for them all, as Revelation and I Peter show, and its demand that the Roman church begin to instruct the other churches would tend to make them look to Rome for what it had to teach.

There is a deep Platonic strain in the thought of Hebrews, derived no doubt by way of Alexandria, where Philo had so thoroughly allegorized Old Testament figures like Melchizedek, making him a symbol of the Logos. The writer of Hebrews is no mere follower of Philo, however, though he owes much to this type of thought, building on slight suggestions of lan-

guage like King of Peace (Salem), and King of Righteousness (Melchi-zedek) and piecing together texts
from Genesis and Psalms 110 to build up his doctrine
of a permanent pre-Levitical priesthood.

Of course allegory was not unknown to Paul (cf.
Gal. 4:21–31), but it makes its most impressive showing in New Testament literature in Hebrews. Allegory
was in wide use in antiquity, having been long and
successfully applied to Homer by his Stoic interpreters.
There is a splendid passage in Epictetus which shows
its power:

Who would Hercules have been, if he had sat at home?
He would have been Eurystheus and not Hercules! Well,
and in his travels through the world, how many intimates
and how many friends had he? But none more his friend
than God, for which reason he came to be considered the
son of God, and so he was! It was in obedience to him that
he went about purging away injustice and violence.[1]

In such terms Stoic preachers were allegorizing the
heroes of Greek mythology in the very days in which
Hebrews was written. The personal touches in 13:18–
25 certainly create a very Pauline atmosphere and owe
much to Paul's collected letters. Wrede thought they
were part of a Pauline disguise and were meant to
make the letter sound like Paul. The mention of
Timothy, whom Paul mentions so often, even oftener
than Titus, suggests that the writer is trying to write
like Paul. And if the letter at first claimed to be the
work of Paul, striking facts about it would be explained: (1) its use of these Pauline touches in 13:18–

[1] *Discourses* ii. 16.

25; (2) its manifest acquaintance with the collected letters of Paul; (3) its need of a name, for, as long as it claimed to be by Paul, it could not be called Romans, as there was already in the corpus a well-known letter of Paul to Rome; (4) its ascription to Paul by the Alexandrians, from Pantaenus down, which would have been natural if it originally bore Paul's name.

Pseudonymity was already coming into use at this very time, as Ephesians just before and I Peter just after clearly show. But the Ann Arbor papyrus, our most ancient witness to the text of Paul, while it includes Hebrews among his letters and even places it second, immediately after Romans, has no mention of Paul at the beginning of the epistle.

LITERATURE

GOODSPEED, EDGAR J. *The Epistle to the Hebrews* (New York, 1908).

MOFFATT, JAMES. *The Epistle to the Hebrews* (New York, 1924).

SCOTT, ERNEST F. *The Epistle to the Hebrews: Its Doctrine and Significance* (New York, 1922).

XVII
THE FIRST EPISTLE OF PETER
✠

Occasion. It is a striking fact that very soon after the writing of Hebrews the Roman church is found undertaking the very kind of Christian service that Hebrews had demanded of it—the instruction of the other churches. I Clement and I Peter may be regarded as the response of the Roman church to this challenge, which might well spur a conscientious Christian body to great exertions: "Although from the length of your Christian experience you ought to be teaching others, you actually need someone to teach you over again the very elements of Christian truth, and you have come to need milk instead of solid food," Heb. 5:12.[1] Certainly the Roman church did respond to this demand, for Ignatius twelve or fifteen years later wrote to the Romans, "You have taught others," Ignatius, *Rom.* 3:1.

The Shepherd of Hermas, written not long after A.D. 100, describes it as the business of "Clement" to send copies of Hermas' visions to other cities, *Vis.* ii. 4. 3,

---

[1] It is true the Roman church had already put forth the Gospel of Mark and done that much to be the teacher of the churches, but that was long before, almost in the times of the apostles, and was chiefly the work of those "former leaders who had brought them God's message," 13:7, not of the Roman church itself.

"for that is his duty."[1] So between the writing of Hebrews and the testimony of Ignatius three writings of great importance to the early church had emanated from Rome: I Clement, I Peter, and *The Shepherd* of Hermas. In fact, the main purpose of the last of these was to modify the doctrine, which Hebrews seemed to teach, that there could be no forgiveness for post-baptismal sin.[2]

The Letter of Clement of Rome to the Corinthians is unquestionably an elaborate effort on the part of the Roman church to instruct another church. That letter shows great familiarity with Hebrews and is influenced by it both in general structure and in detail. It seems a very natural conclusion that I Clement was really written in immediate response to the demand of Hebrews that the church at Rome take up the task of teaching the churches.[3] This becomes all the clearer when one observes the labored character of I Clement. Unable to write a great letter, the writer very obviously seeks to make up for it by writing a long one. It is apparent that he is not altogether self-moved; he is seeking to meet a demand that has been made upon him. If he wrote from some great inward compulsion, out of a full heart, his work could not have been so lifeless and commonplace. Lightfoot described the characteristics

[1] This early date for *The Shepherd* has been established by Dr. W. J. Wilson, "The Career of the Prophet Hermas," *Harvard Theological Review*, XX (1927), 21–62; cf. B. H. Streeter, *The Four Gospels* (New York, 1925), p. 340.

[2] Heb. 6:4–6.

[3] E. J. Goodspeed, *New Solutions of New Testament Problems* (Chicago, 1927), pp. 110–15.

of I Clement as comprehensiveness, sense of order, and moderation.[1] He might have added mediocrity. No one would call it great or very moving. It does not sound at all as though a great afflatus had come upon a man and a great idea had suddenly possessed him demanding to be expressed. It sounds much more as though it were written from a sense of duty, and someone else's sense of duty at that.

This impression is singularly confirmed by the opening lines: "Owing to the sudden and repeated misfortunes and calamities that have befallen us, we suppose we have been too slow[2] in paying attention to the matters under dispute among you, dear friends." This left-handed way of beginning has long perplexed interpreters. It has a very apologetic ring, and yet the writer is not apologizing to the Corinthians, for they have not asked his advice. He is really apologizing to himself and saying in effect, "We realize that we ought to have written you about this matter long ago." But what has made the Roman church realize this? Hebrews, of course. It was Hebrews that first called on the Roman church to teach the churches.

The strange tone of this sentence is further relieved by the fact that, if Hebrews was sent not only to the Roman church but was more widely circulated—in fact, published—the Corinthians might well understand this allusion to a duty the Roman church had neglected but was now beginning to perform.

I Peter is another effort of the Roman church in this

[1] *Clement of Rome*, I, 95.

[2] βράδιον νομίζομεν ἐπιστροφὴν πεποιῆσθαι.

new field. The Revelation had raised the standard of a sublime faith in opposition to the empire's demand for emperor worship. But, like the Hebrew prophets, it did not escape the insidious danger of hating its enemies. The empire was a raging beast, the ally of Satan, and was doomed to fall. The emperor was another Nero, doomed to swift destruction. The prophet rejoiced over the destined overthrow of the persecuting city:

Pay her back in her own coin, and give her double for what she has done. In the cup she mixed for others, give her a double draught. . . . . Gloat over her, heaven! and all you people of God, apostles and prophets, for God has avenged you upon her! [Rev. 18:6, 20].

This was a very different attitude from that of Paul, in Rom. 13:1–7, and tended to make of the church a revolutionary society, praying if not also working for the overthrow of the empire. But worse than that, it threatened a fatal blow to Christianity, making it a religion of hate instead of love. It was a great moment in the World War when Miss Cavell's chaplain published those words which she had written in her prayer-book: "Patriotism is not enough; I now see that I must have no hatred or bitterness for anyone." Yet Christianity did not have to wait for Miss Cavell to make this fundamental moral discovery; it shines through the gospels and finds fresh and timely expression in I Peter.

We may think of I Peter, therefore, as called forth by the demand of Hebrews that the church at Rome should be the teacher of the churches, and as con-

cerned with the very real danger, created by the
Revelation of John, that Christianity might degen-
erate into a religion of hate and Christians become
a band of disloyal revolutionaries waiting for an opportunity to overthrow the empire.

For it is the Roman church that is speaking: "Your
sister church in Babylon, chosen like you, and Mark
my son wish to be remembered to you." This is the
"Babylon" of the Revelation, seated on her seven
hills, Rev. 17:5, 9—an obvious symbol of the persecuting empire and a plain token of the writer's acquaintance with the Book of Revelation.

In the letter written to the Corinthians at almost
the same time (I Clement), there had been no disguise;
"The church of God that sojourns in Rome to the
church of God that sojourns in Corinth," it began.
But that is hardly a sufficient authority to combat an
attitude that claimed the authority of the prophet
John, the amanuensis of Christ himself, Revelation,
chapter 1. And in Christian antiquity an idea pre-
vailed that the church that had witnessed a saint's
martyrdom and had become the custodian of his tomb
might consider itself as in some sense his spokesman.
The church at Rome was probably already cherishing,
as it does today, the memory of two great Christian
leaders who had suffered martyrdom there—Peter and
Paul. It is very probable that the churches that bear
their names really mark the approximate sites of their
martyrdoms—Paul's outside the walls, on the Ostian
Way, and Peter's on the Vatican Hill. As early as the
beginning of the third century, Gaius of Rome wrote

that he could show the trophies (that is, the places of the death and burial) of the apostles (meaning Peter and Paul).[1] Hebrews called on the Roman church to remember its former leaders, who had brought them God's message, and to remember their martyr's deaths and imitate them, 13:7. Clement of Rome, about A.D. 95, speaks of Peter and Paul together, chapter 5, as bearing their testimony—that is, suffering martyrdom. The great leaden seal of the Roman church bears the portraits of the *santi apostoli* with their names, Peter and Paul. They are still its great historic sponsors. Even today the papal see seeks money for its work in Peter's name, as Peter's Pence.

Moreover, Paul's letters had just been collected and published, and the possibilities of the letter as a medium of Christian instruction had through that collection become very clear. We have seen that the Roman church adopted that literary type for its message to Corinth. It is not strange that, in seeking to undo the harm that may have been done by the bitter tone of the Revelation, the same type is used, and used in the name of the other great martyr of the Roman church—Peter. That is to say, the existence of a corpus of letters of Paul, an apostle of Jesus Christ (I Cor. 1:1), would easily suggest to a church that cherished the memory of Paul and Peter together the propriety of a letter in the name of Peter, an apostle of Jesus Christ. With their sense of identification with Peter, this would not be difficult for them; they felt that they did indeed speak for him.

[1] Eusebius *Church History* ii. 25. 7.

Had he not already spoken through them in the Gospel of Mark? This fact not only would impel the Roman church to feel justified in writing in his name but had to some extent accustomed the other churches to think of Rome as Peter's spokesman. Twenty-five years before the first written gospel had arisen in Rome, embodying Rome's memories of Peter's preaching. This connection—Peter, Mark, Rome—is expressly recalled in I Pet. 5:13: "Your sister church in Babylon and Mark my son"—a skilful reminder that once before Peter had spoken through Rome.

So when it came to meeting and counterbalancing the authority of John the prophet of Ephesus, claiming to write at the dictation of Jesus himself, and a great name was demanded, the Roman church very naturally fell back on Peter, the chief of the apostles. In the presence of the emergency created by the appearance of the Revelation, and the necessity of counteracting the bitterness of its tone, the pseudonymity of I Peter becomes readily intelligible. Whether this pseudonymity was serious and really meant to deceive the provincials of Asia Minor into supposing the letter was actually from the hand of Peter, we cannot be sure. We have seen that, only a few years ago, the *Atlantic Monthly* published the "Epistle of Kallikrates," confident that no one would be deceived. Some ancient pseudonymity was no doubt of that kind; some probably was not.

The relation of I Peter to the Revelation throws a greatly needed light not only on its claim of the name and authority of Peter but also on the curious matter of the destination of I Peter. For, if the Revelation had been sent to the seven churches of the Roman province of Asia, the corrective of it might very naturally be sent to Asia and the adjacent provinces of Asia Minor—Pontus, Galatia, Cappadocia, and Bithynia. No other approach to I Peter makes this address so natural. It covers not only the region directly addressed by the Revelation, but the contiguous lands likely to be affected by its dangerous doctrine. As for Macedonia and Greece, the church at Rome is at about the same time writing to their chief Christian center, Corinth, on another matter (I Clement). Taken together, I Clement and I Peter fairly well cover the Christian world of that time, except for Syria, and show unmistakably the effort of the Roman church to respond to the demand of Hebrews that Rome should teach the churches. That is exactly what the Roman church—we may almost say officially—is undertaking to do in I Clement and I Peter, and as that is just what Hebrews calls upon it to do, it is hard to see how anyone can avoid the conclusion that Hebrews was the immediate cause, and I Clement and I Peter were the effects. Furthermore, over against the stinging rebuke of Hebrews 5:12—6:2 we can set the very different remark of Ignatius to the Romans, fifteen or twenty years later: "You have taught others," Rom. 3:1. These facts form a sequence that cannot be gainsaid and is most illuminating for all four of the documents involved.

I Peter is clearly written in times of persecution. Again and again, 1:6; 2:12, 20; 3:14, 15, 17; and especially 4:12–19, we catch glimpses of the perils in the midst of which the Christians were living. This persecution is now world-wide: "Your brotherhood all over the world is having the same experience of suffering," 5:9. The background is in this respect substantially that of the Revelation: the church and the empire are in collision over emperor worship. But the reaction here is very different:

Submit to all human authority, for the Master's sake; to the emperor as supreme, and to governors, as sent by him to punish evil-doers and to encourage those who do right. . . . . Treat everyone with respect. Love the brotherhood, be reverent to God, respect the emperor [2:13–17].

The Christian's duty to the emperor is entirely compatible with his duty to God.

Do not be surprised that a test of fire is being applied to you, ... No one of you must suffer as a murderer or thief or criminal or revolutionist, but if a man suffers for being a Christian, he must not be ashamed of it, but must do honor to God through that name. . . . . Therefore those who suffer by the will of God must intrust their souls to a Creator who is faithful, and continue to do what is right [4:12–19].

Thus with no little tact and pathos the church of Rome, heroic as Hebrews describes it, 10:32–34, substitutes a finer attitude toward persecution for that of the Revelation, disclaims revolutionary positions, and revives Paul's old attitude of loyalty to the empire, Rom. 13:1–7.

The influence of Paul is on every page of I Peter. The opening sentence is a quotation of II Cor. 1:3 and

Eph. 1:3. The series of classes—servants, wives, husbands, 2:18—3:7—recalls a fuller sequence in Col. 3:18—4:1—wives, husbands; children, fathers; slaves, masters[1]—which is more fully copied in Eph. 5:22—6:9. The influence of Galatians is clear (1:5; cf. Gal. 3:23; 2:16; cf. Gal. 5:13, etc.), and that of Romans is even more considerable. The mention of Silvanus (like that of Timothy in Heb. 13:23) is an epistolary touch, reminiscent of II Cor. 1:19 and I and II Thess. 1:1. One can hardly doubt that the writer possesses the Pauline corpus. Barnett's examination of I Peter reveals certain use of Romans and Ephesians and a reasonable probability of the use of II Corinthians, Galatians, and II Thessalonians.[2]

Another epistolary touch is the remark, "I have written you this short letter" (lit. "briefly"[3]), 5:12. Who would think a letter of eighteen hundred words a short letter? Only someone familiar with the Pauline corpus of letters, and writing to people familiar with it. That corpus is the indispensable background of this remark. Of course, it immediately recalls the similar expression in Heb. 13:22, "I have written you but briefly,"[4] which may have suggested it. I Peter is evidently related to Hebrews, not only in general but in detail.

[1] Weidinger's appeal to ancient *Haustafeln* to explain this seems unnecessary and inadequately supported by ancient documents (*Die Haustafeln* [Leipzig, 1928]). The facts are capable of a simple literary explanation—Ephesians imitating Colossians, and I Peter imitating them both.

[2] A. E. Barnett, "The Use of the Letters of Paul in Pre-Catholic Christian Literature" (unpublished dissertation; Chicago, 1932), p. 612; *University of Chicago Abstracts of Theses* ("Humanistic Series"), IX (1934), 509.

[3] δι' ὀλίγων.   [4] διὰ βραχέων.

The "chief shepherd"[1] of I Pet. 5:4 recalls the "Great Shepherd" of Heb. 13:20 (cf. I Pet. 2:25; 5:2), and its references to priesthood and sacrifice find reflection here (an unblemished, spotless lamb, 1:19; a consecrated priesthood, 2:5; "You are the chosen race, the royal priesthood, the consecrated nation," 2:9).

Contents. The writer's religious feeling is at once lofty and practical. Persecution has awakened in him a great gentleness and a noble submission to the will of God. Christians are not to be betrayed by the terrible stress of persecution into base or reckless attitudes. The Christian's life is a life of hope, a ground of unfailing joy. Christians already enjoy a salvation of unutterable worth, and they have awaiting them in heaven an imperishable inheritance, 1:3–12. (This insistence upon the great worth of the Christian salvation is occasioned by the danger of apostasy and marks Ephesians and Hebrews as well.) They must live lives of goodness, reverence, and love, 1:13–25. Freed from deceit and malice, they must build themselves up into a spiritual temple (cf. Eph. 2:22) where a consecrated priesthood can offer spiritual sacrifices, for they are the new Israel, the true heirs of the promises of God, 2:1–10.

As in Hebrews and I Clement, Christians are aliens, exiles, foreigners in this world—all the more need to live uprightly among the heathen, respecting the emperor and obeying his laws, 2:11–17. All groups of Christians—servants, wives, husbands—have their

[1] ἀρχιποιμήν.

special responsibilities as Christians, 2:18—3:7, but all must be harmonious, loving, tenderhearted, "not returning evil for evil or abuse for abuse, but blessing people instead"—a mild corrective of Revelation. If the Christian must suffer, let it be for doing right, not for doing wrong; Christ himself, upright though he was, suffered death to bring men to God, 3:8–22.

Christians must live the new life he has opened to them, not their old gross heathen life of sin. They must arm themselves with Christ's resolve to suffer. They must be serious, loving, hospitable, and helpful to one another, 4:1–11. The test of fire opens to them a way of sharing in Christ's sufferings, and if they must suffer, let them intrust their souls to a Creator who is faithful and go on doing what is right, 4:12–19.

The Christian elders are to be true shepherds of the flock of God with no base thought of gain and in no tyrannical spirit. All must submit humbly to God's mighty hand. The brotherhood all over the world is having the same experience of suffering. They must stand fast, 5:1–14.

The reflections of church and social conditions in I Peter are significant. Baptism is a saving ordinance, though spiritually understood, 3:21, 22. But there is a constant and serious emphasis on moral behavior all through the letter. Women are to avoid the attractions of hair dressing, jewelry, and dress; evidently the church now includes people sufficiently well to do to indulge in these luxuries. Christianity has a clearly marked spiritual character in I Peter.

The Christian pastor is to be faithful and devoted. and free from any mercenary motive; he is in a measure a salaried officer, and evidently money passes through his hands. The writer appeals especially to the elders of the church and speaks of himself as their fellow-elder, 5:1. This is an extraordinary link with I Clement, the main purpose of which is to urge upon the Corinthian church the duty of respecting its elders.

The Christian elder as a church officer first meets us in the Acts, 11:30 and 14:23. The apostles and elders are often mentioned later in the Acts as the church authorities in Jerusalem. Paul never uses the word "elder." In I Clement the authority of the elders is the main point at issue: the Corinthians are not respecting it; the Roman church asserts it. And in I Peter, written from Rome in almost the same breath with I Clement, the dignity of the presbyters is again asserted: Peter is their fellow-elder, which of course makes them his fellow-elders. They must accordingly be shown proper deference. This attitude is another link between I Clement and I Peter which, however unequal in spiritual power, are yet companion pieces in time and place. It was inevitable that the major interest of the companion letter, I Clement, should be reflected somewhere in I Peter, and here it is, strangely enough too, for who had ever thought of Peter as a presbyter—an elder?

The mention of Mark is evidently an allusion to the reputed connection of Mark with Peter as his interpreter, 5:13, who wrote down his recollections in the Gospel of Mark. Peter is further identified as a witness to what Christ had suffered, meaning that he could bear witness to the passion but also alluding to his own death by martyrdom. This coupling of Peter's martyrdom with a glorious future—"a martyr [witness] . . . . to share in the glory that is to be revealed," 5:1—resembles the account of Peter in I Clem. 5:4, "Peter . . . . having suffered martyrdom [given his testimony] went to the place of glory that was his due."

Problems. One of the best of recent Introductions[1] declares that "to write under the apostle's name and yet to refer to his martyrdom would be a self-contradiction and a blunder too great for any writer to commit." But this is precisely what the writer of II Peter does:

Yet I think it right as long as I live in my present tent, to arouse you by a reminder, for I know that I must soon put it away, as our Lord Jesus Christ has shown me. I will also take care that after I am gone, you will be able at any time to call these things to mind [II Pet. 1:13–15].

Here is a precisely similar allusion to Peter's martyrdom, and to his having sponsored the Gospel of Mark, in a letter claiming to be by Peter.

McNeile's remark does not do justice to ancient pseudonymity. For either the letter was put forth as having been actually written by Peter in his lifetime, and having passed hitherto unnoticed, or it is just a way of calling very serious attention to its contents as worthy of Peter himself. In the former case, Peter might well be described as having had forebod-

[1] A. H. McNeile, *Introduction to the Study of the New Testament* (Oxford, 1927), p. 209.

ings of martyrdom, as Jesus had so often had, and as Paul is described as having had, Acts 20:25, 38. In the latter, if the pseudonymity of the letter was understood, the allusion to Peter's martyrdom would of course be expected, and even inevitable.

It is also urged[1] that "any writer producing a work under Peter's name, towards the end of the first century, would almost certainly have colored the personality of the apostle to suit not only the tradition (cf. Mt. 16:18 f.; Clem. Rom., 40–41) but the contemporary status of his office." But those conditions are fully met in I Peter, which speaks of Peter as an apostle, 1:1, authorized to address the Christians of five provinces; a martyr, 5:1; and the sponsor for the Gospel of Mark, 5:13—for the combination Mark-Rome-Peter spells the Gospel of Mark and nothing else. That Peter is not more highly exalted is because his figure must be used to dignify the office of presbyter, 5:1—a subject just then of such importance in the eyes of the Roman church that it devoted a whole letter six times as long as I Peter to it. Of course, no one had yet thought of calling Peter the first bishop of Rome; that does not appear until after Irenaeus, *ca.* A.D. 185, had written down his list of Roman bishops, beginning with Linus.[2]

The purpose of I Peter is not to add luster to the great name of Peter; that was unnecessary. It was to make use of his great name for certain pressing situa-

[1] J. Moffatt, *Introduction to the Literature of the New Testament* (New York, (1911), p. 340.

[2] *Refutation* iii. 3. 3.

tions in the church. And how could his greatness be more conspicuously recognized than in using his authority to counteract the influence of the prophet John, who wrote as the inspired amanuensis of Jesus himself?

I Peter is one of the most moving pieces of persecution literature. It is written in very good Greek, somewhat colored by the language of the Septuagint version of the Hebrew Bible. Its picture of the Christian life is lofty and noble. Its attitude to persecution is in the best early tradition, patience and forgiveness, in contrast with the bitterness and hate which so color the Revelation. This contrast is so marked that to present it was probably the immediate purpose of the writing of the letter. Nothing could have been more disastrous for Christianity than for the attitude of Revelation toward the persecutors of the church to have taken root and spread. I Peter definitely opposes just that attitude and was probably written for the express purpose of doing it. This fully explains its pseudonymity and its address (otherwise so mysterious) to the Christians scattered as foreigners over Pontus, Galatia, Cappadocia, Asia, and Bithynia— just the regions where the Revelation would be likely to be felt.

This address has a good deal of importance for the date of I Peter. Those who put the epistle into the reign of Trajan can make little of the address, and usually pass lightly over it. As a matter of fact, it is integral to the epistle. It is, however, claimed that the letter cannot have been written in Domitian's time because it is not until Trajan that we hear of Christians suffering "for the name," 4:14.

Not until then, it is urged, was being a Christian recognized as a crime. But Christianity, of course, was not a *religio licita*, a permitted religion, and from the very beginning was punishable on that ground; it did not need Trajan to point this out.

The correspondence of Pliny with Trajan which is usually appealed to in this connection really seems to reflect a reluctant holdover from an earlier persecution policy rather than a fresh and vigorous attack upon the church. Pliny as governor of Bithynia is half-hearted about it, and the emperor is rather perfunctory. Neither betrays any zeal for hunting out the Christians and disposing of them. As governor of Bithynia, *ca.* A.D. 112, Pliny was in doubt whether the mere name (*nomen ipsum*) without any crimes, or the crimes attaching to the name (*flagitia cohaerentia nomini*), should be punished. But this has little to do with the use of "the name" in I Pet. 4:14, 16—certainly less than the use of that expression in the Acts.

The Acts, which first mentions the name "Christian," 11:26, also speaks of bearing disgrace "for the name,"[1] 5:41. The gospels speak constantly of the name of Christ, Mark 9:41. "Blessed are you when people hate you, ... and spurn the name you bear as evil," Luke 6:22. "They will hand you over to persecution and they will put you to death, and you

---

[1] ὑπὲρ τοῦ ὀνόματος.

will be hated by all the heathen because you bear my name,"[1] Matt. 24:9; Luke 21:17.

Tacitus, in his account of Nero's attack upon the Christians of Rome, says that, after the burning of Rome, Nero, who was popularly held responsible for it,

to suppress the rumor, falsely charged with the guilt . . . . the persons commonly called Christians, who were hated for their enormities. . . . . Accordingly first those were seized who confessed they were Christians; next, on their information a vast multitude were convicted, not so much on the charge of burning the city as of hating the human race [*Annals* xv. 44].

Undoubtedly it was a crime in Trajan's day to be a Christian; but so it was in the times of Tiberius, Gaius, Nero, Domitian. All Trajan says, in effect, to Pliny is that the imperial law (against unlicensed religions) must of course be enforced, and the truth is he says it with very little enthusiasm: "If indeed they should be brought before you and the crime is proved, they must be punished," unless, he goes on to say, they deny it and invoke the Roman gods, in which case they may be pardoned (*Letters* x. 97. 98).

The claim that the geographical address in 1:1 is not easier to understand in the time of Domitian than in a letter actually "written by Silvanus for Peter"[2] is fully met by the fact that I Peter seeks to correct a false attitude presented in the Revelation and would therefore naturally be addressed to the wider circle of the

[1] διὰ τὸ ὄνομά μου.

[2] Moffatt, *Introduction to the Literature of the New Testament*, p. 340.

Revelation's influence—those who are scattered as foreigners over Pontus, Galatia, Cappadocia, Asia, and Bithynia. This whole address, so strangely vague, may be no more than a way of reaching the churches of Asia without being too pointed about it. Certainly it can be understood only if I Peter is recognized as written in reaction to the Revelation.

Moffatt's claim that absence of motive weighs most strongly against the idea of pseudonymity is fully answered by the very strong motive the Roman church, spurred on by Hebrews, would have for seeking a great authority to set against John, the amanuensis of Jesus himself, to correct such a gospel of hate as was likely to be derived from the Revelation, with its bold claim of divine inspiration.

And when would such a limited encyclical be more natural than in the days of the limited encyclical of the Revelation (to seven churches) and of Ephesians, which was, of course, an encyclical addressed to Christians everywhere? That period, in short, supplies everything necessary to the understanding of the letter: Hebrews has challenged the Roman church to become the teacher of the churches; I Clement is an illustration of its acceptance of that role; Revelation has created a dangerous moral situation in the church in the chief Christian center of Asia Minor—the danger that the church while meeting persecution heroically might nevertheless be betrayed into the very human error of hating its enemies; the Pauline corpus has exhibited Paul as a writer of letters to churches, and Ephesians has shown the possibilities of the encyclical; the Roman church has another great name at its command, in its patron Peter, memories of whose gospel-preaching Rome had published twenty-five years before and for whom it can claim to speak just as authentically as Ephesus in the Revelation spoke for Christ—taken altogether, these conditions supply every element implied in the writing of I Peter. The atmosphere—persecution, the Christians aliens in the world, the church honeycombed with apathy, undervaluing its own faith—is just that of Ephesians, Revelation, and Hebrews. We cannot agree that "the further down we go the object of the writing becomes less and less obvious."[1] After Revelation and Hebrews, I Peter becomes almost a necessity. We may therefore confidently date I Peter about A.D. 95, soon after the appearance of the Revelation and Hebrews and very near in date to I Clement, another product of the same movement in the same church.

That I Peter reads like an address is only natural if it was to be read aloud before every Christian church in five provinces of Asia Minor. The writer of course does his utmost to project himself into the actual situation which he has in view. The suggestion that 1:3—4:11 is an address to newly baptized persons[2] fits with some obvious aspects of the letter: "Now that by obeying the truth you have purified your souls for sincere love of the brotherhood . . . ," 1:22; "like newborn babes crave the pure spiritual milk that will make you grow up to salvation . . . ," 2:2; "Bap-

[1] Moffatt, *Introduction to the Literature of the New Testament*, p. 340.

[2] B. H. Streeter, *The Primitive Church* (New York, 1929), pp. 121–41.

tism . . . . now saves you also," 3:21; compare also 4:4.

But there are other elements in this part of the letter that do not fit so well with the suggestion. The address to servants, wives, and husbands and especially to preachers and deacons, 4:11, combined with the call to hospitality, 4:9, hardly suits a group of new converts. The time to free one's self from malice, deceit, hypocrisy, envy, and slander would seem to be before, rather than after, accepting Christian baptism. The persecution atmosphere pervades both the supposed parts of the letter, 2:12, cf. 4:15, 16, as does the warning against lawbreaking. 4:12–19 repeats and elaborates 2:11–17. The tone of 4:12—5:14 does not differ from that of 1:3—4:11. The idea of treating 1:3—4:11 as a separate document is based on the doxology at 4:11, which seems to mark a stop. But in a document so strongly colored by Pauline phraseology the natural explanation of this little doxology is to be sought not in the gratuitous hypothesis of a previous document but in the parallel doxology of Eph. 3:20, 21, especially as I Peter's debt to Ephesians is at other points so great.

The striking emphasis upon loyalty to the emperor, even in a time of persecution, which is the leading trait of I Peter and was so needful when the bitterly hostile attitude of the Revelation to him, 17:7–14, was fresh in Christian minds, seems a little superfluous in an address to the newly baptized; unless taught otherwise by the Revelation, they would hardly need to be twice admonished to honor the emperor, 2:13, 17.

286 INTRODUCTION TO THE NEW TESTAMENT

At best the baptism-address theory deals with only a fraction of the letter and never grapples with the main problem: Why was I Peter, as we know it, written? Written in the name of Peter? And written to the people it is addressed to? The theory leaves these questions untouched and focuses attention on minor aspects of the letter while neglecting major ones.

And, after all, is not this just the way in which Peter would be represented as addressing the believers from the heathen provinces of Asia Minor? He is made to address them as converts from heathenism, newly escaped from the brutal wickedness of an idolatrous world. To the chief of the apostles they would all appear babes in Christ, 2:2, who need spiritual milk—perhaps another gentler reflection of Heb. 5:12. He might well welcome them into the Christian fellowship after the laxity and dissipation of their old life, 4:3. Certainly, it cannot be denied that the letter in its broad aspects has more affinity with the Ephesians–Revelation–Hebrews–I Clement literature than with the Johannine-Ignatian. There is far less specific concern about sects, for one thing. And if we must treat the document as two—one an address to the newly baptized of a church or group of churches and, second, the reshaping of this into an encyclical letter for publication—the important question will still be: What was the occasion of the latter?

LITERATURE

HORT, F. J. A. *The First Epistle of St. Peter* (London, 1898).

XVIII

THE EPISTLE OF JAMES

✛

Occasion. We so commonly think of religion as expressed in sermons that it would be strange if there were not one sermon among the books of the New Testament. Of course there are sermons in the Gospel of Matthew and in Luke-Acts. Some would say that Hebrews is a sermon made into a letter. But we have seen that it is better described as a letter cast in the form of a public address, for the very good reason that the writer knew that it was in that way that it would be read, that is, in public before the Christian congregations of his day. In the Letter of James, however, we have a genuine sermon, afterward published as a letter to Christians everywhere.

The ancient world was full of preachers. Some of them were Stoics—men in rough cloaks who would stand on street corners and gather a little audience, half curious, out of the passing crowd, holding them as best they could with their easy familiar conversational style as they spoke of piety, sincerity, and duty. We find something like this in the *Discourses* of Epictetus, whose lectures were often really sermons. Here is an example of his preaching:

Have you not God? Do you seek any other while you have him? Or will he tell you any other than these things?

If you were a statue of Phidias, either Zeus or Athena, you would remember both yourself and the artist, and if you had any sense you would endeavor to do nothing unworthy of him who formed you or of yourself, nor to appear in an unbecoming manner to spectators. And are you now careless how you appear, because you are the workmanship of Zeus? And yet what comparison is there either between the artists or the things they have formed? . . . .

Being then the creation of such an artist, will you dishonor him, especially when he has not only formed you, but intrusted and given to you the guardianship of yourself? Will you not only be forgetful of this but actually dishonor the trust? If God had committed some orphan to your charge, would you have been so careless of him? He has committed yourself to your care, and says, "I had no one fitter to be trusted than you. Preserve this person for me such as he is by nature; modest, faithful, sublime, unterrified, dispassionate, tranquil." And will you not preserve him?[1]

These vigorous and searching rhetorical questions remind us of I Corinthians, chapter 9, where there are sixteen of them in the first thirteen verses. Indeed, there is no doubt that Paul's style was much influenced by his habit of extempore preaching. This is what gives such rapidity and vigor to his writing. In the public square at Athens, Paul engaged in this kind of conversational preaching;[2] in fact, the Greek word for sermon is *homilia*, which means "conversation" and hence "instruction." It was there that Paul came into conflict with some of these Stoic preachers. A later student of Stoicism, Justin Martyr, became a

[1] *Discourses* ii. 8. [2] Acts 17:17, 18.

Christian and tells in the *Dialogue with Trypho* how he
continued to practice this way of preaching on the
promenade at Ephesus.[1] These informal Stoic discussions were called "diatribes."

Vivid bits of dialogue with imagined questioners
(I Cor. 15:35, 36) and fondness for paradox (I Cor.
1:25) are marked characteristics of Paul as they are of
the diatribe, and the Epistle of James abounds in them.

The ancient epistle and the modern sermon usually
deal with a single theme, which gives them some degree, at least, of unity. But the ancient sermon sought
the exact opposite. It aimed at variety, as though to
make sure that, if one line of thought did not move
the hearer, another might, and so everybody in the
audience would gain something from the discourse.
This is strikingly true of the Epistle of James.

A somewhat developed Christianity underlies James.
There had been a time when Christian interest was
absorbed in Jesus—his life, teaching, and sacrifice.
But a time came when the Christian emphasis shifted
more and more to the Christian's duties and responsibilities, his weaknesses and failings. Christian preaching had always strongly emphasized moral conduct
and life, but now this almost engrossed the preacher.

Like the Stoic diatribe James mingles scorn and
humor in its appeals. The rich man cordially welcomed to church while the poor man is coldly neglected is an inimitable picture, never out of date. The
calm dismissal of the needy, with a heartless "Goodbye, keep warm and have plenty to eat," is exposed

[1] *Dialogue* i f.

with unsparing humor. The misunderstanding that had grown up of Paul's doctrine of faith, evidently derived from his letters, is covered with ridicule, 2:14–26. The boundless possibilities of the tongue for evil are set forth in unforgettable terms, 3:1–12.

Religion is an eminently practical matter in James, yet it never becomes wholly concrete and external. Its basis is still clearly seen to be in the inner life. God yearns jealously over the spirit he has put in our hearts. There must be no bitter feelings in them, 3:14—4:10.

James is full of gems of religious thought. The question is: How are these related? The work has been compared to a chain, each link related to the one before it and the one after it. Others have compared its contents to beads on a string. Of course, the thought of the Christian life runs through it all, but that is too general a subject to give much coherence to contents so varied as these. Perhaps James is not so much a chain of thought, or beads on a string, as it is just a handful of pearls, dropped one by one into the hearer's mind.

James reflects no definite situation, so it is not a letter. It does not deal with any single theme or group of themes, so it is not an epistle. It is simply an ancient sermon, of the varied and conversational kind popular in the early church. The appeal in 1:22, "Obey the message; do not merely listen to it," confirms this impression. The people are listening to a sermon in church.

Contents. The trials of life should be received with joy, for they develop character, 1:2–4. A steadfast faith is essential to effectual prayer, 1:5–8. Poverty is no misfortune, 1:9–11. Trial really comes from our desires, not from God; all his gifts are good ones, 1:12–18.

We must open our hearts to the message and not only listen to it but obey it, 1:19–27. There must be no partiality shown to the rich and great, 2:1–13. Faith without works is dead, 2:14–26. What harm the tongue can do! 3:1–12. There must be no bitterness or jealousy in our hearts, 3:13–18. We must have pure hearts and motives, 4:1–10. We must not judge others, 4:11, 12. Pride and self-confidence must be avoided, 4:13–17.

The wicked rich are denounced, 5:1–6. We must have patience like the prophets, 5:7–11. There must be no swearing, 5:12. The power of prayer is great, 5:13–20.

Problems. James occasionally reminds us of Matthew, especially the Sermon on the Mount: 1:13 reads almost like a discussion of Matt. 6:13, "Do not subject us to temptation"; 4:12 reminds us of Matt. 7:1; and 5:12 of Matt. 5:33–37, on avoiding oaths. It may be that James knew the Gospel of Matthew. A whole series of parallels with Luke has also been developed. His acquaintance with the letters of Paul is clear from his discussion of a current abuse of their doctrine of faith, 2:14–26. He shows use of Romans, I Corinthians, and Galatians and probably used Ephesians and Philippians. He knows Hebrews, too, for his representation of Rahab as made upright for her good deeds, not simply her faith, 2:25, seems to be intended to modify the view taken of her in Heb. 11:31.

But the most interesting of James's literary contacts are those with I Peter. There are a dozen points of contact between them, and it is clear that James is using I Peter.

The address of the letter, "Greeting to the twelve tribes that are scattered over the world," strongly resembles that of I Peter, "To those who are scattered as foreigners over Pontus, Galatia, etc." The expression of greeting is better Greek, however, than the salutation in any other New Testament letter, except the two in the Acts, 15:23; 23:26, where the same infinitive construction,[1] regularly found in Greek papyrus letters, is used.

Of course, this is simply a way of addressing Christians everywhere. The church is the new Israel, and the scattered believers form a new Diaspora—Dispersion—like that of the Jews. The only way to deliver the "letter" would be to publish it and circulate it just as widely as possible. It is this that makes it probable that the salutation was added to the sermon when it was published as an encyclical. Such an act of course implies the existence of previous encyclicals, for there must have been some precedent for going about the publication of the sermon in this way. Ephesians was such an encyclical—the only one known to us from this early date. So whether

[1] χαίρειν.

Ephesians was known to the composer of the sermon or not (and it probably was), it was known to those who put the sermon into circulation by publishing it with this address.

The name of James may have been suggested by the apparent opposition to Paul in 2:14–26, taken in conjunction with Paul's own reference to James in Gal. 2:12, where the identification of James with the anti-Pauline group in Jerusalem is suggested. In any case the reference is, of course, to the brother of Jesus, Matt. 13:55, not to the apostle James, who had been put to death long before Galatians was written, Acts 12:2. The mention of the elders of the church, 5:14, and the warning against letting too many of the brothers become teachers, 3:1, also point to a developed church life. The writer is himself a "teacher" ("we who teach," 3:1). Luke-Acts speaks of elders and teachers, 11:30; 13:1; 14:23, etc.

The apparent use of a considerable Christian literature in James (Matthew, Luke, the Pauline corpus, Hebrews, I Peter) points to a date probably early in the second century.[1] The absence of the homily from

---

[1] The supposed dependence of Hermas upon James (the parallels may be found in Moffatt, *Introduction to the Literature of the New Testament*, p. 467) would help very much toward fixing a definite date between 95 and 100 for James, if it could be established, for Wilson's recent studies have shown that *The Shepherd* was written at the very beginning of the second century, not thirty to forty years later. But these resemblances are for the most part so slight and loose that they are probably due to the common forms of popular preaching—the paraenesis—of the day. Jas. 4:7 = Mandates xii. 2. 4, xii. 4. 7, xii. 5. 2 (the devil will flee from you) is probably the closest; but the idea is not unusual (cf. Tob. 8:3). Yet it is not impossible that such literary dependence as there is may have been the other way as Pfleiderer

early Christian canons (Origen, A.D. 185–254, is the first writer to show acquaintance with it) confirms the impression that it is a work of the second century, though probably of its early years.

Its resemblance to Greek literary forms (the diatribe), together with the excellence of its Greek and the ease with which the author uses a somewhat elaborate vocabulary, shows that it was a work of some Greek Christian "teacher," addressing Greek Christians rather than Hellenistic Christians of Palestine, as some have argued.[1] Its writer was indeed familiar with the Septuagint Greek version of the Jewish scriptures, like most Christians of his day—such as the writer of I Clement before him, or Justin Martyr perhaps a generation afterward (cf. *Apology* 37–40, 50, 51). The apparent transposition of the Sixth and Seventh commandments (2:11) probably reflects the use of the Septuagint, since the Vatican Codex reads in that way in Exod. 20:13, 15. The only express quotation, however—"Do you suppose the Scripture means nothing when it says, 'He yearns jealously over the Spirit he has put in our hearts'?" 4:5—cannot be found in either the Greek or the Hebrew Old Testament, and comes probably from one of the lost books which was included in the Greek version of the Jewish scriptures.

It is difficult to say where James was written,

---

thought, and James may have made some slight use of Hermas. On the whole, nothing can be built on the trifling coincidences between James and Hermas.

[1] J. H. Ropes, *Epistle of St. James* (New York, 1916), p. 48.

though it can hardly have been, as Ropes supposed, for Greek-speaking Jewish Christians of Palestine; its Greek is too elaborately good for that, and such groups had probably disappeared by the time it was written. But its emphasis upon Christianity as primarily moral behavior aligns it with Matthew and with the primitive form of the Didache—"The Teaching of the Lord through the Twelve Apostles to the Heathen." The primitive Didache is reflected in the brief Latin *Doctrina apostolorum*, in Didache, chapters 1–6, and in the Epistle of Barnabas, chapters 18–21. There seems to have been a strong impulse in the Antioch circle to promote the new Christian ethic as evidenced by Matthew, the primitive Didache, Barnabas, and the expanded Didache—all probably of Syrian origin. These affinities, therefore, point rather in the direction of Antioch as the probable place of origin for James.

LITERATURE

Ropes, J. H. *The Epistle of St. James* (New York, 1916).

XIX
THE GOSPEL OF JOHN

✚

Occasion. By the early years of the second century the Christian movement had reached a point where it had become clear that the field of Christianity was the Greek world. Its public was to be the men and women not necessarily of Greek blood but of Greek speech and Greek culture. The long discipline of Greek civilization had prepared a people capable of appreciating the inward and spiritual values of the new religion. These people had, in fact, in no small degree already helped to shape its thought and life. To them, at any rate, Christianity was now addressing itself.

It is usually held that the Greek genius found its highest expression in the great days of the Athens of Pericles and Plato. But it was another great service of that same genius that it adopted the struggling Christian faith and became its standard-bearer for a thousand years.

There were, no doubt, among those of Latin speech and stock persons like the younger Pliny and Paetus and Arria[1] whose sensibilities were fine, but the whole trend of Roman life was the other way. While the Greek devoted his leisure to athletic sports, as he has taught us to do, and to witnessing great plays of

[1] Pliny *Letters* iii. 16.

296

Sophocles or Euripides or even Aristophanes in the theater, the Roman found his entertainment in the brutal spectacles of the amphitheater, where men fought with wild animals or with one another until they died.[1] It was not until two generations later that Christianity began to find a Latin public.

To meet the needs of this Greek public some adjustment had to be made. Christianity was addressing it in Jewish terms. A Greek who felt like becoming a Christian was called upon to accept Jesus as the Christ, the Messiah. He would naturally ask what this meant and would have to be given a short course in Jewish apocalyptic messianic thought. Was there no way in which he might be introduced directly to the values of the Christian salvation without being forever routed, we might even say detoured, through Judaism? Must Christianity always speak in a Jewish vocabulary?

The old books of Christianity were unsuited to this new situation. There was, of course, the great Gospel of Matthew. But how unpromising its beginning would be to a Greek! The great masterpieces of Greek literature knew so well the importance of the opening sentence. "I have often wondered," the *Memorabilia of Socrates* began, "by what possible arguments the accusers of Socrates persuaded the people that he deserved death at their hands." Here was an opening sentence the world has never been able to forget. The opening lines of the *Iliad* and of the *Odyssey* lay before

---

[1] In his *Res gestae* ("Achievements") 22, Augustus boasts that, in the eight gladiatorial exhibitions he had given, ten thousand men had fought.

the reader the great theme of each poem in a short paragraph. This was the kind of approach the Greek mind demanded. Twenty-five or thirty lines of Jewish genealogy made quite a different impression upon the Greek inquirer, just as they do upon us. Was there no way in which Christian truth could be stated in forms that would be immediately intelligible and welcome to the Greek mind? The times demanded that Christianity be transplanted to Greek soil and translated into universal terms.[1] The Gospel of John is the response to this demand.

Contents. The Jew, once possessed of a truth, said that revelation had given it to him. The Greek, when he gained possession of one, said he had reached it by reason. Which was right? What would we say? We would say there was a truth in both. And so thought the author of the Gospel of John. Jesus is more than the Messiah of Jewish nationalistic expectation; he is the Logos—the Word of Revelation that came upon the prophets, and also that Reason by which Stoic philosophy found its way to truth. In this one word, which has both meanings and which John uses in both senses at once,[2] he performs the wedding of reason and revelation, of philosophy and religion.

In the Gospel of John the function of Jesus is not so much sacrificial as to bring life and impart it: "I have come to let them have life," 10:10. "I am Way and

---

[1] Definite apologetic interests have recently been discerned in John (E. C. Colwell, *John Defends the Gospel* [Chicago, 1936]), but these were certainly subordinate to the broader, deeper needs and uses outlined above.

[2] As he does ἄνωθεν, "again," "from above," in John 3:3, 7.

Truth and Life," 14:6. "I myself am Resurrection and Life," 11:25. Salvation is, in fact, eternal life. Salvation is closely related to knowledge. Plato faced the question whether a man could be really good without also being wise. In John, Jesus is the Light of the World, the Light that makes knowledge possible, 8:12. But knowledge of what? Of the truth. "You will know the Truth, and the Truth will set you free," 8:31. Life, light, truth, freedom, knowledge—this is the atmosphere we know, and this is the atmosphere of the Gospel of John.

Jesus' work on earth is finished, not postponed. Paul, viewing Jesus as the Messiah of Jewish expectation and believing that the supreme function of the Messiah was to judge the world, concluded that Jesus would return to complete his messianic work. But in the Gospel of John Jesus declares that he has completed the work God had given him to do, 17:4, and his last words on the cross are, "It is finished!" 19:30.

Jesus' death has little of its old sacrificial meaning of which Paul made so much. Here it is the sign of his unfaltering, utter devotion to his followers: "He loved those who were his own . . . . to the last," 13:1. It is also to be the signal for his followers in all the world to rally to his standard: "If I am lifted up from the ground, I will draw all men to myself," 12:32.

But what then becomes of his expected return of which Paul had spoken so confidently? It has already been realized. He was himself Resurrection and Life, 11:25. In John, Resurrection, Second Coming, and the gift of the Spirit are made one. John substantially returns to Matthew's picture of Jesus restored as a spiritual presence to his disciples.

This is the meaning of the "little while" so repeatedly emphasized in 16:16–19, where the expression occurs seven times. "In a little while you will not see me any longer, and a little while after, you will see me again." There is to be no long absence, only a short one—a few hours or days comparable with the interval between his last discourse and his death the next afternoon. Jesus himself after the Resurrection imparts the holy Spirit to the disciples, 20:22, in contrast with Luke's account, where it comes upon them after the Ascension at Pentecost, Acts 2:4. So Resurrection, Return, and the gift of the Spirit are identified.

What, then, becomes of Judgment, of which Paul had made so much as a messianic function? We remember Matthew's gigantic canvas of the general Judgment, so stupendously pictured in the final parable of Jesus' last discourse. It disappears as a future expectation, to be replaced by another profounder kind of judgment within the human soul. "God did not send his son into the world to pass judgment upon the world, but that through him the world might be saved," 3:17. "No one who believes in him has to come up for judgment," 3:18a. "He has committed the judgment entirely to the Son," 5:22b. "He has given him the authority to act as judge, because he is a son of man," 5:27. "I have come into this world to judge men," 9:39a. "The judgment of this world is now in progress," 12:31.

Judgment is just a terrible, perpetual, automatic process by which men by their own choices convict or acquit themselves. It is particularly for the sin of unbelief: "The helper will bring conviction to the world about sin, ... as shown in their not believing" in Christ, 15:9. Sin in John is rather shadowy, at least as compared with Paul's idea of it. With Paul it was a terrible reality, haunting his life with a deep sense of guilt. "What a wretched man I am," he cried. "Who can save me from this doomed body?" Rom. 7:24. With John sin is chiefly unbelief.

For in John faith has become belief. It means intellectual assent; the old mystic side—trust, *fiducia*—has fallen away from it. With Paul it had both aspects; now it has only the intellectual meaning. And with this comes the creation of an intellectual approach to Christianity that was of enormous value to the church. For the Gospel of John set the new religion upon the rails of thought and theology upon which it was to run for a thousand years. The Greeks called it the Gospel of John the Divine[1]—the Theologian—as we speak of the "Great Divines." So clearly did they recognize this great quality in it.

But great as was the service of the Gospel of John to theology, its service to Christian devotion was no less. If we pause to consider what are the world's great classics of devotion, we think at once of certain Psalms, notably the twenty-third. What has the New Testament to set beside it? Nothing in Paul; he is always too argumentative for that mood, even in I Co-

[1] ὁ θεολόγος.

rinthians, chapter 13 or 15. Not the Sermon on the Mount; it is too didactic. But when we turn to the Upper Room discourses in John, chapters 14–17, we are satisfied. Of all New Testament literature they alone possess that great devotional quality: "Your minds must not be troubled; you must believe in God and believe in me."

This balance, this poise, is a marked characteristic of John. Just as his sacrifice of the old idea of a Final Judgment was for the Greek mind, and for the modern mind, more than compensated for by his doctrine of the inner judgment through our own choices, so his apparent neglect of one side of faith is fully made up by his splendid development of the mystical side of religion. He has here, in fact, in Greek fashion simply analyzed the older experience of faith into its two great aspects: the intellectual and the mystical, belief and trust.

On the ethical side the gospel has its great doctrine of love as a Christian virtue and of the love of God. Christians are to love one another. "I give you a new command: Love one another. Just as I have loved you, you must love one another. By this they will all know that you are my disciples—by your love for one another," 13:34, 35; compare 14:15, 21, 24. The great text of 3:16 only restates the thought of Rom. 5:1–11: "God loved the world so much that he gave his only Son, so that no one who believes in him should be lost, but that they should all have eternal life." All this, of course, culminates in the great climax in the First Epistle: "Whoever does not love does not know

God, for God is love," 4:8. "God is love, and whoever continues to love keeps in union with God and
God with him," 4:16*b*. "There is no fear in love but
perfect love drives out fear. . . . . We love because
he loved us first," 4:18*a*, 19*a*.

John never mentions the church or its officers, but
no gospel lays more stress on both. The Good Shepherd, willing to lay down his life rather than lose a
single sheep, is the pattern for all Christian shepherds
(Lat. *pastor*) who must enter the sheepfold through
him who is also the door—that is, through a vital
sharing of his experience of complete devotion to the
protection and welfare of the sheep. The responsibility of the Christian ministry has never been more finely
set forth, 10:8–16.

While the church is never mentioned in John, it is
symbolized in Jesus' circle of personal followers and
in the group of disciples in the Upper Room, chapters
13 f. It is shown silhouetted against the dark background of the brutal and hostile world: "It is because
you do not belong to the world, but I have selected
you from the world, that the world hates you,"
15:19. "In the world you have trouble; but take courage! I have conquered the world," 16:33. "They do
not belong to the world any more than I belong to the
world," 17:16.

The church is also sharply distinguished from the
Jews. Of course, Jesus and all his personal followers
were Jews, but John constantly pictures him and his
followers as standing over against "the Jews" who
oppose and misunderstand him. This is so foregone a

conclusion, indeed, that it sometimes seems that Jesus does not wish or expect them to understand him. "Why do I even talk to you at all?" 8:26a. More than sixty times in the gospel "the Jews" appear as the opponents and enemies of Jesus. Their animosity to him and the animosity felt by the evangelist for them plainly reveal the stage of opposition that had developed between church and synagogue when the Gospel of John was written. Church and synagogue are at war.

The church is sharply distinguished not only from the world and the Jews but from the sects which were now emerging into clearer light. The Docetists who held that Jesus was too divine to suffer agony and death are opposed in the gospel's insistence upon the reality of Jesus' death. The soldier's spear thrust left no room for doubt on that point, 19:33, 34. Yet Docetic notions of his immateriality continued to appear in the Gospel of Peter and the Acts of John.[1] There were still those who regarded John the Baptist as the Messiah, or at least as the new Elijah of Mal. 4:5, like the men Paul found at Ephesus, Acts 19:1–7. Justin mentions Baptists among the Jewish sects, *Dialogue* lxxx. 4, and in the third century the *Clementine Recognitions* speaks of people who declare John to be the Messiah. Against this view of John, the gospel repeatedly emphasizes his subordination to Jesus: "He who was to come after me is now ahead of me, for he existed before me," 1:15. "He admitted—he

[1] M. R. James, *The Apocryphal New Testament* (Oxford, 1924), pp. 91, 251, 252, 254.

made no attempt to deny it—he admitted that he was not the Christ," 1:20. Of Jesus, John says, "He must grow greater and greater, but I less and less," 3:30.

The warning against the sects culminates in the Intercessory Prayer, which forms the climax of the Upper Room discourse, chapter 17. The one request Jesus makes for his followers is that they may be one, 17:11. For them and for all who through their message later come to believe, Jesus prays again, "Let them all be one," 17:21. "That they may be one just as we are, ... so that they may be perfectly unified," 17:22, 23. This repeated emphasis upon the need of unity among believers points unmistakably to the time, early in the second century, when the sects were beginning to honeycomb the churches.

The approach to the gospel reflects the characteristic Greek disposition to announce the theme of a book in its opening lines. In a lofty and somewhat abstract Prologue the writer seeks to place Jesus in philosophical, eternal, and cosmic relationships. He is the Word of Revelation, the Reason of Philosophy. It was to him that God said, "Let us make man." He is that divine Wisdom through which creation was effected. He was the light of mankind, the bringer of life to men. These are no mere narrow national terms; they are so broad that they have never been outgrown.

Dr. Henry B. Sharman used to say that the Gospel of John is a book of a few great ideas to which the writer returns again and again. These ideas are laid before the reader in the Prologue. They are Revelation, Incarnation, Regeneration, the Impartation of

Life. It is to present them that the gospel is written. They are of more importance in the writer's mind than mere historical facts. He is, in short, one of those men who care more for truth than for fact. The eye-witness testimony to what happened here or there is subordinated to the testimony of religious experience. Jesus says to Thomas, "Is it because you have seen me that you believe? Blessed be those who believe without having seen me!" 20:29. It is the inward appreciation of Jesus that supremely matters. It is written on behalf of those mystic later followers, those beloved disciples, who may enter more deeply into Jesus' life and spirit than did the eyewitnesses themselves.

The form in which this Christian theologian-mystic put his teaching was a gospel narrative. In form it is the story of Jesus' revelation of himself to his disciples and his followers.

The new narrative differed from the older ones in many details. In it Jesus' ministry falls almost wholly in Judea instead of in Galilee and seems to cover three years instead of one. The cleansing of the Temple stands at the beginning instead of at the end of his work. Nothing is said of his baptism, temptation, or agony in the garden. His human qualities disappear, and he moves through the successive scenes of the gospel perfect master of every situation, until at the end he goes of his own accord to his crucifixion and death. He does not teach in parables, and his teaching deals, not as in the earlier gospels with the

Kingdom of God, but with his own nature and his inward relation to God.

In his debates with the Jews he defends his union with the Father, his pre-existence, and his sinlessness. He welcomes the interest shown by Greeks in his message, 12:20-23, prays for the unity of the future church, chapter 17, and interprets the Lord's Supper even before he establishes it, 6:48-58. His cures and wonders, which in the earlier gospels seem primarily the expression of his overflowing spirit of sympathy and helpfulness, now become signs or proofs to support his high claims. The writer has, in short, read back the Jesus of experience into the Jesus of history. Jesus is made to declare, in what has been termed the "I style," the church's developing views of his nature and person.

√ The gospel contains no parable like those of the Synoptists, unless, as Professor Moulton said, the Vine and the Branches is to be considered one. But in a sense the gospel is itself, much of it, parable. Much of it is so disturbing and difficult historically and so luminous figuratively. Certainly, no one can carry through a literal interpretation of the whole gospel; such efforts invariably shatter on the command to eat the flesh and drink the blood of the Son of Man, 6:53, 54.

It is not simply the physical difficulties with the Johannine wonders that perplex us; it is their moral difficulty. The water made wine—if fact, what a use of supernatural power—to replenish the refreshments at a party; as if there were no crushing burdens and dreadful sores on the world's life that such power might have been used to heal! Taken symbolically, however (and that is the way in which everybody really takes it), the story teaches the gospel's power to transform and enrich human life.

While the Gospel of John is a narrative, yet, when it is properly paragraphed in the modern fashion, the fact emerges that it is very largely dialogue. It is mostly conversation. This broad literary fact about it (which all standard English forms of it completely obscure) is of great significance, for it at once places it as a literary type in the tradition of the most characteristic form of Greek philosophical literature—the dialogue. This is just what the author intended it to be—a combination of gospel and dialogue. As such it may be regarded as standing between the Platonic dialogues and the dialogues between Jews and Christians of which Ariston of Pella (*ca.* A.D. 140) wrote the earliest example known to us and Justin Martyr (*ca.* A.D. 160) the earliest that is extant.

This trait stamps the Gospel of John again as distinctly Greek in feeling and method. In fact, the gospel may be said to be intensely Greek from Prologue to Epilogue in every fiber of both thought and language.[1] Paul looked down the long vista of existence and saw a trial before the court of Christ awaiting every man, II Cor. 5:10; John saw reunion in a Father's house, 14:2. Paul declared himself the slave of Christ, Phil. 1:1 etc.; but Jesus says in John, "I do not call you

[1] On the language cf. E. C. Colwell, *The Greek of the Fourth Gospel* (Chicago, 1931).

slaves any longer, ... now I call you friends,"
15:15. This is the substitution of the Greek idea of
religion as friendship for the oriental idea of religion
as servitude. Before the Christian believer stretched
a broadening way to larger powers and fuller knowledge: Jesus' followers are to do greater works than
his, 14:12; their helper, the Spirit of truth, will guide
them into the full truth, 16:13.

√The Gospel of John is a charter of Christian experience. For the evangelist, to know Christ through
inner experience matters more than to have seen him
face to face in Galilee. "Blessed be those who believe
without having seen me," 20:29. What supremely
matters in religion is not so much what men said or
did, here or there, but the power of the Christian
experience to create itself anew in the human heart, no
matter where or when. Without that what would all
the dogmas, all the liturgies, and all the literatures be
worth to us?

Our mistake has been that we have dealt with John
as though it were just another Mark or Matthew. It
cannot be measured by those standards. It is something altogether apart. It is a great creative work of
religious genius that has lighted the way for Greek
Christianity and for universal Christianity ever since.
Its theology may not be ours, for it was a bridge between its faith and its world-view, just as ours must
be. Historically, it is less convincing than Mark;
ethically it is less exalted than Matthew. Yet it
strikes beyond any of these to the very heart of

Christianity, as above all an inner spiritual life of sonship to God and friendship with Christ.

Problems. Modern learning has sometimes felt that, by a few judicious transpositions, the narrative of John and particularly the movements of Jesus might be made somewhat more plausible. These transpositions—such as that of 7:15–24 to the end of chapter 5; of 10:19–29 to the end of chapter 9; of chapters 15 and 16 to the middle of 13:31; and of 18:19–24 with 18:15–18—are conveniently exhibited in the text of Moffatt's *The New Testament: A New Translation*. There can be no doubt that such rearrangements, which have long been advocated by Burton, Warburton Lewis, and others, relieve the narrative of John of certain material difficulties. But it must be remembered that topography and chronology were among the least of the author's concerns. His head was among the stars. He was seeking to determine the place of Jesus in the spiritual universe and his relations to eternal realities. These were the matters that interested and absorbed him, not itineraries and timetables, so that practical mundane considerations that might apply to Mark, Matthew, or Luke have little significance for his work. Nor has any probable explanation been offered for the origin of these supposed disarrangements.

The "I style" so characteristic of the Gospel of John is a way of stating ancient belief about Jesus in a fashion well known in antiquity. Various inscriptions exhibit the same use of the first person in describing Isis:

I am Isis, the mistress of every land. . . . . I gave and ordained laws, ... I divided the earth from the heaven. I
showed the path of the stars. I ordered the course of the
sun and moon. I devised business in the sea. I made strong
the right. I brought woman and man together. . . . . I revealed mysteries to men. . . . .[1]

There is, therefore, something almost liturgical in
sentences like "I am the bread that gives life," "I am
the Good Shepherd," "I am the door," "I am the
Light of the World," "I am Resurrection and Life,"
"I am Way and Truth and Life." They are in the
religious style of the mystery religions.

The gospel begins with the very phrase that began
the Greek version of the Jewish scriptures, "In the
beginning." It gradually rises to lofty liturgical
levels, chapters 14–16, and culminates in the Intercessory Prayer. It is the most considerable prayer in
point of length in the New Testament and possesses a
liturgical quality so potent that it actually obscures
for most readers the main point of the prayer—union
against the sects. There is thus an unmistakable literary crescendo about the gospel from the point of view
of liturgical values.

The place of the gospel's origin has generally been
recognized as Ephesus, and everything seems to confirm this opinion. It shows acquaintance with the collected letters of Paul—Romans, I and II Corinthians,
Galatians, Ephesians, Colossians, and probably Philip-

---

[1] A. Deissmann, *Light from the Ancient East* (rev. ed.; New York, 1927),
pp. 139, 140.

pians, Philemon, and I and II Thessalonians[1]—as well as with Mark and Luke-Acts; perhaps also with Matthew, but that is much less certain. (It is an anachronism to talk of its use of Luke; Luke was not yet separated from its companion-volume Acts, and it was Luke-Acts that John used.) Its opposition to Docetism and the sects and its great concern for a unified Christianity remind us forcibly of the interest of Ignatius of Antioch in just these matters when he passed through Asia Minor sometime between 107 and 117 on his way to martyrdom at Rome. It was here in the province of Asia that he wrote his seven letters, vehemently urging unity against the sects, and especially against the Docetists, upon the churches of Ephesus, Magnesia, Tralles, Philadelphia, Smyrna, and even upon the far-off church at Rome where he was soon to appear. There is every reason to believe that the Gospel of John belongs to the same place and period that witnessed the writing of Ignatius' letters, that is, Ephesus or the vicinity of Ephesus about A.D. 110.

The Gospel of John ends with the twentieth chapter, which closes with what is manifestly the Finis of the gospel:

There were many other signs which Jesus showed before his disciples which are not recorded in this book. But these have been recorded so that you may believe that Jesus is the Christ, the Son of God, and through believing you may have life as his followers.

[1] A. E. Barnett, "The Use of the Letters of Paul in Pre-Catholic Christian Literature" (unpublished dissertation; Chicago, 1932), p. 612; *University of Chicago Abstracts of Theses* ("Humanistic Series"), IX, 509. I add Philemon to Dr. Barnett's list, comparing vs. 16 with John 15:15.

Chapter 21 forms an epilogue later added to the completed gospel, probably when it was combined with the Gospels of Matthew, Mark, and Luke to form the great quartet of gospels which soon became the Scripture of the churches and later the nucleus of the New Testament. Verse 24 shows that the writer of the Epilogue, who must have been one of the editors of the Fourfold Gospel collection, is not identical with the author of the gospel. In the gospel the beloved disciple is an ideal figure—such a follower of Jesus as would have seen him in his true greatness and in his larger relationships. But in the Epilogue the author, who has evidently passed away, is identified with this beloved disciple: "It is this disciple who testifies to these things and who wrote them down, and we know that his testimony is true." The new conclusion that now ends the book, verse 25, is even more appropriate as the Finis of the Fourfold Gospel: "There are many other things that Jesus did, so many in fact that if they were all written out, I do not suppose that the world itself would hold the books that would have to be written." It said, in effect, to those previously attached to one gospel or another: "Do not be surprised to find in this collection words and acts of Jesus that you never heard of before. He did more than even these four narratives contain, and if all he did were recorded, the books would fill the world."

The Epilogue is added to meet objections to the new gospel, to bring it more into harmony with its companion gospels, to commend it to their adherents, and to enforce its message by a strong indorsement. In harmony with Matthew an account of a Galilean re-appearance of Jesus is now added, 21:1–14. The miraculous catch of fish and the breaking of bread recall scenes in Luke, 5:1–10; 24:30–35. The second half of the Epilogue, 21:15–25, includes a recognition of the leadership and pastoral office of Peter more in line with the Synoptic representation and fitted to commend the gospel to those who cherished his memory; an allusion to his martyrdom as foretold by Jesus, like those of James and John, 21:18, 19 (cf. Mark 10:39); and a reference to the beloved disciple as once supposed to be destined to survive until Jesus' coming. Such a disciple—a man with such insight and sympathy—the writer of the Epilogue declares was the author of the Gospel of John, 21:24.

From the time of Irenaeus (A.D. 180–89) certainly, and probably from the time of the making of the Fourfold Gospel corpus (115–25), the name of John has been attached to the gospel, doubtless from the fact that John the Elder was the writer of II and III John and very probably of I John, also. The question of the identity and personality of John the Elder belongs, however, to the discussion of the Johannine letters.

But the thoroughly Greek character of the thought and interest of the gospel, its literary (dialogue) cast, its thoroughly Greek style, its comparatively limited use of the Jewish scriptures (roughly about one-fifth of Matthew's), its definite purpose to strip Christianity of its Jewish swaddling clothes, its intense anti-Jewish feeling, and its great debt to the mystery re-

ligions[1]—combine to show that its author was a
Greek, not a Jew.[2] In the Gospel of John the Greek
genius returns to religion.

LITERATURE

BACON, B. W. *The Fourth Gospel in Research and Debate* (New
York, 1910).

ROBINSON, B. W. *The Gospel of John* (New York, 1925).

SCOTT, E. F. *The Fourth Gospel: Its Purpose and Theology*
(Edinburgh, 1906).

[1] Cf. H. R. Willoughby, *Pagan Regeneration* (Chicago, 1929). chaps.
v–viii.

[2] Yet the contrary position is affirmed by B. H. Streeter, *The Four Gospels*,
pp. 418, 419.

XX

THE EPISTLES OF JOHN

+

Occasion. About the beginning of the second century there lived in the vicinity of Ephesus a Christian elder of such eminence and reputation that he could style himself simply "The Elder" in his letters. Tradition has called him John. He is spoken of by Papias of Hierapolis, *ca.* A.D. 130–40, and by Eusebius of Caesarea, A.D. 326. Papias speaks of John the Elder (or Presbyter) as one of the disciples of the Lord and, as Eusebius points out,[1] distinguishes him from the apostle of the same name.

A disagreement had arisen among the Christians of Asia about the reality of Jesus' life and death. How could a divine being, the Son of God, possessed of a nature so utterly removed from matter, have lived a life of human limitation and suffered an agonizing and shameful death?

It was a prevalent idea among the ancients that the material universe was, to say the least, unfavorable to the spiritual life, if not itself actually intrinsically evil. God himself, being wholly good, could only indirectly be brought into relation with this material universe. Since Jesus was believed to participate in God's nature, however, he must be relieved as far as

[1] *Church History* iii. 39. 4, 5.

possible from this defiling contact with matter. This was accomplished in the thinking of some by supposing that his divine nature or messiahship descended upon him at his baptism and left him just before his death upon the cross. They held that his sufferings were only seeming and not real, and hence were known as Docetists or "Seemists." Their views found expression some years later in the Gospel of Peter, A.D. 125–50, and in the Acts of John, *ca.* A.D. 160. In the Gospel of Peter, Jesus on the cross "held his peace, as though he felt no pain." His last cry was, "My power, my Power, you have forsaken me!" In the Acts of John, John says: "Sometimes when I would lay hold of him, I met with a material and solid body, and at other times again when I felt him, the substance was immaterial and as if it existed not at all." His feet left no footprints on the ground, chapter 93. He seemed sometimes tall, sometimes short. His breast was sometimes hard, sometimes tender, chapter 89. While he was apparently being crucified down in Jerusalem, John saw him and talked with him in a cave high above the city, and Jesus said to him, "John, unto the multitude down below in Jerusalem I am being crucified, and pierced with lances and reeds, and gall and vinegar are given to me to drink. But I am speaking to you, and listen to what I say," chapter 97. "Nothing therefore of the things they will say of me have I suffered," chapter 101.

It was one of the purposes of the Gospel of John as it was of the Letters of Ignatius to repel such views. Ignatius writes to the Trallians, A.D. 107–17, "But if,

as some affirm who are without God, that is, are unbelievers, his suffering was only a semblance (though
it is they who are merely a semblance), why am I a
prisoner?" Trallians, chapter 10.

The profession of these semiphilosophical views of
Christ's life and death separated these people from ordinary Christians, and this separation was aggravated
by their claims of higher enlightenment, mystic fellowship with God, clearer knowledge of truth, and
freedom from sin. Expressions like "I have fellowship
with God," "I know him," "I have no sin," "I am in
the light" were often on their lips. These spiritual
pretensions, combined with their fantastic views of
Christ, made them an unwholesome element in the
life of the churches of Asia, as people of similar pretensions had been at Colossae half a century before.

The Elder was deeply concerned over these views.
He was sending out missionaries over Asia to preach
the gospel to the Greek-speaking people, but so sharp
was the issue of the hour that some Christians refused
ordinary Christian hospitality to his emissaries and
went so far as to threaten any who entertained them
with exclusion from the church.

Contents. In this situation the Elder wrote three
letters. One, known to us as III John, is addressed to
a certain Gaius, to acknowledge the support he has
given the missionary cause, to encourage him to continue it, and to warn him against the party of Di-
otrephes, who refuses to co-operate with the Elder.
Demetrius is the missionary whom the Elder is in-
dorsing and hopes Gaius will support. As the Elder's

missionaries accept nothing from the heathen for their preaching, it is essential to the mission that Christians give them the necessary entertainment wherever they appear. The picture is that of Matt. 10:8, 11:40: "Do not accept gold or silver or copper money. . . . . Whatever town or village you come to, inquire for some suitable person, and stay with him till you leave the place. . . . . Whoever welcomes you welcomes me."

At the same time the Elder writes another short letter, our II John, to the church to which Gaius belongs, "the chosen lady and her children"; compare I Pet. 5:13, "Your sister church in Babylon, chosen like you." He urges its members to love one another and live in harmony, and warns them against the deceivers who do not acknowledge the coming of Jesus Christ in human form, that is, the Docetists. The Elder declares such people the agents of Antichrist himself—not, of course, in the old Jewish sense, but to express the intensity of his abhorrence of their views. The advocates of such views Gaius is to let severely alone, refusing them even the salutations of ordinary courtesy or common Christian hospitality. They are not to admit such people to their houses—that is, probably, when they are holding church in them.

There is little or nothing in these two brief notes to explain their preservation, not to mention their inclusion in the New Testament, except as covering letters for I John. A little reflection will show how improbable it is that either of them could have survived by itself or in combination only with the other. They were written to accompany I John, and without it they could have had little or no meaning. For as Demetrius and his associates went about Asia, completing the evangelization of it, they carried with them and read to the churches they visited a longer message from the Elder's pen in which the same pressing matters were more fully dealt with. We have seen that the short letters were without his name; the long letter—it is really a pastoral—does not bear even his title. It would hardly need it if it was to be carried by his messengers and read by them as a message from him to the assembled local church in each community.

This longer letter, which we know as I John, deals with the same matter as II John and puts it with the same confident authority. The only difference is that in III John the Docetists are trying to drive other Christians out of the church, verse 10, while in I John 2:19 they are themselves leaving the church. These are probably no more than two ways of stating the same thing. If the Docetists could not drive the non-Docetists out, they would probably be driven out themselves; compare II John, verse 11.

In language that recalls the opening words of the Gospel of John and out of the heart of his own experience, the writer brings one of the great ideas that characterize the Gospel—the Revelation of Life. God was historically manifested in the life of Christ, and the Christian experience of fellowship with God and Christ is sufficient for anyone's spiritual needs, 1:1-4.

That experience is one of Light and Truth, of Repentance and Forgiveness. The Docetic pretensions to peculiar spiritual privilege and attainment are false, 1:5-10. The claim of knowing Christ is meaningless apart from obedience to his commands, and sinners have in him an intercessor and an atoning sacrifice, 2:1-6. The old command of love is always new, for it is being newly experienced and realized, and living in the light means living in love, 2:7-11.

The Elder's reason for writing to his friends is that they have laid the foundation of a real Christian experience, and he wishes to warn them against sinking back into a life of worldliness and sin, 2:12-17. The Docetists have no place or part in the church; they are just so many Antichrists. It is right that they should leave the church as they are doing, 2:18-21. Christians must hold fast their faith in Jesus as the revealer of the Father and not be misled. Their experience of the Spirit in their hearts will protect them from being led astray, 2:22-29.

Through the love of God the Christian is God's child, with all the hopes and duties of such sonship. Sin can have no place in his life. The children of God can always be known from the fact that they love one another, 3:1-12.

Love is the law of their new life; hatred and selfishness mean death, 3:13-18. Prayer must be offered with a clear conscience in a spirit of obedience to God, of faith in Jesus as his Son, and of love for one another. Obedience keeps us in union with him, and his Spirit in our hearts shows his union with us, 3:19-24.

Some Docetists claim that the Spirit has indorsed their teaching, but it does not indorse it. Only inspired utterances that acknowledge that Jesus Christ has come in human form are from God. Those that deny him are of the world and of Antichrist, which is already at work in the world, 4:1–3. The Elder declares that he is on God's side, and whoever belongs to God will listen to him and not to the Docetists, 4:4–6.

Love is the bond in their great spiritual fellowship. Love is of God, and God is love. Christ is the gift of his love. If God has loved us so, we ought to love one another. The way to union with him is through love and the recognition of Jesus as his Son. Love frees us from the fear of judgment. God's love awakens love in our hearts not only for him but for all our brothers, 4:7–21.

Loving God means loving his children too. Faith in Jesus as the Son of God makes us victorious over the world. Jesus' sonship is witnessed not only by his human life and death but by the Spirit in our hearts; the three are at one in bearing witness that God has given us eternal life, and that this life is in his Son, 5:1–12. In words recalling the conclusion of the Gospel of John, the Elder declares his purpose in writing this letter to be that his readers who believe in the Son of God may know that they have eternal life. Christians must pray for one another, except in the matter of the "deadly sin," by which apostasy is probably meant, 5:13–17; compare Heb. 6:4–6, etc.

In a final paragraph of almost credal dignity the main positions of the letter are restated. Sonship to

God means renunciation of Sin. The Christian has an inward assurance that he belongs to God who is revealed in the historical Jesus, 5:18-21.

Problems. A few touches mark this little work definitely as a pastoral—"I am writing to you, dear children, ... I am writing to you, fathers, ... I am writing to you, young men, ... I write to you, children, ... I write to you, fathers, ... I write to you, young men," 2:12-14, "I have written this," 5:13, but aside from them it might easily pass for a sermon or a homily, except that it is so entirely concerned with combating a particular error—the Docetic view of Christ. These traits all become intelligible and natural when it is perceived that it is a pastoral letter, carried about among the churches of Asia to save them from the Docetic views that were threatening the churches of Asia in the early years of the second century, as we know from Ignatius.

Efforts have been made to show that differences exist between the style of I John and the style of II and III John. But the singular style of the general letter and the gospel, of course, would be quite inappropriate to what were really simply the covering letters, almost business letters, that accompanied the former. These would never have survived unless buoyed up by the great religious value of the first letter. Yet II John is as necessary to I John as I John is to II John. In short, the three were written and organized, and must be approached, as a corpus if they are to be understood. An atomistic treatment is unsuited to the problem they present.

The fact that some early Church Fathers seem to mention only one letter of John, or only two, simply means that they regarded the three as forming a single letter, or two letters. Thus Irenaeus in his *Refutation of Gnosticism*, usually called *Against Heresies*, iii. 16. 7, quotes II John, verses 7, 8, and in the next sentence I John 4:1, 2, as from "the Letter of John," evidently having both and regarding them as one letter, just as we ordinarily treat the letter of introduction for Phoebe in Romans, chapter 16, as a part of Romans.

The ancients not improperly thought of I, II, and III John now as one letter (Irenaeus), now as two (the Muratorian writer at Rome about A.D. 200, and Clement of Alexandria about the same time), and now as three (the Clermont List, probably reflecting Christian practice in Egypt about A.D. 300). These varied testimonies are not to be understood as meaning that one writer had one letter and another two, but that all possessed the full corpus of three letters, one long and two very short, and designated them differently, as well they might, since in a very real sense they might be regarded as one letter with two covering notes, or two letters with a covering note (III John); for I John, having no address or author's name, really needed II, or II and III, to complete it and make it intelligible as a letter. There is no valid reason for supposing that any one of them ever circulated without the others before the Peshitto Syriac canon of A.D. 411.

The great words of I John—life, light, love, freedom, witness—are also characteristic of the Gospel of John, as we have seen, and the strange style, so simple and yet so almost hypnotic in its use of repetition, binds the two works together.[1] Certainly they come from the same circle, and in all probability from the same writer. Our only clue to his identity, since his works are all anonymous, is in his designation of himself as "the Elder" in II and III John, combined with the evidence from Papias and Eusebius (*Church History* iii. 39. 5) as to the existence of an elder named John in the Asian circle, early in the second century. It is reasonable to conclude that the tradition is right and that John the Elder was the author of gospel and letters. Papias, who knew him personally, speaks of him as John the Elder (Presbyter), the disciple of the Lord, and sometimes simply as "the Elder." It was from him that Papias gained his information about the origin of the Gospel of Mark.[2]

Later tradition loosely identified John the apostle, John the prophet, who wrote the Revelation, and John the Elder, locating them all at Ephesus. The last two certainly belonged there, but hardly the first. In our earliest gospel Jesus predicts the martyrdom of James and John, Mark 10:39, 40, and they become the objects of general indignation for their self-seeking and inconsiderate demand that they be given preference over all the other apostles. Luke reports that Herod had James beheaded, Acts 12:2; and John was put to death by the Jews, according to Papias, whose

[1] Professor C. H. Dodd argues that the writer of I John is no such philosophical thinker or religious genius as the author of the gospel, but is a diligent student of his work, and forms his style upon its model, *Bulletin of the John Rylands Library*, XXI (1937), pp. 21–56.

[2] Eusebius *Church History*, iii. 39. 5, 7, 14, 15.

words are quoted by Philip of Side, in the fifth century, and Georgius Hamartolus, in the ninth.[1] This twofold testimony leaves no doubt that Papias really made this statement in the second book of his famous work, *Interpretations of the Sayings of the Lord*. Nor do the glimpses we have of John, the son of Zebedee, in the gospels especially favor the identification of him with the author of the Fourth Gospel; he does, indeed, with Peter and James form the inner circle of the Twelve, but he wishes to call down fire on the inhospitable Samaritan village, Luke 9:54, and when Jesus is full of foreboding about his approaching visit to Jerusalem, James and John are so blind to his anxieties that they thrust their personal claims to preferment upon him, Mark 10:32–35. Upon his arrest the apostles all left him and made their escape, Mark 14:50, James and John with the rest. Peter is the only one near enough during the trial even to deny him.

And of course the thoroughly Greek character of the Gospel of John, both in language—so steadily parallel to the idiom of the vernacular papyri—and in thought, shows that it cannot reasonably be considered the original work of a Galilean fishermen, whose language was Aramaic, or the translation of such a work, supposing any Palestinian Jew to have been capable of thinking in terms so characteristically Greek.[2]

LITERATURE

BROOKE, A. E. *The Johannine Epistles* (New York, 1912).

[1] The fragments of Papias can be consulted in Lightfoot's *Apostolic Fathers*, pp. 527–35.

[2] E. C. Colwell, *The Greek of the Fourth Gospel* (Chicago, 1931).

XXI

THE EPISTLES TO TIMOTHY AND TITUS

+

Occasion. As the years went by and Christianity grew, it became more and more evident that Paul's conception of its work as a short, intensive campaign in preparation for the Lord's return must give way to a longer perspective. The church must take the long look and gird itself for a long, long conflict. It must adjust itself to an extended, perhaps even a permanent, activity in the world. So the churches must be definitely organized with responsible officers having specific qualifications and duties.

Christian leaders had come to realize that their officers must be people of good reputation not only within but outside the church. Money had to be collected, handled, and dispensed, and this must be scrupulously done. There must be no financial or other scandals in the conduct of Christian bodies. Provision for the needy in the churches, at first made spasmodically or as occasion arose, needed to be regulated and organized, especially in the matter of those Christian widows who had no means of support.

The sects which we have seen first obscurely referred to in the Acts (20:29, 30), the Revelation (2:6, 15), and Ephesians (4:3-6, 14) became more and more active through the first half of the second century, and by 150 were, to use Harnack's figure, in full bloom. By 139, Marcion of Sinope, in Pontus, reached Rome, where he tried to win the church to his views. He thought the creator-God of the Jewish scriptures a different being from the merciful Father revealed by Jesus and rejected the whole Jewish scripture, which had been almost from the first the Bible of the church. Marcion put in place of it the Gospel of Luke and ten letters of Paul, and worked vigorously to persuade the churches to adopt a Christian scripture. He added a book of his own, the *Antitheses*, or *Contradictions*. But the Roman church refused his advances, and in 144 he withdrew from it. Yet such was his success that Justin could say in his *Apology*, *ca.* A.D. 150, that he had many followers in every nation of mankind (xxvi. 5).

As the Docetic and Johannist sects had clouded the sky of the beginning of the second century, Marcionism and Gnosticism overhung its middle decades. Cerinthus, Cerdo, Valentinus, and Basilides were leading Gnostic teachers. Cerinthus flourished early in the century, Cerdo about 137, and the others around 150. So the atmosphere of the middle of the century was murky with sectarian movements, Marcionism and Gnosticism in particular being at their height.

From the point of view of standard non-sectarian Christianity, it was unfortunate that Marcion had made himself the champion of Paul. Paul's letters composed more than half of his new Scripture. This is the explanation of the curious reticence about Paul that characterizes Justin in the two works of his that

have come down to us: the *Apology* and the *Dialogue*.
He uses Paul freely in them, it is true, but never once
mentions his name. It is instructive to compare with
this the mention of Paul and his letters in II Pet. 3:15
(a document contemporary with Justin), where it is
accompanied by what is almost a quaint apology, certainly an explanation; the writer clearly feels that, if
he is to mention Paul, he must at once safeguard himself from being classed with Paul's principal adherents, the Marcionites:

Look upon our Lord's patience as salvation, just as our
dear brother Paul, with the wisdom that God gave him,
wrote you to do, speaking of it as he does in all his letters.
There are some things in them hard to understand, which
ignorant, unsteadfast people twist to their own ruin, just
as they do the rest of the scriptures.

There were four elements, therefore, in the Christian situation that underlay the writing of the Pastoral
Epistles: (1) the lack of efficient church organization;
(2) the menace of the sects; (3) the undermining of the
old Scripture; and (4) the misuse of Paul. It was to
meet these needs and perils that the letters to Timothy
and Titus were written. They are addressed to two of
Paul's closest lieutenants, well known to readers of
the ten letters of the first Pauline corpus, in which
Titus is mentioned eleven times (nine in II Corinthians, twice in Galatians), and Timothy twelve times.
Timothy is also spoken of six times in the Acts, but it
was probably the frequency of these mentions in Paul's
letters that suggested the names for the missionary
leaders to be addressed in these Pastoral Letters, so

called from the fact that they are largely concerned with the qualifications and duties of Christian pastors, being really addressed to Christian ministers, as represented under the guise of historic representatives of their class.[1] They were, therefore, the men to whom Paul might most naturally be expected to have written, and who might most naturally represent the first Christian ministry in the Greek world.

This situation behind the writing of the letters explains the fact that they form a corpus, conceived and executed at one time and by one hand, obviously as a supplement to the Pauline corpus. Hardly a generation later, Irenaeus begins his great *Refutation of Gnosticism* in language drawn from them, using I Tim. 1:4, which he ascribes to "the Apostle." In fact, the very title of Irenaeus' work, *The Refutation of What Is Falsely Called Knowledge* [*Gnosis*], is based on a well-known phrase in I Tim. 6:20.

I Timothy represents Paul as writing from Macedonia or Greece after leaving Timothy at Ephesus, 1:3. We may assume that he has been released from his Roman prison and is once more a free man. In II Timothy, Paul is again in prison, evidently at Rome, 1:17; 4:21, facing sentence or execution, 4:6–18. His emissaries have gone to various provinces and cities— Galatia, Dalmatia, Asia (Ephesus). Paul has visited Miletus, Troas, and Corinth.

In Titus, however, Paul is at liberty, so that Titus is meant either to precede the other two or, more prob-

---

[1] Silas is mentioned more often than either of them in the Acts, but only four times in Paul's letters.

ably, to come between them. He is planning to winter in Nicopolis where he wishes Titus, whom he has left in Crete, to join him, 3:12.

It would seem that the movements here implied are to be understood not as among those reported in the Acts but as subsequent to them, the writer assuming that Paul was acquitted at Rome and only after extended travels in the East rearrested, taken there, and condemned. This is quite in line with the view and procedure of the author of the Acts of Paul, writing in Asia a few years later, *ca*. 160–70, who finds room for extended wanderings on the part of Paul after his supposed release from his Roman imprisonment. He may have taken this hint from the Pastorals.

Contents. I Timothy opens in the name of Paul, "an apostle of Christ Jesus," natural enough if the intention is to claim his authority for what follows, but very strange if the letter were in fact addressed to his closest associate, who would need no assertion of apostolic authority to make him heed a message from Paul.

Timothy is addressed as the representative of all Christian pastors and teachers. He is warned against Gnosticism, strange views, fictions, interminable pedigrees—fruitless talk from people who have missed the heart of the Christian experience—purity, sincerity, and faith, 1:3–7. The old problem of the Christian use of the Law is dealt with, the Law being dismissed as applicable to violent, lower beings who have not the exalted Christian attitude, 1:8–11. Paul is pictured, as in I Cor. 15:9 ("not fit to be called an apostle, because I once persecuted God's church'') and Eph. 3:8 ("the least of all his people") as rescued from the depths of unbelief by the mercy of God, 1:12–17.

The instructions that follow are to help Timothy in his Christian warfare, and to save him from falling into sectarian errors, 1:18–20. All Christians should pray for their rulers, emperors, and governors, 2:1–4 (the loyal attitude of Romans, already expressed in I Peter). There is but one God (not two, as Marcion seemed to think) and one intermediary—the man Christ Jesus, 2:5–7. Public prayer is to be offered by men, not women; women are to dress simply and live piously. They are not to teach but to subordinate themselves to their husbands, 2:8—3:1a.

Superintendents and assistants must have certain definite qualifications for these offices, 3:1b–13. The church is of great importance, for it is nothing less than the household of God, the pedestal on which is mounted a religion of divine truth. A few lines of a Christian hymn, of almost credal quality, are quoted in support of this, 3:14–16.

Not only its officers but its doctrines are therefore of great importance. Heretical teachers, inspired by demons (cf. Justin *Apology* xxvi. 4, 5, where Menander of Samaria and Marcion of Pontus are said to be actuated by demons), inculcate a false asceticism, 4:1–5. The principles of the faith and the traditional teaching of the church are to be preferred to the worldly fictions and old wives' tales of the Gnostics. Physical training is good, but the training for the religious life is what matters most, 4:6–10.

The Christian minister must be an example of behavior. He must read the Scripture, preach, and teach, devoting himself to such activities, 4:11-16. Elderly widows who have been useful in the church and are now dependent must be looked after, under proper restrictions, 5:1-16. Elders must be held in high respect. They should not be ordained until they have shown their fitness. Ascetic practices should be avoided, 5:17-25. Slaves must serve their masters faithfully, 6:1, 2.

The heretical leaders are mercenary and self-seeking, but love of money is a fruitful source of evil, 6:3-10. The Christian minister must hold to the highest ideals, 6:11-16. The rich must do good with their money, 6:17-19. The minister must be on his guard against the pretensions of Gnosticism; the mention of "Contradictions" ("Antitheses") looks like an express warning against Marcion's book of that name, 6:20, 21.

Titus in its salutation describes Paul as a slave of God (cf. Phil. 1:1) as well as an apostle of Jesus Christ. Both God and Christ are spoken of as Savior (a word used by Paul only in Phil. 3:20), 1:1-4.

Titus, in Crete, is to appoint elders (cf. Acts 14:23) who must as God's overseers have certain qualifications and characteristics, 1:5-9. Heretical teachings, which seem to have a Jewish base, must be corrected, 1:10-16. Old and young, men and women, slaves and freemen, have their several Christian duties, 2:1-14. Christians must obey the laws and be useful members of society. They have been saved, baptized, and renewed by the holy Spirit, and they must make it their business to do good and avoid the schismatics and the fruitless follies of the sects, 2:15—3:11. Personal messages and instructions conclude the letter, 3:12–15.

II Timothy is written from Rome where Paul is again in prison, 1:8, 12, 17; 2:9; 4:6, 16, 17. Paul rejoices in Timothy's faith and urges him to follow his example of courage in standing up for the gospel, as Onesiphorus has done, 1:1–18. Timothy is to communicate the gospel to suitable men who will teach it to others. Paul's example will strengthen them to meet hardship as he has done, 2:1–13. The idle arguments and foolish speculations of the sects are to be avoided. The Christian minister must pursue uprightness, faith, love, and peace, 2:14–26. He must be prepared to meet all sorts of wickedness on the part of the schismatics; he must expect persecution but must imitate Paul's example and stand by the Scriptures and what he has been taught, 3:1–17. The duties of the Christian minister are again contrasted with the practices of the schismatics, 4:1–5.

Paul's work is at an end; he has run his race, he has preserved the faith, he has won the victor's crown, 4:6–8. Echoes of his trial, the movements of his aids, and personal messages conclude the letter, 4:9–22.

Problems. These are very different interests from those that absorbed Paul and are reflected in his genuine letters. They find their appropriate setting in the middle of the second century, when Marcionism and Gnosticism confronted the church, Paul was being discredited through Marcion's adoption of him as his patron saint, the Christian use of the Jewish scripture was being undermined, and church organization needed to be standardized. These are precisely the matters with which the Pastoral Letters are principally concerned, and with them in mind every paragraph of these three letters is seen to be significant and timely.

It is not so much that style, vocabulary, and idiom in these letters are unlike those of Paul; what matters most is that the interests and attitudes of the writer are so far removed from those Paul reveals in his own letters. Paul was an inspirer, a prophet; the writer of the Pastorals is an organizer, a conserver of the values achieved by the prophet—in short, a priest. No less useful in his own way, but in a very different and much less lofty and unusual way. The difference is that between the dynamic and the static in religion. It was not like Paul to belabor opposition without defining it; Titus 1:12 is an incredible utterance for him.[1] On the other hand, a man writing in the name of Paul almost a century after his death might well hesitate to be too explicit in pushing back into Paul's time the sectarian views of his own day, and his polemic might well be loose and vague, as that of the Pastorals is.

In the Pastorals faith is no longer the great vital inward experience that Paul described; it has become *the* faith, a set of beliefs and principles received from the past to be preserved and transmitted. Paul's great epitaph, II Tim. 4:7, comes much more naturally and

---

[1] Probably quoting Epimenides *On Oracles* 6.

suitably from a later Paulinist than from Paul himself, and Paul would never have said it. For him faith was not "the faith," something to be scrupulously preserved against adulteration; it was the controlling inner experience of his life. The whole outlook of the Pastorals, planning the organization of the officers of the church and its charities, faces a long future, quite unlike that before the author of I Cor. 7:26–31, with his immediate apocalyptic expectation. To quote the gospels (Luke 10:7) as Scripture side by side with Deut. 25:4 (I Tim. 5:18) is hardly possible much before A.D. 150. And, finally, the historical background, disclosed by the letters, of rampant sectarian movements with strange doctrinal perversions cannot be matched until a hundred years after Paul wrote his first extant letter in A.D. 50.

But about 150 every element falls into place.

1. The vague polemic against heresy and schism, which is on every page of the Pastorals, is fully satisfied by the ravages of the Marcionite and Gnostic sects. "Endless genealogies," I Tim. 1:4, sounds like the aeon speculations of the Valentinian Gnostics (Irenaeus *Refutation* i. 11; cf. Titus 3:9). But it would be difficult to refer to Marcionism and Gnosticism more explicitly than is done in the last lines of I Timothy, "Keep away from the worldly, empty phrases and contradictions [Antitheses] of what they falsely call Knowledge [Gnosis]." Gnosis was the name of the chief prevalent heresy, and *The Antitheses* was the name of Marcion's one book. These alone would not prove the point, but taken in conjunction

with all the evidence of date and occasion supplied by the letters themselves, they must be given more decisive weight than has hitherto been allowed them.

2. The need of standardization in church organization is met in the Pastorals by the recognition of a twofold ministry—overseers (or presbyters) and deacons, for each of which definite qualifications are laid down. Against the ascetic sects, marriage is recognized, but there must be no remarriage for those who are to serve as officers or to be enrolled as widows and provided for by the church. It is true that Ignatius of Antioch, in A.D. 107–17, advocated a threefold ministry, but that did not become standard procedure until the founding of the Catholic church, toward 180. It is the absence of this fully developed polity in the Pastorals that shows us that they are earlier than the founding of the Catholic church.

3. Marcion's repudiation of the Jewish scripture, which had long been the Bible of the church, leads to the reassertion of its authority; the consecrating effect of its use in prayer, I Tim. 4:5; the duty of reading it publicly before the church, 4:13; and above all the great assertion of II Tim. 3:16: "All scripture is divinely inspired, and useful in teaching, in reproof, in correcting faults, and in training in uprightness." This is a denial of one of Marcion's most emphatic tenets, and much more; it is the extension to the whole of the Greek Old Testament of the doctrine of verbal inspiration, which Palestinian Judaism had applied only to the five books of the Law—a step that brought allegorical interpretation in its wake.

4. Most important of all, the danger that the influence of Paul's letters would be reduced and even destroyed by their appropriation by Marcion gives us the explanation of the otherwise inexplicable composition of this group of letters in the name of Paul. Marcion had made himself the champion of Paulinism, as he understood it, and had elevated Paul's letters to the position of Scripture. He was clearly the first to do this. They had been collected and published perhaps fifty years before his time, but there is no recognition of them as a part of Scripture before Marcion, A.D. 140–50. Justin (about 150) does not recognize them as Scripture; it is only "the memoirs of the apostles [the gospels] or the writings of the prophets" that are read in Christian meetings, "as long as time permits," *Apology* lxvii. 3. Indeed, as we have seen, he does not mention Paul or his letters though he shows no little familiarity with them.

The writer of the Pastorals grasps the situation boldly. For the people of his day, as someone has pointed out, it was as natural to write a letter in the name of Paul as it was to compose a speech or a sermon and put it in his mouth. Paul is being made a tool of Marcionism, and he must be rescued, and recovered for the uses of the church. The Pastoral Letters accomplish this. They disown Marcion and his chief positions in the name of Paul; "There is but one God," I Tim. 2:5; "All scripture is divinely inspired," II Tim. 3:16. "Keep away from the . . . . contradictions [Antitheses]," I Tim. 6:20. In this way Paul himself is made to disclaim Marcion.

This is effected not by a single letter but by a corpus of letters. It is a mistake to approach the Pastorals atomistically and seek to determine which is earlier and which later. They are to be understood as a unit. The same situation and the same purposes run through them all. The same errors are again and again attacked and denounced. The same reforms of organization are set forth. It was as a corpus that they were produced and put forth, for they mutually buttress and support one another. In fact, as we have seen, Titus is made to intervene chronologically between I and II Timothy, thus integrating the three inseparably. They are personal in form, though not in purpose, for it was too late to offer another church letter of Paul's. And by this time Titus and Timothy belonged to everybody and had become suitable symbols of the Christian minister of the Pauline type. Through them the contemporary Christian ministry could be addressed and guided.

The new corpus is no independent unit, however; it is to be a supplement to the existing Pauline literature. That is just what it became, as Irenaeus' use of it a generation later shows, *Refutation*, Preface. It effected just the recovery of Paul for standard Christianity that was intended; indeed, its influence upon polity was less than its effect upon canonization, for it swept not only Paul but itself into Christian scripture. When the first New Testament was organized some twenty-five years later, it included thirteen letters of Paul (just the number of Plato's letters), and thenceforth no Christian canon contained less.

The Pastoral corpus met a critical situation and met it with signal success. It reflects an attitude like Justin's as to the demonic inspiration of the schismatics; it successfully opposes the rising disposition to let women teach in church, evidenced by the Acts of Paul a dozen or twenty years later[1] and the Montanist movement a little later still.[2] Like Justin (*Apology* lxvii. 3), it recognizes the gospels as Scripture, for in I Tim. 5:18, "The workman deserves his wages" (from Luke 10:7) is quoted as Scripture side by side with Deut. 25:4, "You must not muzzle an ox when it is treading out the grain." The mention of Pontius Pilate, I Tim. 6:13, also suggests Lucan influence, for he alone gives Pilate's nomen, or gentilic name, Luke 3:1; Acts 4:27.

Efforts have been made to identify scraps of genuine Pauline material in the Pastorals, but these invariably include just the things that Paul can hardly be imagined to have written, such as his own great epitaph, II Tim. 4:7. The idea that "many of the details, e.g., the references to Paul's cloak and books (II Tim. 4:12, 13), are too circumstantial and concrete to be explained" on the hypothesis "that these writings were nothing more than the products of a later Paulinist's inventive imagination and reverence"[3] shatters upon the fact that just such details characterize the Acts

---

[1] M. R. James, *The Apocryphal New Testament* (Oxford, 1924), pp. 270–99.

[2] Eusebius *Church History* v. 14. Montanus, Maximilla, and Priscilla were the chief prophets of Montanism.

[3] Moffatt, *Introduction to the Literature of the New Testament* (New York, 1911), p. 399.

of Paul, written a dozen or twenty years later. For example, the description of Paul—"a small-sized man with thin hair and crooked legs, of vigorous physique, with eyebrows meeting and a hooked nose, but full of grace"—is quite as circumstantial and concrete as the reference to Paul's cloak and books but can hardly be accepted on that account as an authentic portrait of Paul. Such touches really belong, of course, to the very rudiments of fiction. Both are simply attempts at verisimilitude.

But the chief point in the art of the Pastorals lies in this—that instead of being encyclicals they are focused upon individuals. Their author means them for the whole church (the encyclical intention shows itself for an instant in the "everywhere" of I Tim. 2:8), but he addresses them to Timothy and Titus, two individuals often mentioned by Paul, but really little known apart from him. The pseudonymity is, as it were, double; both author and recipient are assumed. The result of this was greatly to enhance the interest and effect of the letters. Not only did they gain in probability, for private letters were much more likely to have lain long unnoticed than church letters, but they possessed the interest of private and, as it were, confidential letters, so much greater than that of semi-public communications to a body of people. This is a trait in the art of the Pastorals that has not been fully appreciated.

Not only did the letters gain in interest but they actually gained in authority from this personal address in each of them. They seemed to come with the authority not only of Paul but of his chief lieutenants, the men closest to him in his missionary travels. These men became the medium through which he could speak to the pastors and teachers of the later day. They were like an inheritance not only from Paul the apostle but from my brother Titus (II Cor. 2:13) and our brother Timothy (Col. 1:1). An author capable of such a brilliant reversal of the familiar encyclical technique may certainly be credited with such small literary details as the cloak and books left at Troas.

The influence of the Pauline corpus is, of course, strong in the Pastorals (all ten letters are reflected[1]), as is that of the Acts, II Tim. 1:5, compare Acts 16:1; II Tim. 3:11, compare Acts 13:13—14:28; 16:1. Of ten places mentioned in the Pastorals nine are spoken of in the Acts—all but Nicopolis. The four provinces or countries mentioned—Asia, Galatia, Crete, Dalmatia—all appear in Paul or the Acts, the last under the name of Illyricum of which it was really the southern part. Of twenty-seven persons named, ten are known to us from Paul's letters. Pudens, Linus, and Claudia are appropriately located at Rome, where Linus was afterward recognized as the first bishop (Irenaeus *Refutation* iii. 3. 3).

The regulative tone of the letters with their definite statements of the requisite qualifications for church superintendents, assistants, assistants' wives, I Tim. 3:11, and dependent widows suggests the atmosphere

---

[1] A. E. Barnett, "The Use of the Pauline Letters in Pre-Catholic Christian Literature," p. 612; *University of Chicago Abstracts of Theses* ("Humanistic Series"), IX, 509.

of Rome rather than that of Ephesus. The conflict with the sects seems to have been hottest at Rome. Cerdo, Marcion, and Valentinus appeared there in person, no doubt seeking to dominate the Roman church as the strategic center of the Christian movement. There, too, the feminism which was advancing in the province of Asia (cf. Thecla in the Acts of Paul, *ca.* A.D. 160–70, and the high position of Priscilla and Maximilla in Montanism not long after) would be sternly repressed, I Tim. 2:12. The fact that feminism went on to such lengths in Asia long after the Pastorals were written makes it less likely that they were written there than in Rome, which was definitely anti-feminist (as Tertullian reflects) and was soon to take other steps against Marcion and the contemporary sects in the development of its great baptismal symbol —the Apostles' Creed, almost every clause of which denies some heretical doctrine. Perhaps the words "Everyone in the province of Asia has deserted me," II Tim. 1:15, refers to Asian laxity about the place of women in the church, or to the general neglect of Paul on the part of Christians of the nonsectarian type there.

We may therefore suppose these letters to have been written in Rome, about the middle of the second century or soon after, and made a part of a new edition of the Pauline letters for the use of Christians of the non-schismatic type, who followed neither Marcion nor the Gnostics. Our first real witness to them[1] is

---

[1] Unless their influence be detected in the Acts of Paul in the common assumption that he was released from prison and resumed his missionary

Irenaeus of Lyons who grew up in the neighborhood of Smyrna and went to Gaul probably well after 150. The supposed use of the Pastorals in Ignatius and Polycarp must be interpreted the other way, in view of the historical situation so clearly reflected in the Pastorals themselves.

---

travels; that work also mentions Demas and Onesiphorus but can hardly have approved the Pastorals' denial of woman's right to teach. Perhaps it was written, among other things, to correct their reactionary attitude on that point.

XXII

THE EPISTLE OF JUDE AND THE
SECOND EPISTLE OF PETER

JUDE

Occasion. Many ancient thinkers thought of God as by nature far removed from the material world and too pure to have anything directly to do with it. This idea naturally created a chasm between the physical and the spiritual aspects of human experience and led to the dangerous doctrine that the spirit might seek and find fellowship with God while the body followed its own material impulses and passions.

With regard to Jesus, such thinkers separated his human nature from his divine and followed a Docetic type of thought, believing that the divine in him had escaped from him on the cross and only his material body had suffered there. They accordingly saw little spiritual meaning in his death, but they considered themselves so spiritual that they did not need an atonement. Indeed, they felt so secure in their spirituality that they thought it did not much matter what they did physically, and so they permitted themselves all sorts of indulgence without scruple.

Such people could not fail to be a scandal in the churches, and a Christian teacher named Jude burst out against them with a vehement denunciation. It is no local situation that he addresses; his little tract speaks to Christians everywhere, to all who have been called, who are dear to God the Father, and have been kept through union with Jesus Christ. For the Docetists and their immoral practices are everywhere, honeycombing and corrupting the churches.

Contents. Jude feels compelled to appeal to all Christian people to come to the defense of the faith that has once for all been intrusted to them. The activity and success of the schismatics are so great that the truth and purity of the Christian religion are in danger. This was the feeling of many Christian leaders in the early and middle years of the second century, when Docetism, Marcionism, and Gnosticism were invading the churches. Into the churches have come godless people who make the mercy of God an excuse for immoral practices and take a view of Jesus which amounts to a denial of him, verses 3, 4.

In language that recalls the Epistle to the Hebrews and the Book of Enoch (chaps. 17–19), Jude points out the fearful consequences of such disbelief and disobedience, verses 5–7. These Docetic dreamers indulge their animal passions regardless of the divine commands, which they explain away. Arrogance, hatred, venality, and insubordination mark them. At Christian suppers they carouse in cliques, regardless of others. They are rainless clouds, fruitless trees, barren waves, darkened stars, verses 8–13. They are the godless rebels whom Enoch foretold (1:9, etc.), passion-driven, arrogant, mercenary, verses 14–16.

Christian believers must be on their guard against

these unspiritual and animal schismatics. They must build themselves up on the foundation of their most holy faith, pray in the holy Spirit, and keep in the love of God. Some of the schismatics they may still save, but some of them they can only fear and pity, verses 17–23. A stately doxology concludes the tract, verses 24, 25.

Problems. It is clear that Jude is denouncing a schismatic type of high spiritual pretensions but low moral character, which was widespread in his day. The Docetists are first reflected and opposed in the Gospel and Letters of John and the Letters of Ignatius (107–17) and represented by the Gospel of Peter, *ca.* A.D. 125–50. Some things in Jude have parallels in the Pastorals—God our Savior, verse 25; the idea of faith as something once for all intrusted to God's people, verse 3—but it cannot be said to show dependence upon them. Jude clearly looks back upon the age of the apostles, for they had foretold the conditions he now sees existing, verses 17, 18. He quotes with the greatest confidence passages from the Book of Enoch and the Assumption of Moses (toward A.D. 50)—late Jewish writings which he evidently regards as Scripture, verse 6, 9, 14. On the whole, his letter is best understood as written somewhere about A.D. 125. The mere fact that it is encyclical in form—addressed to all Christians everywhere—suggests that that literary form was already familiar through Ephesians, possibly James, and to some extent I Peter, though this last is addressed only to the Christians of five provinces of Asia Minor.

It is a remarkable fact that this little tract (of two pages in our printing) should have made such an impression in the early church. This is all the more striking when it is observed that it was soon absorbed practically entire in II Peter, of which it forms the bulk of the second chapter. Yet it found its way into two of the three earliest lists of New Testament books —those of Tertullian and the Muratorian writer— outstripping James and II Peter and, in the Muratorian List, even I Peter. While its use of apocryphal writings limited its influence (Jerome *De viris illustribus* 4), it must have met a definite and pressing need of second-century Christianity, which found it indispensable.

Who Jude was we cannot tell. We have seen that he looks back upon the age of the apostles, asking his readers to recollect how they had foretold that, as time draws on toward the end, scoffers will appear, verse 17. The words "the brother of James" were probably added to his name by some later copier of his letter who took the writer to be the Judas or Jude mentioned in Mark 6:3 and Matt. 13:55 as a brother of James and of Jesus. Or they may reflect a misunderstanding of the mention of "Judas [son] of James" among the apostles, in Luke 6:16; cf. John 14:22. Yet it is hard to think the ancients would misunderstand the common Greek idiom which regularly followed a man's name with his father's name in the genitive case—the ordinary way in the papyri. Early English translators, Tyndale and Coverdale, understood this idiom correctly in

Luke,[1] but Beza introduced the mistaken "brother of James," Luke 6:16, which found its way through the Geneva Bible of 1560 ("Iudas Iames *brother*") into the King James Version of 1611, where it still appears.

II PETER

Occasion. A generation after Jude's vigorous letter was written, it was taken over almost word for word into what we know as II Peter. By the end of the second century, or soon after, so many books had been written in Christian circles about the apostle Peter, or under his name, that one could have collected a whole New Testament of works bearing his name. There arose a Gospel of Peter, Acts of Peter, The Teaching of Peter, The Preaching of Peter, The Letters of Peter, and The Revelation of Peter. Most of these laid claim to being from the pen of Peter himself.

The one that claims this most insistently is II Peter. It comes from a time when Christians were seriously doubting the Second Coming of Jesus. A hundred years had passed since his ministry and death, and men were saying, "Where is his promised coming? For ever since our forefathers fell asleep, everything has remained as it was from the beginning of creation." Perhaps the Gospel of John had succeeded in replacing the more material expectation with the consciousness of the Spirit's presence and influence. Certainly, the spiritualizing of the Second Coming which that gospel taught did not commend itself to the writer of II Peter, if he perceived it. He prefers to meet the skepticism

[1] Wyclif reads ambiguously "Judas of James."

of his day about the Second Coming with a sturdy insistence upon the old doctrine. In support of it he appeals to the Transfiguration, which he seems to know from the Gospel of Matthew, II Pet. 1:16–18; Matt. 17:5, and to the widespread ancient belief that the universe is to be destroyed by fire, 3:7, 10.

Burning to rebuke in the strongest possible way this spreading doubt about the Second Coming, the writer of II Peter seizes upon Jude's invective against the Gnostic libertines and hurls it with suitable alterations against the deniers of the Second Coming. Jude was thus made to form the basis of the second chapter of II Peter.

Contents. The epistle is an encyclical, addressed to Christians generally. The gifts and promises of God should move us to turn from physical passions and cultivate the divine nature, developing faith, goodness, knowledge, self-control, steadfastness, piety, brotherhood, and love, and so making certain of God's call and choice of us, 1:1–11.

The writer identifies himself with Peter and confirms the truth of the gospel story. It fulfilled the message of the prophets, who spoke as they were inspired by God, 1:12–21.

Like the false prophets of old, heretical teachers will invade the church, introducing immoral ways of life and false views. God will deal with them as he dealt with the fallen angels and the wicked world before the Flood, 2:1–10. They are impudent, vicious, self-seeking, futile deceivers, 2:10b–19. Their followers might better have remained heathen, 2:20–22.

The false teaching is defined as the denial of the Second Coming. But they must remember that, as the world was once destroyed by water, it will finally be destroyed by fire, 3:1–7. The apparent delay in the coming of the Day of the Lord is because God in his patience is giving men time to repent, but it will surely come and destroy heaven and earth, making way for new heavens and the new earth, where uprightness is to prevail, 3:8–13. Christians are to recognize God's patience in this delay as Paul taught and to hold fast to the truth, 3:14–18.

Problems. One of the most interesting and significant things about II Peter is the wide acquaintance of its author with Christian literature. In 1:17 he quotes the Transfiguration oracle in the form given it by Matthew (17:5) who seems to have conflated the Baptism and Transfiguration oracles and used the result in both places.[1] In 1:15 II Peter reflects knowledge of the tradition that Peter was the voucher back of the Gospel of Mark, hinted at in I Pet. 5:13 and preserved in Papias.[2] In 1:17 the writer alludes to the prophecy of Peter's martyrdom given in the Epilogue to John, 21:18. But as this was written to be added to the gospel when it was made a part of the Fourfold Gospel corpus, knowledge of it means knowledge of that corpus, so that the writer of II Peter knew the Fourfold Gospel.

It is also clear that he knew the Pauline corpus of

[1] Cf. II Pet. 2:20 with Matt. 12:45.

[2] Eusebius *Church History* iii. 39. 15.

ten letters at any rate, 3:15, 16. We need not suppose that he knew it in its extended form of thirteen letters. He also knew Jude (cf. II Peter, chap. 2) and I Peter (cf. 3:1). His reference to a new heaven and a new earth may be an allusion to Rev. 21:1 or to Isa. 65:17; 66:22, from which the Revelation doubtless derived it. The stern reference to backsliders and apostates, 2:20, 21, greatly resembles the statements of Hebrews on the same point and was probably influenced by Heb. 6:4–8; 10:26–31, etc.

The use of the Epistle of Barnabas in II Peter is less certain. That "with the Lord . . . . a thousand years are like one day," 3:8, recalls the words of Ps. 90:4: "A thousand years in thy sight are but as yesterday when it is past." The accompanying saying in II Peter, "that with the Lord one day is like a thousand years," greatly resembles Bar. 15:4, except that Barnabas himself seems to be quoting it: "For he himself bears me witness saying, 'Behold, with the Lord a day is like a thousand years.'" Mathematically speaking, one of these sayings might suggest the other, but rhetorically one is the opposite of the other. It is possible that II Peter drew upon Barnabas and the Ninetieth Psalm; or that both Barnabas and II Peter are drawing upon some other source no longer extant.

In any case the writer of II Peter possessed a considerable Christian library—the Four Gospels, Paul's letters, Hebrews, Jude, I Peter, and perhaps Barnabas —and wrote at a time when Paul's letters and the gospels were already being regarded as Scripture. It was the Scilitan martyrs[1] who first, so far as we know, included Paul's letters, apparently along with the gospels, among the books in their church chest, and that was about A.D. 180. Justin Martyr, on the other hand, does not include them among the books read in church, *Apology* lxvii. 3. In its attitude toward Christian scripture, therefore, II Peter falls between these two dates but perhaps nearer to Justin than to the Scilitan martyrs, for it so vividly reflects the Marcionite misuse of Paul, 3:16.

The explicit use of Peter's name and the way in which the epistle links itself with I Pet. 3:1 rather point to Rome as the place of its origin. I Peter was a work of Roman origin and used the Book of Enoch; it should be understood as mentioning Enoch in 3:19 where the allusion to the Book of Enoch, chapters 10, 12, is in any case unmistakable. II Peter, too, must have been written in a circle where such books as Enoch were held in high regard. But while Jude appears in almost our earliest reflections of the New Testament—Tertullian, the Muratorian List (though not in Irenaeus)—II Peter, like James, is nowhere recognized as Scripture before the time of Origen, A.D. 185–254.[2] Jude is therefore first recognized as Scripture in Rome and Carthage.

Four considerations thus favor Rome as the place where II Peter was composed—its use of Jude, of

---

[1] See E. J. Goodspeed, *The Formation of the New Testament* (Chicago, 1926), pp. 62–64.

[2] *Ibid.*, chaps. viii–x.

I Peter, and of Enoch, and its appropriation of the name of Peter. No one of these alone would weigh very greatly, but together they establish a probability in favor of Rome. Its wide acquaintance with Christian writings—gospels, Pauline and catholic letters—would fit well with such a place of origin, for it was the Roman church that within twenty years organized the first New Testament. The reflections of Hebrews in II Peter would not weigh against this: the West knew Hebrews well enough, from I Clement on—Tertullian even mentions it by name—but western Christianity did not, until two centuries after it was written, recognize it as Scripture. Jude, on the other hand, found a place in the Roman New Testament from the first.

While Jude and II Peter are vague in their picture of the particular heresies they attack, they seem to reflect the Marcosians, the followers of Marcus of Asia, whose movement is described in Irenaeus *Refutation* i. 13–17 and in Hippolytus *Refutation* vi. 34–50. Their picture of the immorality, greed, speculations, allegories, and magical practices of the Marcosians makes it probable that that was the sect immediately before the minds of Jude and the writer of II Peter.[1] Strong reaction against schismatic movements found early expression in the West; Justin wrote a *Syntagma* against heresies, now lost, and Irenaeus, Tertullian, and Hippolytus wrote in the West—at Lyons, Carth-

[1] R. B. Swensen, "The Rise of the Sects as an Aspect of Religious Experience" (unpublished dissertation; Chicago, 1934).

age, and Rome. These facts fit very well with the suggestion that these antiheretical epistles were of Roman origin.

LITERATURE

MAYOR, J. B. *The Epistle of St. Jude and the Second Epistle of St. Peter* (London, 1907).

TRANSLATIONS AND INTRODUCTIONS

The Twentieth Century New Testament: A Translation into Modern English. New York, 1900.

GOODSPEED, EDGAR J. *The New Testament: An American Translation.* Chicago, 1923.

MOFFATT, JAMES. *The New Testament: A New Translation.* New York, 1913.

WEYMOUTH, R. F. *The New Testament in Modern Speech.* Rev. ed.; Boston, 1903.

BACON, B. W. *An Introduction to the New Testament.* New York, 1900.

DIBELIUS, MARTIN. *A Fresh Approach to the New Testament and Early Christian Literature.* New York, 1936.

JÜLICHER, ADOLF. *An Introduction to the New Testament.* Translated by Janet Penrose Ward. New York, 1904.

MCNEILE, A. H. *An Introduction to the Study of the New Testament.* Oxford, 1927.

MOFFATT, JAMES. *An Introduction to the Literature of the New Testament.* New York, 1911.

SCOTT, E. F. *The Literature of the New Testament.* New York, 1932.

SODEN, HERMANN VON. *The Writings of the New Testament.* New York, 1906.

INDEX

[PRINTED IN U·S·A·]